The Early Settlers of the Bahamas

and Colonists of North America

A. Talbot Bethell

HERITAGE BOOKS
2008

HERITAGE BOOKS
AN IMPRINT OF HERITAGE BOOKS, INC.

Books, CDs, and more—Worldwide

For our listing of thousands of titles see our website
at
www.HeritageBooks.com

A Facsimile Reprint
Published 2008 by
HERITAGE BOOKS, INC.
Publishing Division
100 Railroad Ave. #104
Westminster, Maryland 21157

Copyright © 1937 A. Talbot Bethell

*Third Edition Revised
1937*

— Publisher's Notice —
In reprints such as this, it is often not possible to remove blemishes from the original. We feel the contents of this book warrant its reissue despite these blemishes and hope you will agree and read it with pleasure.

International Standard Book Number: 978-0-7884-1249-3

THE THIRD EDITION

OF

THE EARLY SETTLERS

INCLUDES AN ACCOUNT OF THE

COLONISTS OF NORTH AMERICA

The History of the Early Settlers of Bahamas is augmented by a brief account of the History of the New World, its Colonization and the Development of the American Colonies, giving events which led up to the American Revolution

PREFACE.

In writing an account of the Early Settlers I have found it somewhat impracticable to trace in detail the gradual growth and development of these historic Islands. Documents relating to the early history of the Colony are few, and those few we have are defective and so time-worn that they have become well nigh illegible. In the early days of the Colony, documents were evidently not carefully preserved, and some were undoubtedly lost during the disturbances caused by unwelcomed visits of pirates and Spaniards.

Great importance is attached to the names of the Early Settlers, a number of whom came direct from the Mother Country, others from Bermuda and South Carolina about the middle of the 17th century.

In the 18th century the Islands became more historical by the loyalists coming from various American Colonies.

The Spaniards occupied the Islands several times after they were settled, but only for short periods.

The inhabitants were frequently attacked by pirates who were finally driven off with the assistance of volunteers from Harbour Island and Eleuthera.

The dreadful hardships endured by the Early Settlers, the lawless and merciless crimes perpetrated by the pirates, present a ghastly picture of human existence in those times. Yet the hands of the Settlers were not folded. They stood firmly upon the ground on which their feet were planted and shaped a Colony.

Much the same conditions prevailed in connection with the early Colonists of America. They were discouraged on every hand before a gleam of hope of their triumphant Colonization was manifested to them.

They persevered under the strength of the religion brought to the Western Continent by the Pilgrim Fathers, and upon that foundation the American people now and will ever stand.

A.T.B.

CONTENTS

	PAGE
HISTORY OF THE NEW WORLD	9
FIRST LEGISLATIVE ASSEMBLY	21
GENERAL WOLFE	31
A BRIEF ACCOUNT OF THE AMERICAN REVOLUTION	34
DECLARATION OF INDEPENDENCE	43
NEW YORK CAMPAIGN	45
TURNING POINT OF THE WAR	51
SIGNING OF PEACE	60
EARLY HISTORY OF THE BAHAMAS	63
VIRGINIA AND THE BAHAMAS	73
INHABITANTS OF NEW PROVIDENCE, 1671	75
ELEUTHERA	82
JOHN BETHELL	88
GOVERNOR WOODE ROGERS	91
AN ACCOUNT OF THE LOYALISTS	99
NAMES OF REFUGEES	101

	PAGE
PUBLIC SERVICES AND GENERAL INFORMATION	110
OFFICERS OF THE GOVERNMENT	110
MEMBERS OF HOUSE OF ASSEMBLY	115
CHURCHES	116
SCHOOLS	118
GEOLOGY	121
LAND SALE	128
APPOINTMENT OF J.P.'S	131
FREEING OF SLAVES	133
GRAVEYARDS AND MONUMENTS	139
THE CHOLERA	145
RUNNING THE BLOCKADE	148
PIRACIES AND PROTESTS	152
PIRACIES AND ROBBERIES	162
GOVERNORS OF THE BAHAMAS (1671-1937)	175
DISTINGUISHED RESIDENTS	177
BIOGRAPHIES OF DESCENDANTS OF THE EARLY SETTLERS, &c.	184
LOYAL ADDRESS TO HIS MAJESTY KING GEORGE VI.	217

HISTORY of the NEW WORLD.

The History of America, or the New World, begins with the arrival upon her shores of natives of Iceland and Greenland.

Biorne, the Norseman, sailed in A.D. 986 down the Straits of Belle Isle, and temporarily settled either in New Brunswick or Nova Scotia.

Lief and Thorwald, natives of Greenland, heard of Biorne's voyage and made arrangements to set out on a similar one.

About 1000 years after Christ, they sailed from Greenland towards the point from which Biorne returned.

Moreover, fishermen from Limerick, Ireland, were said to have been driven westward in a storm where they found a great land. but making no attempt to explore it, returned in safety from whence they came.

There is some tradition that Prince Madoc and his followers came to America from Wales in the middle of the twelfth century; and the Frisland fishermen have been represented as Fourteenth-Century Discoverers of America.

In 1497. King Henry VII. of England instructed Cabot to explore the New Distant Lands, and having prepared himself for the voyage sailed westerly from Bristol for a month, and in this direction reached Cape Breton Island or there about, and came down the coast to Florida, and marked it North America for England.

The Early Settlers.

Again, we have the myth of Atlantis which takes us back to Solon, who learned from Egyptian Priests that there was at one time a Continent greater than "Libya and Asia," and Bacon, in the "New Atlantis," identified it with America.

The world's literature has many references of voyagers to America prior to its discovery by Christopher Columbus, and, during which time, America remained securely hidden from the eye and mind of Europe.

But, with all these previous accounts concerning the New World, to the foresight, sagacity and physical energy of Columbus is attributed the actual discovery of this New World by him in 1492. Then came the Portuguese and Spanish adventurers courageously voyaging in these Western regions with a view to conquest.

At the close of the 15th century, Venice and Genoa were rivals in commerce, in which Venice had greatly the superiority. Christopher Columbus, a native of Genoa, whose knowledge of the true figure of the earth was much superior to the general notions of the age in which he lived, conceived a project of sailing to the East Indies by directing his course Westward. This design was founded upon a mistake of the geographers of those days who placed the eastern parts of Asia too far to the eastward, so that had they been right, the shortest way would have been to sail directly Westward. He applied first to his own country, but being rejected by them he applied to France, where he was laughed at and ridiculed.

He next applied to Henry the VII. of England, but meeting with a disappointment there he made application to Portugal, where he met with the same disheartening reception.

Spain was his next resource, where he finally obtained a fleet in the year 1492.

The largest vessel was commanded by Columbus himself, who gave it the name of "Santa Maria" out of respect of the Blessed Virgin, whom he honoured with singular devotion.

The second was called the "Pinta," and the third the "Nina."

His squadron was victualled for twelve months and had on board 90 men, mostly sailors, with the exception of a few

The Early Settlers.

adventurers, who followed the fortunes of Columbus, and some gentlemen of Queen Isabella's Court, whom she appointed to accompany him on his long voyage.

The undertaking was an expensive one, and was one of the circumstances which alarmed the Court of Spain and retarded the negotiations with Columbus.

The cost of fitting out the squadron was four thousand pounds. Columbus never neglected his religion, and the one great object of his expedition was to advance the Christian faith. In this, he publicly implored the guidance and protection of Heaven. With this view he, together with all those under his command, marched in solemn procession to the Monastery of Rabida, and after confessing their sins and obtaining absolution they received the Holy Sacrament with those whose prayers were offered for the success of his great enterprise.

Next morning, being Friday, the third day of August, in the year 1492, Columbus set sail a little before sunrise in the presence of a vast crowd of spectators, who sent up their supplications to Heaven for the prosperous issue of the voyage which they wished rather than expected. Columbus steered directly for the Canary Islands and arrived there without any occurrence that would have deserved notice on any other occasion. But in a voyage of such expectation and importance every circumstance was marked. The rudder of the "Pinta" broke loose the day after she left the harbour, and that accident alarmed the crew, who viewed it as an ill-omen, foreshadowing the destiny of the expedition. In making the short run to the Canaries the ships behaved badly, which was unpleasant for a long and dangerous voyage. However, Columbus refitted them to his best ability and having supplied himself with fresh provisions, he took his departure from Gomera, one of the most Westerly of the Canary Islands. On the sixth day of September he truly began the voyage of discovery. Columbus, holding his course due west, left the usual track of navigation and stretched into unfrequented seas.

The first day being very calm he made but little way, on the second day he lost sight of the Canaries. His sailors began to be dimayed and beat their breasts and shed tears as if they were never more to behold land.

The Early Settlers.

Columbus comforted them with assurances of success, and the prospect of vast wealth in those opulent regions to which he was conducting them. He superintended and regulated everything by his sole authority, but for the few hours of sleep which he allowed himself he was at all other times upon deck.

As his course lay through seas which had not formerly been visited, the sounding line or instruments for observations were continually in his hands. He was attentive to the motion of the tides and currents, watched the flight of birds, the appearances of fishes, of sea weed, and of everything that floated on the waves, and entered every occurrence with exactness in the journal which he kept.

By the 14th of September the fleet was above 200 leagues to the West of the Canary Islands, a greater distance from land than any Spaniard had ever been before. At this point a strange thing occurred. They observed that the magnetic needle in their compass did not point exactly to the Polar Star, but varied towards the West, and as they proceeded, this variation increased. This appearance filled the companions of Columbus with terror. They were now in a boundless and unknown ocean, far from the usual course of navigation. Nature itself seemed to be altered, and the only guide which they had left was about to fail them. Columbus, with no less quickness than ingenuity, invented a reason for this appearance, which, though it did not satisfy himself, seemed so plausible to them, that it dispelled their fears or silenced their murmurs.

He still continued to steer due West, and on this course he came within the sphere of the trade winds which blow invariably from East to West between the tropics and a few degrees behind them. He advanced rapidly before a strong wind, and when about 400 leagues to the West of the Canaries he found the sea so covered with weeds that it resembled a meadow of vast extent, and in some places they were so thick as to retard the motion of the vessels.

This strange appearance occasioned new alarm and disquietude. The sailors imagined that they had now arrived at the utmost boundary of the navigable ocean; that these floating weeds would obstruct their farther progress; and concealed dangerous rocks or perhaps some large tract of submerged land which they knew not of. Columbus

The Early Settlers

endeavoured to persuade them that that which alarmed them ought rather to encourage them and was to be considered as a sign of approaching land. Birds were seen hovering about the ships and directing their flight towards the West. The crew began to entertain fresh hope, and upon the first of October they were according to reckoning 770 leagues to the West of the Canaries. They had been out three weeks at sea, and had gone far beyond what former navigators had attempted, and all their prognostics from the sight of birds and other circumstances had proved fallacious. The appearance of land which Columbus had flattered his crew with from time to time had been altogether illusive, and their prospect of success seemed no v to be as distant as ever. The contagion of fever spread from ship to ship. They contended that it was necessary to return, being far in an unknown and hopeless course, and should incur no blame for refusing to follow a desperate adventurer to certain destruction. All agreed that Columbus should be compelled by force to adopt a measure on which their common safety depended. Some of the more audacious proposed that the most expeditious and certain method of getting rid at once of his remonstrances, would be to throw him overboard, being persuaded upon their return to Spain that the death of an unsuccessful projector would excite little concern.

Columbus was now in a perilous situation. He saw his crew ready to burst out into open mutiny, but in the face of it all he retained perfect presence of mind and pretended to be ignorant of their machinations. His countenance was always cheerful as a man fully satisfied with his progess, and confident of success. Sometimes he appeared persuasive and tried his endeavours to work upon the ambition of his men by a magnificent description of the fame and wealth which they were about to acquire. At other times he assumed a tone of authority and threatened vengeance from their Sovereign if their dastardly behaviour should defeat the noble effort to promote the glory of God and to exalt the Spanish name above that of every other nation. His words were weighty, and not only did he restrain them from those violent excesses which they had been meditating, but prevailed with them to accompany their commander for some time longer.

The Early Settlers

As they proceeded, the indications of approaching land seemed to be more certain and excited hope in proportion. The birds began to appear in flocks, making towards the South-west. Columbus, in imitation of the Portuguese navigators, who had been guided in several of their discoveries by the motion of birds, altered his course from due west towards that quarter whither they pointed their flight.

They held on for several days in this direction, without any better success than formerly. They saw no object for thirty days but sea and sky. His companions again lost hope. Their fears revived with additional force. Impatience, rage, and despair appeared on every countenance. All sense of subordination was lost. The officers who had hitherto supported Columbus in his opinions and upheld his authority now took part with the ordinary seamen. They assembled tumultuously on deck, expostulated with their commander, mingled threats with their expostulations, and required him instantly to tack about and to return to Europe. Columbus perceived that they all had lost heart and every generous sentiment which they had previously shown was extinguished. He could use no more of his former arts to soothe their passions, but for the last time, he solemnly promised his men that he would be ready to comply with their request provided they would accompany him and obey his commands for three days longer, and at the expiration of that time he would abandon the enterprise and return to Spain.

Although enraged, his sailors accepted this proposition as somewhat reasonable. The presages of discovering land were now numerous, and, which he deemed infallible. For some days the sounding line reached the bottom, and the soil which it brought up indicated land to be at no great distance. The flocks of birds increased, and were composed not only of sea-fowl, but of such land birds as could not be supposed to fly far from the shore. The crew of the "Pinta" saw a cane floating which seemed to be newly cut, and likewise a piece of timber artificially carved. The sailors aboard the "Nina" took up the branch of a tree with red berries perfectly fresh. The clouds around the setting sun assumed a new appearance, the air was more mild and warm, and during the night the wind became unequal and variable. From all these appearances, Colum-

The Early Settlers

bus was so confident of being near land that on the evening of the 11th of October, after public prayers for success, he ordered the sails to be furled, and the ships to lie by, keeping strict watch lest they should be driven ashore in the night. During this interval of suspense and expectation, no man shut his eyes, all kept upon deck, gazing intently toward the quarter where they expected to discover the land which had so long been the object of their wishes. About two hours before midnight Columbus, standing on the forecastle, observed a light at a distance, and privately pointed it out to Pedro Guttierez. He perceived it and called to Salcedo, Comptroller of the Fleet, when all three saw it in motion, as if it were carried from place to place. A little after midnight the joyful sound of "Land! Land!" was heard from the "Pinta," which kept always ahead of the other ships. But being so often deceived by fallacious appearances, every man was slow of belief, and waited in all the anguish of uncertainty for the return of day.

As soon as morning dawned, all doubts and fears were dispelled. From every ship, an island was seen about two leagues distant, whose flat and verdant fields, well stored with woods and watered with many rivulets presented the aspect of a delightful country. The crew of the "Pinta" instantly began the "Te Deum" as a hymn of thanksgiving to God and were joined by those of the other ships. With joy mingled with tears they threw themselves at the feet of Columbus, with feelings of self-condemnation and a deep expression of reverence and implored him to pardon their ignorance, incredulity and insolence which had caused him so much uneasiness, and had so often obstructed the prosecution of his well-concerted plan. And passing in the warmth of their admiration, from one extreme to another, they now pronounced the man whom they had so lately reviled and threatened, to be a person inspired by Heaven with sagacity and fortitude more than human, to have accomplished a design so far beyond the ideas and conceptions of all former ages.

As soon as the sun arose, all their boats were manned and armed. They rowed towards the island with their colours displayed, with warlike music and other martial pomp. As they approached the coast, they saw it covered with a multitude of people, whose attitude and gestures

The Early Settlers

expressed wonder and astonishment at the strange objects which presented themselves to their view. He landed in a rich dress, and with a naked sword in his hand. His men followed, and kneeling down, they all kissed the ground, as a spot venerated and which they had so long desired to see. They next erected a cross, and, prostrating themselves before it, returned thanks to God for bringing their voyage to such a happy issue. They took possession of the land in the name of their Catholic Majesty and called it San Salvador—which has lately been set down as Watlings Island in the Bahamas.

The object of Columbus, in his first voyage, was to arrive at the East Indies by sailing directly West.

His discovery of the New World commenced an era of geographical exploration. The main motive of these voyages of adventure was to discover or seize gold, silver and precious stones which the adventurers might happen to find.

The extreme East was abounding in mineral and jewels, and for this reason Columbus named the Islands he discovered the Indies, thinking that he had reached the East India Archipelago.

The Spaniards quickly followed up the discovery of Columbus, and in a few years had conquered Mexico and a considerable proportion of South America. They plundered and robbed the native population of all their valuables which they sent back to Spain in their stately Galleons or Treasure Ships, which were the only vessels at that time on the Carribean Sea. England was not yet a maritime power. It was not until Cabot's suggestion in 1551, that a company of merchant adventurers was formed for the discovery of the Island dominions in the western regions; from then on English ships began to find their way to West Indies and greatly interfered with the progress of the Spaniards in their plunder.

Among the names of merchant adventurers newly formed were Frobisher, John Davis, John Hawkins and the Slave Trader, Francis Drake, Humphrey Gilbert and Sir Richard Grenville. The latter, in his little ship "The Revenge." fought fifty-one Spanish ships from evening till the morning of the next day, and died at his post.

The Early Settlers

Martin Frobisher and John Davis were the seekers of a North West passage, hence the name of Davis Straights. John Hawkins was a famous Slave Trader.

Francis Drake, the Dragon of the Ocean, as he was sometimes called, lived on the ocean striking at the Spanish treasure fleets with unrivalled gallantry and with great success.

He took from one ship, the "Cacafuego," 20 tons of silver bullion, 13 chests of silver-coin and eighty pounds of gold.

The Spanish Government estimated its loss from this ship to be about three million dollars. Drake accomplished this with one single vessel and about 85 men.

While this adventure of English Sea Rovers was going on in the Western Ocean with signal success, supreme test of their daring, pluck and courage came in 1588, when Phillip's Vast Armada was destroyed in the English Channel and the North Sea.

The overwhelming defeat of the Spaniards was followed by a succession of lesser defeats, and in 1596 Raleigh, with the Earl of Essex and Lord Thomas Howard, shattered the remaining Spanish fleet at Cadiz.

Humphrey Gilbert, the half brother of Raleigh, sailed in 1582 to found a Colony on the mainland of America. He landed in Newfoundland and took possession of it in the name of Queen Elizabeth. He proceeded South in search of a place with a milder climate. His ship was swamped in a storm and he was drowned.

In 1584, Walter Raleigh, being the favourite of Queen Elizabeth. received a Knighthood. In 1585, he sent two ships under command of Captains Amidas and Barlow to explore America. They landed on an Island called Wocoken in the inlet of Pimlico Sound. then proceeded to the Island of Roanoke at the mouth of Albemarle Sound in North Carolina. where they were well received by the natives.

Having freighted their ships with furs and cedar, they returned to England, giving a glowing account of the marvellous beauty of the country, speaking highly of the fertility of the soil and the mildness of the country and the innocence of the natives.

The Early Settlers.

Queen Elizabeth, so elated with the description he gave of the country, called it Virginia, as a memorial; because, that country had been discovered during her reign.

In 1585, a fleet of seven vessels sailed from Plymouth, England, under the command of Sir H. Granville with one hundred and fifty colonists.

On board was John White, Esquire, who had been appointed Governor of Virginia, and eighty-nine men and seventeen women. Of the women, one was Eleanor Dale, daughter of the Governor and wife of one of the Magistrates.

Soon after her arrival she gave birth to a female child who was named Virginia, being the first child born in the United States of English parents.

When the ships were ready to depart for England, the emigrants became very gloomy with apprehensions and implored the Governor, who was returning, to hasten back with supplies. He embarked, and soon after his arrival in England, the Spanish war broke out which caused the Colony of Roanoke to be forgotten.

After the defeat of the Spanish Armada, Raleigh was unable to send any assistance to the Colonies, and it was nearly three years before White returned, and when he did arrive, not one of the Colonists was there, whether they had been killed or captured by the Indians or died from starvation no one knew, and it may be said that these fruitless adventures withdrew the attention of the English from these regions for several years.

In April, 1602, Bartholomew made a voyage to America. He steered his ship directly West from England, thus shortening his voyage and arrived in May on the coast of Massachusetts.

He discovered a headland, and taking a great quantity of fish nearby, called it Cape Cod. After trading a while with the Indians he returned to England.

The report made by Gosnold revived the spirit of adventure, and in 1603, and 1605, two voyages were made in the same directions, and Penobscot Bay, Massachusetts Bay, and the rivers between them were discovered.

Navigators confirmed the report of Gosnold which naturally led to a more extensive scheme of further colonization.

The Early Settlers.

Richard Hakluyt took the most active part in this scheme. By his persuasion an Association of Gentlemen in different parts of England was formed for the purpose of sending Colonists to America.

Upon their making application to King James, he, by Letters Patent dated in 1606, divided the country of Virginia then considered extending from the Southern boundary of North Carolina to the Northern boundary of Maine into two Districts and constituted two companies for planting colonies within them.

The Southern was granted to Sir Thomas Yates and his association, chiefly residents of London, and was styled the London Company.

The Northern District was granted to Thomas Hanham and his associates and was styled the Plymouth Company; supposedly the principal members resided in that city.

This district extended from near the Southern boundary of New York to the Bay of Passamaquoddy, and the two districts were called North and South Virginia.

The members of these two companies were principally merchants. Their object was the extension of commerce and the discovery of mines of metal which were supposed to abound in North as well as South America.

For the supreme government of these colonies a grand council was instituted, the members of which were to reside in England and were to be guided by its instructions.

To the emigrants and their descendants were secured the employment of all the rights of citizens in the same manner, and to the same extent as if they had remained or been born in England.

The London Company, in 1606, sent out 103 men, mechanics and others, and among them was the famous John Smith, who was by far the most able man in the country.

The expedition entered Chesapeake Bay and founded Jamestown, and while many were busy building and settling down, John Smith made a short voyage up the St. James River. When he returned he found the Colony going to ruin for want of a strong hand and will over them.

He came to the rescue, and having restored peace and order, again set off into the interior to trade for corn.

The Early Settlers.

He was taken prisoner and was treated well till he was handed over to the King—Powhatan.

He was sentenced to death, but through the intercession of the King's daughter, Pocahantas, he was saved.

On his return to Jamestown, he found the settlers greatly reduced in number, and those whom he found had decided to abandon the country, but by Smith's persuasion they were induced to stay and to relinquish their design. Smith brought supplies of provisions which he obtained from the Indians through the influence of the Princess Pocahantes, and which were the means of preserving the Colony from famine. She personally sent him such articles as were most needed by them.

The settlers were thus enabled to subsist until Capt. Newport arrived at Jamestown with a large quantity of provisions and one hundred and twenty persons who came to reside in the Colony.

While Smith was absent exploring the coast of Chesapeake Bay, the people again became discontented and turbulent.

Upon his return he was made President, and under his administration peace and plenty smiled upon the Colony.

In 1608, Newport again arrived at Jamestown and brought with him seventy emigrants, among them were two females, Mrs. Forrest, and Ann Burras, her maid.

Soon after, Ann Burras married John Laydon, and this, it is said, was the first marriage of Europeans celebrated in America.

The attention of the English people, and especially eminent men, had been attracted to the Colony.

In 1609, a New Charter was issued to a powerful company which included such well known men as the Earls of Southampton, Lincoln and Dorset, Robert Peel, Sir Edward Sandip, and Richard Hakluyt.

The territory was increased, and Lord Delaware appointed Governor of the new Colony, and Sir Thomas Gates Lieutenant-Governor. The latter, with Sir George Somers, sailed with another party including several women and chldren, but were unfortunately wrecked at Bermuda.

Meanwhile Smith had left the country owing to a gun accident, and the Colony, no longer controlled by a strong authority, went headlong to ruin.

The Early Settlers

In six months the four hundred and ninety inhabitants were reduced by indolence, vice and famine to sixty.

When Gates arrived from Bermuda, he took them on board to be carried back to England, when he was met by Lord Delaware who persuaded them to remain while he re-organized the Colony and started it on the right road.

Owing to ill-health, Lord Delaware had to resign his position and was succeeded by Sir Thomas Dale.

The new Governor ruled firmly, recognizing the truth of what Smith said " nothing is to be expected but by labour," he therefore forced the Colonists to work hard and severely flogged the lazy and the indolent.

Dale wrote home for new recruits. " Let me," he said, " commend unto your carefulness the pursuit of this business, take four of the best Kingdoms in Christendom and put them altogether, they would in no way compare with this Country, either for commodities or goodness of soil."

Sir Thomas Gates was sent over with six ships with 300 emigrants and 100 head of cattle. He was appointed to succeed Governor Dale.

In 1612, Pocahontas was taken prisoner by Capt. Argal and later married a young man by the name of Wolfe, a tobacco Planter.

As time went on, Wolfe and his Princess sailed for England where she was received by the King and Queen with the attention due to her rank. For her virtue and disinterested service she was universally beloved and respected.

She died when about to return to America, having one son from whom are described some of the most respected families of Virginia.

THE FIRST LEGISLATIVE ASSEMBLY.

The year 1619 was an important one for the Colony, for on the 30th July the first Legislative Assembly met and drafted a Code of Laws and regulations for the State, and two years later a written constitution was granted.

But the young nation had no sooner attained this dignity than it suffered a severe set-back. The Colonists had been living in peace with the Indians and had scattered themselves over a large district.

The Early Settlers

At mid-day, March 4th, 1622, the Indians rose and massacred all the whites whom they could lay hands on, and only by timely warning was Jamestown saved, but before the insurrection could be checked, 1500 settlers had been killed.

From this severe blow the recovery was slow. Many of the inhabitants left for England.

Public Works were abandoned, and the public spirit was temporarily paralysed.

In 1624, the Charter to the London Company was withdrawn, but the Colony steadily grew in wealth and population, and was always the leading state.

FRENCH SETTLERS OF CANADA.

Many voyages which have not been herein mentioned were made to the coast of North America by the French.

The banks of New Foundland were frequently visited by Fishermen of Brittany and Normandy. James Cartier discovered the St. Lawrence River, and in a subsequent voyage reached Montreal and built a Fort at Quebec.

In 1604, Henry IV., of France, granted to the Sieur de Monts all the country between the 40th and 46th degrees of North Latitude, or between New Jersey and Nova Scotia.

By virtue of this grant a settlement was made on the South Eastern Side of the Bay of Fundy, which they called Port Royal.

In 1608, Champlaim founded Quebec and populated by the French.

The French settlers mingled with the savages and obtained over them an influence greater than those of any other nation; and whenever war existed between France and England, and at other times the Indians made incursions from their settlement into New England and New York' and, on the frontier were often found cattle slain, and men, women and children massacred.

VIRGINIA.

The first attempt at a settlement in America was made by Sir Walter Raleigh in 1585, as already noted. It was on an Island at the mouth of Roanoke River.

The Early Settlers

The English Colony of Jamestown, Virginia, was settled in 1607, and almost at once the Anglo Saxon desire for self government was clearly shown.

The Royal Charter promised the Colonists "all the liberties, franchise and immunities enjoyed by their brother Englishmen at home."

These phrases, however, when interpreted in the light of English History, contained the promise of a large measure of liberty confering upon such Colonies as should be established within the Imperial expanse of what was then Virginia, the rich inheritance of Anglo-Saxon liberty.

Acting in the spirit of this grant, the Jamestown Colonists asserted the right to select their own rulers. They therefore replaced the King's Governor and appointed John Smith as their ruler. This was practically a revolutionary act.

By 1619, the Jamestown Colony was entitled to consider itself established and permanent, consequently, there comes into operation by them the Chartered Privileges which had been reaffirmed by the two Charters of 1609 and 1612. They instructed a Representative Assembly, elected by the people of the eleven places which now boasted of its inhabitants.

The Assembly was organised on June 30th, 1619, in a Wooden Church, the members arranged in order of rank and wearing hats as was then the custom in the English House of Commons.

The meeting was opened by prayer, when afterward the Oath of Supremacy was made to the burgesses.

The law-makers then provided for the establishment of the Church of England, commanding all persons to attend services morning and evening, and to bring their offerings. Excess of apparel was discouraged. The law provided that "if a man be single, he shall be taxed according to his appearance of his outer clothing, or if he be married, according to h's own or his wife's."

These and other laws, similarly executed, were put into operation without previous ratification, without any power in England, and thus Virginia began to overn herself more than a year before the "Mayflower" sailed from the shores of England with the Pilgrim Fathers on board,

The Early Settlers

Virginia prospered under the laws so enacted. The ordinance and constitution was definitely authorised by the Virginia Company in London (1621). It was a model of fine government which all the other Colonies in America followed, and was regarded as the embodiment of the kind of government which English subjects in America had a right to enjoy, and Royal Governors of whatever Colony who sought to deny it found themselves face to face with a crisis.

Sir John Harvey ventured to slight the Virginia General Assembly. The result was that on the 28th April, 1635, he was thrust out of office, and Capt. John West acted as Governor till the King's Pleasure was known.

This was practically another revolutionary act, and its spirit appears and re-appears in the thirteen colonies in America. Each of them asserted the right of Government by an Assembly similar to that of Virginia.

NEW ENGLAND.

The emigrants that came to Virginia under the auspices of the Virginian Companies have done so for adventure or in hope of gain, but it was another and more powerful motive which drove the Pilgrim Fathers from their homes, friends and dear ones in England—it was an earnest desire, pure and simple, for religious freedom.

The English Puritans, smarting under the tolerance of the age, yearned for a land where they could worship as they thought fit.

In 1609, many left England for Holland, and in 1620 about 50 of these and 50 from England, embarked in the "Mayflower" for the New World.

They landed at Plymouth, and though they had suffered from sickness and want, they felt a certain degree of happiness in the fact that they had left behind them great persecutions against the banner of religion; however, they had come to stay, and so settled down to work, with a will.

Later, they were joined by others from England and Holland, and in 1628, the Massachusetts Company was formed and controlled by the Puritan Party.

The Early Settlers

Two years later, John Winthrop took about 1,000 emigrants and settled at Boston, and for many years there was a continued stream of Exiles for Religion's sake to the new land of Promise.

But though the Colonists had left England because of religious intolerance, they were far from tolerant themselves, indeed, they were the most bigotted of Sectarians.

Disputes arose among them which led to their separation and sought new states, for example: The followers of Annie Hutcheson went off and settled in Rhode Island. Thomas Hooker, a Minister, founded Towns in Connecticut. Roger Williams was banished from Boston for his damnable heretical opinions and settled with a party in Narraganset Bay.

New Haven and New Hampshire were peopled as an outcome of these disputes. The stern belief in what they considered right took precedence of all the deeper feelings of life, parental, conjugal or filial, and so deep was it, that to the present day the New England conscience is a source in American politics.

Men of such stern intentions made excellent colonists, and the various settlements formed by them steadily progressed.

The Puritans were fairly kind to the Indians, but always kept their eyes on them and did not hesitate to use force against them when necessary, they had very little pity when roused.

The redoubtable Miles Standish who went out in the "Mayflower" was a typical example.

In 1636, the New England Colonists commenced a war against the Pequot Indians of Connecticut, and after several reverses, John Mason, with about eighty men, attacked their stronghold and massacred nearly seven hundred of them.

In 1670, another war broke out, the death of a chief occured immediately after a visit to one of the towns and was ascribed to witchcraft.

The Indians arose, and for four years a pitiless warfare raged, during which time the natives were practically exterminated, and henceforth there was a lasting peace,

The Early Settlers.

MARYLAND.

In 1632, Charles I. granted George Calvert, Lord Baltimore, an Irish Peer, who had attempted to form a settlement in Avalon, all the land now included in Maryland and Delaware, at a yearly rental of two Indian Arrows, and one-fifth of all the gold and silver found there.

Lord Baltimore having died soon after, his son Cecil carried on the work. The land was named Maryland in honour of Henrietta Maria.

In 1633, Leonard Calvert, the brother of Cecil, Lord Baltimore, sailed from England with a body of Colonists consisting mainly of labouring men, only twenty gentlemen officials were on board.

They landed safely, sailed up the Potomac and founded St. Mary's, on land which they bought from the Indians.

Some of the land had been previously granted to the Virginian Companies and there were a few Virginian Settlers holding to their claims, notably among them was a man named Claybourne. This led to a long dispute and lawsuit which was ultimately settled in favour of Maryland.

Although the Civil War in England caused some confusion, the tide of prosperity flowed steadily on, meanwhile, refugees from the continent of Europe who suffered from religious intolerance, came over in great numbers.

In 1692, Maryland became a Royal Province.

The English nation was not the only one to foresee the great development of the New World, other nations were also attracted to its possibilities, and made strenuous efforts to secure for themselves footholds in the name of their Sovereignties.

The Spaniards settled in Florida, the French in Canada, and Holland along the Atlantic Sea Coast.

In 1609, Henry Hudson, an Englishman in the service of the Dutch East India Company, visited Newfoundland and the coast of New England and proceeded as far as Chesapeake Bay. When returning he explored Delaware Bay and sailed up the Hudson River which bears his name.

The reports which he brought back to his employer led to a considerable trade between Holland and America, with the result that a New Netherland Company was formed in 1615, which lasted three years,

The Early Settlers.

In 1623, the first permanent settlements were made- Albany on the Hudson, and New Amsterdam at its mouth on Manhattan Island, the site of New York.

In 1664, the Dutch were dispossessed by the English, and Charles II. made a present of the District to his brother the Duke of York, hence New Amsterdam became New York.

The Duke of York gave these Estates to two of his followers, Lords Berkeley and Cateret; the latter had defended Jersey against the Parliament, and in memory of that fact called his share New Jersey.

The State was peopled largely by Scotch Emigrants.

The English possession was confirmed by the Peace of Breda, 1665.

Six years later the Dutch again occupied New York, but only for a year. Hudson, on a subsequent voyage, discovered Hudson Bay, here his crew mutined and turned him adrift in a boat with some sick men, they were never heard of again.

NORTH CAROLINA AND SOUTH CAROLINA.

The First Settlement of the Carolinas was the result of a scheme, and more of an experiment.

Charles II., in 1663, made a large concession of land South of Virginia to eight gentlemen, among whom were Lords Clarendon and Shaftesbury. The latter, in conjunction with John Locke, the Philosopher, drew up a highly ornamental but far from practical constitution. It was an attempt to revive feudalism. There were to be three classes of Nobles, Palatines, Landgraves and Caciques. To these were assigned Territories of various extent on which the colonists were to settle, paying tribute to their feudal Superiors who in turn sent a share of it home to the Proprietors. But the Colonists ridiculed the idea— they settled lands for themselves, and these great men were left without subjects.

The Yoke of the Lords Proprietors was thus thrown off in 1719, and in 1729, the Carolinas became Crown Colonies.

NOTE.—The land was originally called Carolana, derived from Carolus the latin for Charles. Charlestown was founded in 1680.

The Early Settlers.

PENNSYLVANIA.

As the Colonization of New England arose out of the persecution of the Puritans, so was the founding of Pennsylvania the result of intolerance towards the Quakers.

This Sect was disliked more than any other, and with least cause.

They were the followers of George Fox; affected extreme simplicity in dress and speech, refused to remove their hats to any one, and though assailed by the bitterest words and deeds, nothing could shake their patience. They called themselves the Society of Friends. The term "Quaker" was singularly inappropriated since they quaked at nothing.

One of the few men of any position among them was William Penn, son of Admiral Penn, to whom Charles II. owed a considerable sum of money.

Instead of money, William Penn obtained a grant of land on the west side of the Delaware, and sent out his first emigrants in 1681.

Others soon followed, not only from England, but from the other States where religious tolerance was unknown.

The land was free, all forms of religion were permitted, and there was no other over-Lord but Penn himself.

Penn had no trouble with the Indians, and what he did was to make a treaty with them which was faithfully kept. This Colony was administered by the Penn family till the War of Independence.

The capital was Philadelphia, meaning "Brotherly Love."

GEORGIA.

This State was formed south of Carolina through the exertions of General Oglethorpe.

He being distressed at the dreadful state of the debtors in the English Prisons, and moved by pity for those Germans who were then suffering persecution for the sake of their religion in Salzburg, proposed to find a Colony to which these people might go and start life anew under more favourable circumstances.

George II. gave him a grant of land from Savannah to Florida, and the new Colony was called Georgia in honour of the King.

The Early Settlers

Parliament voted him £10,000, and in 1733, the first party of Colonists landed and founded Savannah.

Two years later 200 more came, and in 1738, in view of the dispute of Spain, Oglethorpe arrived with a regiment of 600 men.

In 1741, he repelled an attack made upon the Colony by the Spaniards.

The idea of the founder was that the settlement should be communistic, the members to be of good character, that no man should be richer than the other, that no slavery or sale of intoxicating liquors should be tolerated, and that the production of silk should be the staple industry. However, the colonists were anxious to become rich and clamoured for slaves and freedom from restrictions, and this had ultimately to be granted.

Dissensions arose, and a popular Preacher, John Wesley, had to leave for England where a greater work awaited him.

Charges were brought against Oglethorpe, and in 1743, he left the Colony and went back to England.

In 1752, the Charter was surrendered, and Georgia became a Crown Colony.

THE GROWTH OF THE COLONIES.

During the seventeenth century the whole of the seaboard from Maine to Savannah was occupied, and at the end of the century all the Colonies were making steady advance. The settlers were not English only, but French, Dutch, Germans, Swedes, Scotch, Irish and Welsh. The reasons for their emigration were as varied as their nationality. Some were free-settlers sent out by the various companies, some came from religious motives, and some because they had no choice, for it was recognised that prosperity came only from labour, that labourers were few, and that some means must be found of supplying the deficiency. Hence waifs and strays were sent out from England largely and made up for labour shortage. Negro slaves were imported from Africa in large numbers. These slaves were usally satisfied, especially where they found kindness shown towards them by their masters and families.

The wealth of the Colonies consisted of agricultural produce, especially tobacco, rice and corn.

The Early Settlers

POPULATION IN 1749.

An estimate of the number of inhabitants in 1749, including slaves, were 1,046,000.

New Hampshire	30,000
Massacheusettes	220,000
Rhode Island	35,000
Connecticut	100,000
New York	100,000
Jersey	60,000
Pennsylvania and Delaware	250,000
Maryland	85,000
Virginia	85,000
North Carolina	45,000
South Carolina	30,000
Georgia	6,000

CANADA.

The victory of Wolfe on the Plains of Abraham caused the cession to England of a vast tract of country, the boundaries of which were at that time unknown.

The term "Canada" was applied to the basin of the St. Lawrence River, and this district was then colonized by the French who regarded the English as their implacable enemies.

But there were no grounds for such fear. The proclamation when read by the English General showed that there would be equal rights to all. However, the French were far from being convinced that these promises would be carried out.

The English allowed the French civil laws to continue, while the English criminal law was introduced.

Indeed, they all settled down in content watching events. But it was not long before they found that they had acquired a greater freedom than they had formerly enjoyed. Hence the feeling of resentment passed away and was replaced by staunch loyalty to England.

In the meanwhile, the Indians happened to give the British some trouble, but at length were quieted down and remained loyal to England during the War of Independence.

The Early Settlers

GENERAL WOLFE.

General Wolfe—the hero of the War in America, the man whose energy and ability gave Canada to the British, was James Wolfe. His career had been so interesting that it deserves some detail mention.

In 1740, when only thirteen and a half years old, he had volunteered against the Spaniards; but not till he was nearly fifteen did he receive his Commission and went to fight on the Rhine.

At the age of seventeen he was a Captain, and his promotion was due entirely to his merit.

He assisted in crushing the rebellion of 1745, and fought at Culloden, and after another campaign against the French, returned to England at the age of twenty-one, already a Veteran.

In 1756, went as Brigadier-General in an expedition against the coast of France and his services then attracted the attention of Pitt. Two years later (1758) he went with General Amherst to attack Louisburg on Cape Breton Island. After a vigorous resistance the place was taken largely through Wolfe's energy. The next year (1759) Pitt determined to make a bold attack on Canada in three directions.

Wolfe, with 9,000 men, was to ascend the St. Lawrence. Amherst was to proceed by Lake Champlain and the River Richelieu, while the other force was to reduce the Forts on Lake Ontario and come down the St. Lawrence, and the united forces were then to take Quebec. As it happened, Wolfe was the only one to reach the rendezvous. Amherst was too slow and cautious.

On the 26th June, 1759, Wolfe's Fleet arrived before the Forts of Quebec and landed on the Isle of Orleans. On the North side of the River lay a French Army, 14,000 strong, in a strong position and rendered more so by earthworks and batteries.

To the West lay the Town itself, backed by the heights of Abraham which formed an apparently insurmountable obstacle in that direction.

The Early Settlers

Only three months remained before the coming of winter, when operations would be suspended.

The French were confident of success and did not delay operations.

On the very first night a fleet of Fireships came drifting towards the English Squadron, but the time was badly arranged, and the ships burned themselves out before the English line was reached, and a harmless display of fireworks was the sole result.

Wolfe commenced operations by taking Point Levis which overlooked the Town from the opposite side of the river, and establishing a battery there, by which much damage was done.

The first attack on the French position North of the river was made from the East and South, one body being told off to cross the Montgomery and turn the French flank, while the other attacked them in the front.

The English troops detailed for this frontal attack could not wait till the proper time, but made a premature attempt to scale the heights only to be driven back in utter confusion.

Wolfe fell ill, and for several days was on the point of death. When he recovered, he had conceived another and bolder plan.

Quebec was not to be taken from the East, winter was fast approaching, and Wolfe had determined never to return without success, to be exposed to the censure and reproach of an ignorant populace.

West of Quebec were the heights of Abraham, a Plateau whose sides sank precipitously to the river.

Montcalm felt sure that no attack could come that way, unless, as he said, the invaders had wings. Nevertheless, it was in this direction that Wolfe determined to strike. Under a heavy fire from his guns on the Southern bank, his ships dashed up stream, having on board 4,000 of his troops in readiness for the decisive moment. An opportunity presented itself—a fleet of provision boats was expected down the river by the French, and Wolfe embarked his men in the flat-bottom boats and dropped down the stream under the shadow of the over-hanging cliffs.

The Early Settlers

When challenged by Sentries, answers were given in French, and they were taken to be the expected provision boats. At last a little cove was reached from which a narrow path led to the summit.

The English landed in silence, clambered up the path, and in the morning the whole force of 4,500 men—British troops and Indian allies—were marching towards Quebec.

Montcalm, when he heard the news, could hardly believe it. He hurried what forces he could across the St. Charles River and boldly attacked.

The English reserved their fire until the French were within forty yards, and then fired a volley which, by its terrible effect, practically won the battle.

The French line stagggered, and Wolfe gave the order to advance, and this movement was carried out with such determination that the French were swept away.

The battle was won, but the gallant English Commander was killed, also his opponent, Montcalm.

A monument has since been erected in honour of both.

Though a small battle, it decided once and for all that the Anglo-Saxon race was to rule in North America, and the dream of Empire by the French was rendered impossible.

Quebec surrendered at once, and was occupied by the English who wintered there.

The next spring the French came down from Montreal and the English, sallying forth, were defeated with the loss of 1,000 men. But when, three weeks later, English ships sailed up the river with reinforcements and supplies, the position was changed.

Advance was made to Montreal, and the English, with a force 17,000 strong, demanded the surrender of Montreal. After a little hesitation the place capitulated on September 8th, 1760, and French power in Canada was at an end. In 1763, the treaty of Paris finally gave Canada, Nova Scotia and Cape Breton to the British.

A BRIEF ACCOUNT

of the

AMERICAN REVOLUTION.

In the year 1770, the great controversy between American Colonists and England began to arouse serious attention at home; causing, at the same time, great anxiety on both sides of the Atlantic. Moral and intellectual forces that had been previously dormant were called into activity, while indications of a change of thought and feeling were seen in the number of speeches that were delivered and pamphlets that were issued, dealing with the burning question of the hour.

"TAXATION WITHOUT REPRESENTATION."

Hundreds of meetings were held in the principal towns of America, to protest against the proposed taxation. This strife went on for ten years, and finally, transmuted into actual warfare.

The Early Settlers.

THE BOSTON TEA PARTY.

In the same year the Townshend Acts had been repealed, with the exception of a small tax on tea. George III. insisted that the Tea Tax be kept as a proof of his power to tax the Colonies, and as an opening wedge for further taxation. The Colonists saw through this ruse, and refused to buy the tea. Everyone gave up tea drinking, and steps were taken to prevent the stuff being landed in America. In Philadelphia, New York, Charleston and Anapolis the tea was either turned back to England or destroyed. In Charleston the tea was seized and stored in damp cellars, where it soon spoiled. In Anapolis the ship "Peggy Stuart" was burned in broad daylight.

In 1773, several ships of the British East India Company arrived in Boston with cargoes of tea. The citizens asked Governor Hutchinson to order them to leave the port, Hutchinson declined; whereupon the people decided to settle the matter themselves, and secretly met in an old meeting house to make their plans. On the night of December the 16th, 1773, a band of Provincials, dressed as Indians, and acting under the direction of Samuel Adams, boarded the Tea Ship, overpowered the crew, and emptied the tea chests into Boston harbour. This bold stroke became famous as the "Boston Tea Party."

THE INTOLERABLE ACTS.

When the startling news of the "Boston Tea Party" reached England the angry King and Parliament took steps to punish Boston, which they looked upon as a hot-bed of rebellion. As a result, four Acts intended to force the Americans into submission were proposed and, although disapproved by William Pitt (Lord Chancellor) and Edward Burke, were passed in March, 1774.

The Acts were as follows:—

(a) The Boston Port Bill, which closed the Port to commerce until the townspeople had paid for the destroyed tea.

The Early Settlers.

(b) The Regulating Act, which took away all liberal features from the Massachusetts Charter.

(c) The Administration of Justice Act, which provided for the quartering of troops and trial in England for offenders.

(d) The Quebec Act, extended the boundaries of that Province to prevent Americans settling in the West.

The Colonies looked upon these Acts, which they called the Intolerable Acts, as the last straw, and found themselves faced by a choice of abject submission or war. The blow to Boston paralized the commerce of New England, and was felt in the other Colonies. In May, 1774, four regiments of British regulars were sent to Boston. General Gage succeeded Hutchinson as Governor, and the town was put under Martial Law. The Blockade of Boston reduced the inhabitants to dire straits, and had it not been for the relief, smuggled into the town past the British outposts, from the surrounding country, many might have starved.

The spirit of the Boston people spread rapidly, and in a short time resistance to British oppression was preached by earnest patriots.

The Whigs grew in power, and while, as yet there was no desire to sever themselves from Great Britain, they were determined to stand for their rights as British subjects.

The first armed rising occurred in 1771, when the North Carolinians took up arms against the despotic Governor Tyron. In the Battle of Alamance the Colonials were defeated, and Tyron hanged seven patriots as "rebels."

In 1772, the revenue cutter "Gaspee," while in pursuit of an American schooner, ran aground on the Rhode Island shore. The British skipper was a noted bully, and, in revenge, a party of Colonials burned the vessel. Later the Chief Justice, a patriot, refused to give the offenders up to the British for trial in England.

That same year the King tried to gain complete control of the Colonial public officials by putting them in the pay of the Crown. To offset this, Samuel Adams, at a meeting in Faniel Hall, proposed a committee of correspondence to guard the interests of the Americans; like committees were appointed in other Colonies.

The Early Settlers

THE WAR SPIRIT OF THE COLONIES.

The first constituted Congress had the result of uniting various Colonies for concerted action, and a wave of patriotic feeling swept the land. Many Whigs, who had been opposed to separating from England, now changed their views and urged complete Independence. Meanwhile, Pitt and Burke, friends of the Colonies, urged the British Parliament to adopt conciliatory means towards the Americans.

Lord North, the Prime Minister, offered to exempt any Colony that would raise its quota, but this plan was a failure.

On February the 26th, 1775, General Gage sent a force of Red Coats to seize some cannon which he heard the Provincials had stored at Salem; but finding they were blocked by "Minutemen," under Colonel Pickering, the British retired without bloodshed.

Infused by the war spirit,
Patrick Henry exclaimed:—
" Why stand we here idle?
Is peace so sweet as to be
Purchased at the price of Chains
And slavery? . . . I know not
What course others may take, but give
Me Liberty or Death! "

In March, 1775, Patrick Henry roused the Virginia Burgesses to a high pitch of enthusiasm by a fiery speech, in which he declared that the hour had come for Colonials to rally and fight for freedom. His words " Liberty or Death " became the slogan of the Virginia riflemen.

SULLIVAN SEIZES FORT WILLIAM AND MARY.

John Sullivan was the captain of a company of New Hampshire " Minute-men," who were training in Durham to bear arms in defence of the Colonies. In December, 1774, a courier brought word that two British regiments were on their way to Portsmouth, to occupy Fort William and Mary.

Sullivan determined at once to take the Fort, and seize the powder store there, before the coming of the reinforcements. That night he set out in a small sail boat,

The Early Settlers

with a handful of Patriots. Advancing stealthily, the little band of "Minute-men" surprised the astonished garrison, who surrendered without resistance.

Searching the Fort, the Provincials found one hundred kegs of powder and a quantity of muskets. The munitions captured at Fort William and Mary were taken to Durham, and hidden in the Church. Later they were sent to the Army of General Washington. Sullivan afterwards became a Major-General.

PAUL REVERE'S FURIOUS RIDE.

On the night of April the 18th, 1775, General Gage secretly despatched a force of 800 Red Coats from Boston to march to the neighbouring towns of Lexington and Concord to capture the powder stored there by the Patriots. Major Pitcairn also bore a warrant for the arrest of the "Rebels" Handcock and Adams. Learning of Gage's plans, and informed of the departure of the British by signal light from the belfry of old North Church, Paul Revere, Courier of the Committee of Safety, who was waiting on the Charleston shore, galloped off to warn the "Minute-men." Riding furiously through the night he roused the Colonial Militia with a cry "To Arms! The British are coming!" Samuel Adams and John Handcock were located at Concord, and fled across the field to make their escape. Awake to the fact that the time had come to strike the blow for freedom, the "Minute-men" sprang to arms and ran to rally around their leader to oppose the advancing British.

CONCORD AND LEXINGTON.

At dawn, April 19th, 1775, when the Red Coats reached Lexington they found their way barred by a line of Provincial Militia, drawn up on the Common, under Captain Parker. Riding to the front of his men, Major Pitcairn, the British Commander, called to the Americans, "Disperse! Ye Rebels, Disperse!"

The British numbered 800, the "Minute-men" 70. When the "Minute-men" failed to retire the Red Coats fired a volley into the midst of them, seven Patriots fell. Captain Parker then ordered his men to give way, firing a

The Early Settlers

ragged answering volley as they left the field. The British marched on Concord, where they destroyed some munitions. By this time the "Minute-men" had gathered from the countryside like a swarm of angry bees. The 70 Provincials increased to 400, and met the Red Coats at Concord Bridge. Here the first shot was fired, the British Regulars were repulsed, and began a hasty retreat to Boston. The retreating Red Coats suffered heavy losses. Every fence, post, rock and tree sheltered a Colonial marksman, and many a British soldier fell on the road. The fleeing force reached Boston with a loss of nearly 300 men.

THE SIEGE OF BOSTON.

Pressing the advantage gained by the retreat of the British from Concord and Lexington, the New England "Minute-men," under the leadership of John Stark, Israel Putman, Arnold and Green, gathered in great numbers and laid seige to Boston. Speedy despatch riders carried reports of the fighting to the other Colonies, and everywhere the news was received with great patriotic demonstrations, which set on foot immediate preparations for the coming struggle.

When the tidings of War reached Mecklenburg, North Carolina, the Patriots there deposed all civil and military officials, and formed a Provisional Government "subject to any laws that might be passed by the Continental Congress."

Meanwhile a stream of Provincial troops from every New England Colony kept flowing into Cambridge, and before long General Gage, with 4.000 Red Coats, found himself trapped in Boston, being hemmed in by a Colonial army of 15,000.

SECOND CONGRESS.

On May 10th, 1775 (the day on which Ethan Allan captured Ticonderoga), the second Continental Congress met in Philadelphia. This body drew up a resolution showing why the Colonies must fight. They sent a last petition to the King and authorised a Continental army, which was to be commanded by Washington.

The Early Settlers

That same month General Gage was reinforced by the arrival of 6,000 British Regulars, under General Howe and General Clinton.

In June the King issued a proclamation, warning that all Rebels would be hanged, and offering pardon to all who would submit to the Crown.

In Cambridge the work of developing the raw Militia into an army of well drilled and disciplined troops went on. Marksmen practiced at a target on which was painted a rude likeness of General Gage, which gave rise to the expression, "Now, General Gage, look out for your nose."

General Gage, now confident that he had a force at his command large enough to cope with the "Rebel" army, decided to seize the hills back of Charleston, across the bay, which, if occupied by the Americans, would menace the town of Boston. Knowing that the British intended to seize the heights behind Charleston, the American leaders planned to make the first move, and fortified Bunker Hill themselves.

On the night of April 16th, Colonel Prescott was sent with one thousand two hundred men to occupy the hill, and be prepared to defend it. Under cover of the darkness, Prescott's men laboured all night, throwing up a low rampart of earth across the top of the hill, and before morning the slight fortification was completed.

On the morning General Gage, looking through his spy-glasses, was astonished to see the earthworks on the hill, and the form of Colonel Prescott walking about on the crest. When he was told that Prescott would fight as long "as a drop of blood is left in his veins," Gage decided to take the hill by assault.

Three thousand Red Coats, under the command of General Howe, were sent over to Charleston with orders to take the hills that lay beyond the town, at all costs. Their advance was guarded by the fire of the British warships in the harbour.

THE BATTLE OF BUNKER HILL.

On April 17th, at noon, Lord Howe's Red Coats formed in line of battle and advanced steadily toward the crest of the hill. The Americans awaited their movements calmly,

The Early Settlers

holding their fire until the enemy came within easy range. With beating drums and shining bayonets the British swept up towards the top to meet a withering volley which drove them back with terrible losses.

At the bottom of the hill the Red Coats formed and charged again; only to be repulsed with more casualties. When the third charge reached the top the Americans had completely exhausted their supply of ammunition, and the British took the position at the point of the bayonet. The Americans were forced to retreat with a loss of four hundred and forty men, the British one thousand. This victory appears to have been very dearly bought by the British Regulars.

GEORGE WASHINGTON AS COMMANDER IN CHIEF OF THE CONTINENTAL ARMY.

In July, 1775, George Washington arrived at Cambridge to assume his duties as Commander in Chief of the Continental Army, and was welcomed by the American leaders. He accepts commission on the condition that he be allowed to serve without pay, other than his expenses. Taking immediate command of the forces, his army soon became sufficiently trained and disciplined to face the British on the battlefield.

MONTGOMERY'S EXPEDITION.

In the Fall of 1775 word was brought to Washington at Cambridge that General Carleton, commanding the British troops in Canada, was preparing to invade New York, with the aid of the Tories and the Iroquois Indian tribes.

Washington at once despatched an expedition to block the British advance. The Continental Force was to have been led by General Philip Schuyler, but due to his illness the command was given to General Montgomery, a young but able soldier. Starting northward from Fort Ticonderoga, Montgomery, by a series of brilliant strokes, captured Forts Chambly, St. John, and Montreal. Great quantities of powder and arms were taken in these engagements.

When the news of Montgomery's success reached Cambridge there was much rejoicing in the Patriot army, while the added supply of gunpowder put the Americans on a firmer footing.

The Early Settlers.

BOSTON EVACUATED BY THE BRITISH.

In March, 1776, Washington decided on a bold stroke—confident that he now had enough powder and cannon. His plan was to seize and fortify Dorchester Heights, which lay to the South of Boston. By a secret night march the Americans reached the hill, dug shallow earthworks, and had their guns in position before dawn.

In the morning the British found the town and the fleet at the mercy of the Continental artillery. Realizing that he was caught in a trap, and knowing that it would be folly to storm the heights, General Howe evacuated Boston, and set sail for Halifax, Nova Scotia, with his troops and eleven hundred Tories, who were afraid to be left behind.

On March 18th, 1776, General Washington rode into Boston at the head of his victorious soldiers. Boston has ever since been free of the British.

THE BRITISH ATTACK THE CAROLINAS.

Before Howe evacuated Boston he sent a British fleet southward to co-operate with the Tories of the region in conquering North Carolina. The Tories rallied, and under Donald McDonald set out, with one thousand six hundred strong, to join General Clinton at Wilmington. Learning of this move, a thousand North Carolina patriots marched to head them off. The two forces met at Moore's Creek, and in a bloody battle the Loyalists were cut to pieces and scattered.

Clinton changed his plans, and sailing to Charlestown, South Carolina, attacked the defences on Sullivan's Island in the harbour. The shells of the British warships made but little impression on the Palmetto bags of the Fort; While the fire of Colonel Moultrie and his men did so much damage that the Red Coats were driven off.

The outstanding act of heroism at the defence of Fort Moultrie was that of Sergeant Jasper, who, when the Fort's colours were shot down, rescued the flag through a galling fire from the British and planted it on the ramparts, amid the cheers of his comrades.

The Early Settlers

The Declaration of Independence.

Now that the fight for Colonial rights was in progress the people of the Colonies became convinced that the aim of the war should be a complete separation from England.

In January, 1776, Thomas Payne published a pamphlet called " Common Sense," which voiced the sentiments of all Americans and paved the way for the " Declaration of Independence."

On June 7th, 1776, Richard Henry Lee, of Virginia, in a speech before the Continentals Congress, proposed that the American Colonies should declare themselves a free and independent nation. Many members urged its immediate adoption, and a committee led by Thomas Jefferson was appointed to draw up a Declaration of Independence. Jefferson did most of the work of preparing this document.

On July 2nd, 1776, Congress voted in favour of the " Declaration," and on July 4th it was formally adopted, and signed by Hanocck, the President of the Congress. It was not signed by all the members of Congress until August 2nd, when sixty-six signatures, representing the thirteen Colonies, were obtained.

SYNOPSIS OF THE DECLARATION.

" When in the course of human events it becomes necessary for our people to dissolve the political bonds which have connected them with one another, and to assume among the Powers of the Earth, the separate and equal stations to which the laws of nature, and of

The Early Settlers.

nature's God entitles them; a decent respect to the opinions of mankind requires that they should declare the causes which impel them to the separation."
(Then follows a list of the King's Tyrannical Acts).

The fruitless appeals which had been made to the people of Great Britain are also recounted, but, "they too," concludes this declaration, " have been deaf to the voice of justice and of consanguinity. We must, therefore, acquiesce in the necessity which denounces our separation and hold them as we hold the rest of mankind, enemies of war, in peace friends," and continues: " We therefore, the representatives of the United States of America, in General Congress assembled, appealing to the Supreme Judge for the rectitude of our intentions, do, in the name, and by the authority of the good people of these Colonies, solemnly publish and declare that these United Colonies are, and of right ought to be, Free and Independent States; that they are absolved from all allegiance to the British Crown, and that all political connection between them and the State of Great Britain is, and ought to be, totally dissolved; and that as Free and Independent States, they have full power to levy war, conclude peace, contract alliances, establish commerce, and do all other acts and things which Independent States may of right do. And for the support of this declaration, with a firm reliance on the protection of Divine Providence, we mutually pledge to each other our lives, our fortunes, and our sacred honour."

RECEPTION OF THE DECLARATION.

The Couriers from Congress, hearing the news, found Washington with his army in New York, where he had moved soon after the British evacuation of Boston.

On July 9th, 1776, the "Declaration" was read to all the troops, who now became the National Army. In New York that night a band of patriots gathered in Bowling Green and pulled down a lead statue of King George, which they melted into bullets for the rifles of General Washington's army.

Everywhere in all the Colonies the joyful news of the Declaration was greeted with great patriotic demonstrations. Huge bonfires, ringing of bells, and the roar of cannon; all felt vastly proud of the new nation.

The Early Settlers.

The New York Campaign.

Lord Howe, after deserting Boston, stayed in Halifax only long enough to get supplies and reinforcements and then sailed South to attack New York, the centre of the American Colonies. The British fleet appeared off Sandy Hook in June, 1776. Early in August Howe had landed 32,000 Red Coats on Station Island, which he intended to use as a base of operations. Here the British Commander was greeted by many Tories, including Governor Tyron, who had fled from New York.

Washington, with his army, had marched from New England to defend the city, and immediately set to work strengthening the fortifications at Paulos Hook, Jersey City, and on Governor's Island. He also built Forts Lee and Washington to command the Hudson above New York.

General Nathaniel Green, with 7,000 men, was sent to fortify Flatbush and Jamaica, and block a possible British advance on New York by way of Long Island.

On August 26th, 1776, General Howe landed a mighty force on Long Island, determined to crush the small American army opposing his advance on New York.

On the 27th, General Howe ordered his troops to attack and sent them forward in three columns. In the absence of General Green, who was ill with fever, the patriots were led by Israel Putman, a brave soldier, but not well enough trained to cope with the veteran General Howe.

On the night of August 26th, the attacking column of the British marched around the left wing of the Americans,

The Early Settlers

and in the morning attacked them from the rear, driving them to Brooklyn with a loss of one thousand five hundred men.

The army of Putman was now in a position that if the British fleet sailed up into the East River the Americans would be caught in a hopeless trap on Long Island. Washington, however, proved himself to be master of the situation. In the early morning of August 29th, under cover of a dense fog, he ferried the troops across the river to safety, to the disappointment of Howe, who had figured to force the surrender of Putman.

THE BRITISH IN NEW YORK.

After the defeat of the Americans at the Battle of Long Island, Washington realising he could not hold New York against the British, retreated from the city, and assembled his forces at Harlem, on the upper Manhattan Island.

Lord Howe, the British Commander, occupied New York in September, 1776. In General Howe's army were many Hessians, German soldiers from Hesse, Anhalt and Brunswick, whom King George had hired at so much a head to fight the Colonists. These mercenaries made themselves particularly obnoxious to the Americans, who spoke of them as the " Dutch Butchers."

Many Americans had been captured by the British in the fighting on Long Island, and these were penned up like wild beasts in the sugar houses of New York, or confined on hulks lying in the Hudson River. Most of these unfortunates died, due to their frightful conditions and lack of nourishing food.

While the American prisoners were starving, and Washington playing a waiting game, the British made merry in New York. The wealthy Tories returned, and there was a continual round of balls and banquets in honour of Lord Howe and the King's officers.

NATHAN HALE.

Washington, eager to know the disposition and strength of the British in New York, asked for a volunteer who would go secretly into the city and get this information for him.

The Early Settlers

Nathan Hale, a young captain from Connecticut, offered himself for this hazardous task; in the disguise of a schoolmaster, he went boldly into New York, and wandered about making sketches of the fortifications, and jotting down notes as to the number of British troops that he saw. Having secured the needed information, Hale was about to return when he was recognised by a Tory and arrested.

Taken to General Howe's headquarters in the Beekman Mansion, he admitted his name, rank and mission, and was delivered to the Provost to be hanged as a spy. The next morning, September, 22nd, 1776, the young patriot was led out to be hanged, the cruel Provost refusing to allow him to send a last message to his mother. Hale met his death bravely, his last words being "I only regret I have but one life to lose for my country."

FIGHTING AROUND NEW YORK.

After a brief period of inactivity, fighting was resumed, and in the early fall of 1776 Lord Howe, by force of numbers, had driven north of White Plains. A British attempt to surround the patriot army was defeated by Colonel Glover, with seven hundred men at Pell's Point, of the four thousand Red Coats in the attack, eight hundred were killed and wounded.

General Howe then attacked along the American front, and at the Battle of White Plains, on October 2nd, Washington was obliged to retreat northward to North Castle. Later, hearing that the British planned to invade New Jersey, Washington crossed the Hudson with half his army, leaving General Lee with seven thousand men at North Castle. Having secured the plans of Fort Washington, which was defended by two thousand six hundred men, Howe made a surprise attack upon that on November 16th, 1776. Overwhelmed by the British, the Fort fell, and most of the garrison were slaughtered by the bayonets of the brutal Hessians.

General Washington, with no course left but to retreat, ordered General Green to abandon Fort Lee on the west bank of the Hudson, and retire to Hackenback. He also sent word to General Lee to join him in New Jersey, but that treacherous officer purposely refused to obey.

The Early Settlers

WASHINGTON RETREATS ACROSS NEW JERSEY.

Washington began his memorable retreat through New Jersey on November 21st, 1776. He was hotly pursued by five thousand Red Coats under Cornwallis, but kept out of reach by destroying all bridges, and by forced marches. The American retreat soon became a race for the Delaware River, the British being so close on their heels that while they were leaving a town the British were entering it on the other side. As Washington retreated southward his army gradually grew smaller by desertions. When he reached New Brunswick three thousand Militiamen, whose terms of enlistment had expired, left for their homes. With only three thousand soldiers left, Washington appealed to Congress for a standing army.

Early in December, 1776, Washington's weary troops got beyond the Delaware and were safe from pursuit. Shortly after Washington re-crossed the Delaware and occupied the town. Here he was confronted by the British, who had concentrated in force under the command of Lord Cornwallis. With superior numbers of the enemy before them, and the frozen river at their backs, the case of the Americans seemed hopeless.

On the night of January 2nd, 1777, Cornwallis looked towards the American lines from his outpost, and seeing the glow of the camp fires felt sure he had Washington at his mercy. "In the morning," he told his officers, "we shall at last bag the old fox." Cornwallis did not know that the fires he saw were being kept burning by a mere handful of men to deceive him, while, at that very moment, the "Old Fox" with his main body of his army was making a wide detour of the British lines to surprise their supply base at Princeton.

Early in the morning of January 3rd the Americans surprised and routed a strong British force at Princeton, much to the astonishment of Cornwallis, who was too far away to aid his fleeing rearguard.

OPENING EVENTS OF 1777.

With the coming of 1777 Lord Germain, the British Colonial Secretary, planned a great campaign for the conquest of the Hudson Valley. His idea was to cut off the Northern Colonies from the Middle and Southern States,

The Early Settlers

The Plan:—
(1) An army under General Burgoyne was to start from Canada and invade New York by Lake Champlain.
(2) An expedition led by General St. Ledger was to land at Oswego, and march on Fort Stanwix and conquer the Mohawk Valley.
(3) A division of Lord Howe's army was to capture the American forts on the Hudson and proceed northward. Albany was to be the final objective of each of these forces.

Washington was in great need of cash with which to increase his army, as the worthless Continental paper money was no inducement to recruits.

On New Year's Day, 1777, Robert Morris, of Philadelphia, went from house to house asking patriotic citizens for coin, and in this manner raised fifty thousand dollars in silver for Washington's army.

In January, 1777, the first flag of the United States was made by Mistress Betsy Ross in Philadelphia and adopted in June. It consisted of thirteen white and red stripes. The first flag of this design was unfurled at the siege of Fort Stanwix, when it was flown as the flag of the nation. July, 1777.

THE BATTLE OF ORISKANY.

Following the British plan of campaign General St. Ledger marched from Oswego with a large force of Red Coats and Iroquois Indians, and laid siege to Fort Stanwix on the upper Mohawk River. General Herkimer, speeding with eight hundred American Militia to the relief of the fort, walked into an ambush laid for him by St. Ledger at Oriskany on August 6th, 1777. When Herkimer opened fire upon the Americans the latter leaped into the bushes and, fighting hand to hand, inflicted heavy losses upon the Tories and Indians.

General Herkimer fell with a severe wound, but with great courage, caused his men to prop him up behind a tree, and from that position calmly gave orders to his soldiers, who drove the enemy from the field. While the battle raged at Oriskany, the garrison of Fort Stanwix made an audaci-

The Early Settlers.

ous raid on St. Ledger's camp, and got several back within the walls with several British flags and enough provisions to last them a long time.

Soon after the battle of Oriskany, Benedict Arnold was on his way with two thousand men of Schuyler's army to raise the siege of Fort Stanwix. The American garrison, cheered by the recent victory, was still holding out bravely against St. Ledger and his Red Coats. As he neared the fort, Arnold decided to use a trick to deceive the British as to the size of his forces. Calling before him Tory lads who had been taken prisoners, Arnold promised to free them if one would warn the British that a vast American army was coming to attack them. The ruse succeeded perfectly. Rushing into the British camp, with his coat torn by bullets, the Tory boy announced that the Americans were coming, " as many of them as the leaves on the trees." At this startling news the Tories and Indians fled in a panic, and the next day St. Ledger began his retreat to Canada. Fort Stanwix was saved, and Arnold returned amidst the cheers of the garrison. With St. Ledger disposed of, Burgoyne, alone, was left to be dealt with.

THE BATTLE OF BEMIS HEIGHTS.

At Fort Edward, Burgoyne's Indians became disgruntled because he would not permit them to raid the settlement, and deserted. Eager to reach Albany, Burgoyne now planned to attack Schuyler at Bemis Heights.

At this time, Schuyler, who had proved to be an able leader, was replaced by Major-General Gates, a poor soldier, but a clever politician, who stood high in favour of Congress. The later success of the campaign was due to the ability of Generals Arnold, Morgan and Lincoln.

Deserted by his Indian Allies and facing American forces, which daily grew in numbers, Burgoyne launched an attack on September 19th, in a desperate attempt to drive off the patriot army and reached Albany. Advancing on Bemis Heights, Burgoyne'e troops were met by the Americans at Freeman's Farm, near Stillwater, and a fierce struggle took place, in which the British lost five hundred men. Neither side won, but the advance of the British was blocked.

The Early Settlers

The Turning Point of the War.

On October 7th, 1777, Burgoyne sent his troops' right wing against Gates' army, and a second desperate battle was fought at Freeman's Farm. This time the British were beaten, more than six hundred Red Coats falling before the deadly fire of Morgan's riflemen. Benedict Arnold led the troops in the last charge, and was badly wounded in the leg. If Burgoyne had fled swiftly he could have reached Fort George in safety. Instead, he fell back slowly to Saratoga, where the Americans speedily closed around him. A week later, seeing that it was useless to resist, he sent out an officer with a white flag to ask terms of surrender.

General Burgoyne capitulated at Saratoga on October 17th, 1777, and his six thousand soldiers became prisoners of war. After the capitulation Burgoyne expressed a desire to be introduced to General Gates. They crossed the Fishkill, and proceeded to headquarters on horseback; General Burgoyne in front, with his Adjutant General and two Aide-de-Camps behind him. Then followed Major-General Phillips, the Baron Riedessel· and the other general officers, and their suites, according to rank.

General Gates being advised of Burgoyne's approach. met him at the head of the American camp. Burgoyne. in a rich Royal uniform, and Gates, in a plain blue frock, approached; when nearly within a sword's length, reined up and halted. Adjutant-General Wilkinson then formally announced the name of the gentleman, whereupon General Burgoyne, raising his hat, most gracefully said, " The

The Early Settlers.

fortune of war, General Gates, has made me your prisoner." "I shall always be ready to bear testimony," promptly replied the conqueror, with a courtly salute, "that it has not been through any fault of your Excellency."

Major-General Phillips then advanced, and he and General Gates saluted and shook hands with the familiarity of old acquaintances. The Baron Riedessel and other officers were introduced in their turn. General Gates, with great delicacy, consented to an arrangement by which the American soldiery were not to be present when the British army underwent the shame and humiliation of piling their arms.

The trophies which were gained by this great victory, besides prisoners, were a train of brass artillery, immensely valuable, consisting of forty-two pieces of brass cannon, besides seven thousand muskets, with seventy-two thousand cartridges, and an ample supply of shot, shells, and clothing for seven thousand men, with a large number of tents, and other military stores. The American army numbered three times that of the enemy.

Throughout America the joy which this victory produced was unbounded. Indeed, the contest between England and the Colonies was believed to be substantially decided. At any rate the great victory had three important results:—

(1) It marked the complete failure of the British plans to conquer New York State.
(2) It won the recognition and aid from France, the old enemy of England.
(3) It gave new hope to the soldiers of the Continental army.

EARLY EVENTS OF 1778.

Since the war had taken a definite shape in favour of the Americans, Benjamin Franklin was sent to plead the cause of the Colonials at the French Court. France was asked to aid them in their war against England. Influenced by Burgoyne's defeat, France made an alliance with America early in 1778, and promised to send ships and men to help her. Foreign officers offered their services to Washington; foremost of these was the Marquis De Lafayette, a young

The Early Settlers.

French noble, who came over at his own expense. He became a Major-General, and served gallantly through the war. Washington and his army had just passed a winter of untold privation and suffering at Valley Forge, near Philadelphia. Out of eight thousand soldiers, "three thousand were barefoot, and otherwise naked," and often the army was at the point of starvation.

In March, 1778, England, alarmed by the French Treaty, tried to make peace with the Colonies by offering to grant all their demands except complete Independence, but the Americans desired liberty more than peace, and consequently the British peace plan failed.

TORY AND INDIAN RAIDS.

In the summer and fall of 1778 the people of the Colonies were stricken with horror by a series of bloody raids by the Iroquois Indians against Western Pennsylvania and New York. These raids were directed by Tory officers as ruthless as the savages under their command.

In July Colonel Butler, with a band of Tories and Senecas, defeated a force of Americans near Wilkesbarre, Pennsylvania, and then went through the Wyoming Valley, plundering and burning. Women and children were shot or tomahawked, and hundreds left homeless.

In November a band of renegades inflicted death and devastation upon Cherry Valley, in New York. Here another massacre occurred. It became known that the British Governor of the North West was paying the Indians for American scalps, and this practise only added to the frightfulness of the war.

An American army, under General Sullivan, was sent the following year, 1779, to punish the Indians. They whipped the Senecas, and drove them west to Niagara with their chief, Joseph Grant.

EXPEDITION OF GEORGE CLARK.

The British controlled the North-West territory by forts at Kaskaskia, Cahokia and Vincennes. These posts were held by Frenchmen, employed by Englishmen, under the direction of Hamilton, the British Governor at Detroit.

The Early Settlers

George Clark, a Virginian, undertook to conquer this region for America. Receiving a Lieutenant-Colonel's commission from Governor Patrick Henry, of Virginia, Clark set out secretly in May, 1778, with a small body of wood-rangers to take Kaskaskia. This little expedition travelled down the Ohio River, nearly a thousand miles, and landed in Illinois.

On July 5th, 1778, Kaskaskia was taken by surprise, and without a shot. The garrison, not expecting an attack, was giving a dance when Clark's riflemen entered the fort. Clark stationed his men outside and went in alone to announce the capture of the post. The Frenchmen were startled at Clark's sudden appearance. "Keep on with your merriment; but remember that you now dance under Virginia, not Great Britain," said Clark. "Further, France is now our ally." Whereupon, they took the oath of allegiance to America and hoisted the stars and stripes.

THE FIRST AMERICAN NAVY.

Late in 1775 Congress authorized the building of thirteen warships, and during the war forty-three more were constructed. Twenty guns was the average number carried by these vessels. The first Continental Navy did but little damage to the British in the Revolution. Not having a navy strong enough to meet the British in battle, the Americans turned to privateering, and preyed on English merchant vessels at sea and on the coast of Europe.

The first American naval officer was Paul Jones, a Scotchman, whose brother had settled in Virginia. He was commissioned a lieutenant in the Navy in December, 1775, and raised the first flag on an American man-of-war, called "The Alfred," the flagship, in 1777. The flag was of yellow silk, bearing the figure of a pine tree and the significant device of a rattlesnake in a field of thirteen stripes with the ominous legend, "Don't tread on me!"

AN ACCOUNT OF A CLASH BETWEEN PAUL JONES AND A FEW ENGLISH SHIPS.

On August 14th, 1779, Jones sailed out from a French port in command of a small squadron, consisting of the

The Early Settlers

"Bon Homme," "The Alliance," "The Pallas," "Cerf," and "The Vengeance," about noon, on the 23rd September, 1779, he met a fleet of forty sails off the coast of Yorkshire. The sails in sight were English merchantmen, under convoy of two warships, the "Serapis" and "Scarborough," and as soon as they saw themselves pursued by Paul Jones they ran inshore, while the convoys, the "Serapis" and "Scarborough," bore off from the land and prepared for an engagement.

The "Bon Homme" set every stitch of sail, but did not come into fighting position until seven o'clock in the evening, at which time darkness had set in, but the moon shone forth with serene brightness and beautiful weather. When within pistol shot the "Serapis" hailed "What ship is that?"; the answer from Paul Jones "I can't hear you." The second hail was a thundering broadside from the "Bon Homme"—a signal that meant the roar of the "British Lion."

Captain Cottinean, of the "Pallas," engaged the "Scar-borough," and took her after an hour's engagement, while the "Bon Homme" engaged the "Serapis." In the earlier part of the action the superior sailing qualities of the "Serapis" enabled her to take several advantageous positions, which the old craft of Paul Jones did not enable him to prevent.

The bowsprit of the "Serapis" sweeping over the "Bon Homme's" lashed the vessels together. They lay yard-arm to yard-arm, the muzzles of both ships actually touching. At the termination of the action both ships were damaged, and both fought well, and from all accounts the prize fell to Paul Jones.

THE SOUTHERN CAMPAIGN WEAKENING.

The failure of the British to win the fight at Cowpens caused Cornwallis to start in pursuit of Morgan's men, hoping to catch them before they joined Green's forces; but being held back by the swollen torrents of the rivers Green was able to unite with Morgan and continued their retreat northward.

On February 14th, 1781, Green crossed the Dan River into Virginia, and was then safe from pursuit. Two days

The Early Settlers

later Cornwallis and his weary men reached the Dan, but finding it unfavourable fell back to Guilford Court House. Although most of his troops were Militia recruits, Green boldly re-crossed the Dan, and in March, 1781, offered battle to Cornwallis, who, with two thousand two hundred British regulars, was at Guilford Court House, North Carolina.

In the excitement of their first battle over one thousand of Green's untrained Militia men fled, while the remainder of his soldiers stood their ground, and bravely faced the charge of Cornwallis' seasoned veterans. After a desperate struggle the Americans withdrew in good order before the attack of the Red Coats and were forced to abandon their artillery to the enemy. In this battle the Americans lost two hundred and sixty-one men, the British five hundred and thirty-two. In spite of having won the day, Cornwallis had sustained such heavy losses that he retreated at once to the coast, where a supply fleet was awaiting him at Wilmington.

Green failed to win a single victory over the British in the South, but his good Generalship is shown in the way he exhuasted and tricked the enemy. Worn out by their efforts to crush Green, the British evacuated many of their inland posts and soon the Carolinas were again in American hands.

Disgusted in his failure in the Carolinas, General Cornwallis marched north into Virginia, reaching Petersburg on May 20th, 1781. During May and June Cornwallis sent out a thousand troops mounted on Virginia racehorses to plunder the countryside. These raiders seized or destroyed about 15,000,000 dollars worth of property. Cornwallis was opposed in Virginia by General Lafayette with a small American force, who kept out of reach and harassed the British at every turn.

Washington, then at West Point, planned to attack Clinton at New York with the aid of a French fleet which was coming from the West Indies, under the command of Admiral De Grasse. Hearing that De Grasse was heading for Chesapeake Bay, Washington suddenly changed his plans, and decided to strike at Cornwallis in Virginia. To deceive Clinton as to his real intentions Washington summoned General Rochambeau, with five thousand French troops from Newport, to feign an attack upon New York,

The Early Settlers

Washington, with six thousand Americans, set out on a long march from West Point to Chesapeake Bay (August, 1781).

END OF SOUTHERN CAMPAIGN.

While Washington was on his way to attack Cornwallis at Yorktown the campaign in the South was rapidly drawing to a close. General Green, after the Battle of Guilford Court House, was strengthening his army and had renewed operations in South Carolina, to the astonishment of the British, who thought that they had permanently disposed of Green. Later Green was attacked at Hobkirk's Hill, near Camden. The British won the fight, but, as Marion had cut their line of communication, they were obliged to flee after burning Camden. Green said, " We fight, get beat, and fight again."

Green then laid siege to the British fort, but the arrival of reinforcements for the garrison forced him to withdraw. Everywhere in the South the British abandoned their inland posts and began a general retirement to the coast. In August, 1781, Green marched against Orangeburg, which the enemy hastily evacuated. Green, with two thousand six hundred men, overtook the retiring Red Coats at Eutaw Springs on September 8th, but was repulsed. After the engagement the British force, led by Colonel Stewart, marched on to Charleston.

THE SIEGE OF YORKTOWN.

General Washington was well on his way to Virginia to attack Cornwallis before Clinton, the British Commander at New York, discovered his real intentions. Then it was too late for Clinton to interfere. Reaching York River, Washington found Lafayette waiting to join him, and the French fleet of De Grasse patrolling the Chesapeake, to prevent British warships from coming to the aid of Yorktown. The American leader at once massed his troops to crush Cornwallis. Reinforcements of French and American troops brought the numbers of Washington's army to 16,000 men, of these 7,000 were French. Cornwallis, with 7,000 Red Coats, found himself hemmed in at Yorktown by the American land forces and the patrolling French fleet. However, he proposed to make his last stand.

The Early Settlers

On September 30th, 1781, the Americans began to throw up earthworks around the town, and day by day the American entrenchments drew nearer the enemy's lines, and on the 8th October, 1781, General Washington fired the first cannon of the siege from an American battery, and on the morning of October 10th the batteries began to play on the enemy lines with visible effect. By October 11th the American guns held the situation. The shells and red-hot balls reached the shipping in the harbour, setting one gunboat and several large transports on fire, which were entirely consumed.

On the morning of October 12th the French and American forces stormed the Red Coats in front of the British lines with stubborn fighting. The British were overcome with a stunning blow to Cornwallis, who made a desperate move of cutting his way through the blockade to prevent a surrender. Unfortunately adverse winds drove the boats, in which Cornwallis was retreating, down the river. Cornwallis, then in mortification, saw his defeat, and expressed a preference for death to the ignominy of a surrender.

After his redoubts had been taken his doom was sealed. His firing had now ceased; then came a flag of truce, requesting a cessation of hostilities for twenty-four hours to arrange terms of capitulation. Washington, fearing some reinforcements might be possible by the arrival of the English fleet, allowed him two hours to transmit his proposals. On October 19th Articles of Capitulation was signed, and this final drama marked the end of British rule in America.

NEWS REACHES ENGLAND.

When the news of Cornwallis' surrender reached England Lord North, the Prime Minister, threw up his hands and exclaimed, "It is all over!" He was right. The war had become unpopular in England, because the British realised the impossibility of subduing the Americans, and that they were only accumulating enormous debts. On March 5th, 1782, the British Parliament passed a Bill authorizing the opening of peace negotiations with the Americans. Lord North resigned on March 20th, and a Whig Ministry was formed under Lord Rockingham, who favoured

The Early Settlers

recognising America as a free and independent nation. Lord Rockingham died in July, but this policy was carried on by Shelborne, his successor.

One by one the towns held by the British in America were evacuated. In January, 1782, the Red Coats abandoned Wilmington, North Carolina; Savannah, Georgia, in July, and Charleston in December. General Clinton continued to hold New York, while awaiting to hear the outcome of the plans for peace, which were being discussed. The loss of the American Colonies was a severe blow to George III. It brought about the downfall of the " King's friends " (Party) and upset the King's plans of a Ministry that he controlled. The new regime of the Whigs was inaugurated on a more liberal policy.

DISCONTENT IN THE ARMY.

While negotiations for peace were being made at Paris, Washington, with his army, was at Newburgh on the Hudson watching the British in New York. Having received no pay for months his soldiers were at the point of revolt, and the pleadings of Washington were all that prevented an outbreak. On one occasion one of Washington's Colonels, displeased with the treatment the army had received from Congress, suggested that Washington, with the aid of his troops, could set himself up as King. Washington spurned the suggestion and contemptuously rebuked the officer. " I know of no one to whom your schemes could be more disagreeable," said Washington in reply.

At another time an anonymous letter was circulated among the American officers, urging that a strong military party should supplant Congress as the governing body of the United States. Washington foiled this plot, and persuaded the officers to remain true to their trust. Later, when all over the Colonies the American forces were being disbanded a body of soldiers in Philadelphia mutinied and paraded the streets shouting for their pay and making threats, but committed no acts of violence. Congress, fearing a general uprising of the troops, fled from Philadelphia to Princeton, but the rioters soon dispersed.

The Early Settlers

The Signing of Peace.

Negotiations for peace between the United States and Great Britain were begun at Paris in the summer of 1782. Benjamin Franklin was already in France, and with him John Jay, John Adams and Henry Laurens were chosen as peace commissioners. England was represented by Oswald, acting under the direction of Shelborne, the British Prime Minister.

The French, while desiring to free Americans from England, did not wish her to become a powerful nation, and to prevent this planned to give the Western lands to her ally Spain, who took no part in the war. Seeing that Verginnes, the French Minister, intended to confine the United States to the same narrow strip on the Atlantic coast, the American commissioners followed Jay's advice, signed a separate peace with England, and thereby secured the Western lands for America.

France, by aiding the Colonists, had thought she could dictate what course to adopt. Failing in her intentions, her feelings were ruffled by the Colonists making a separate peace with England without French approval. A slight diplomatic breach arose, which was smoothed over by the shrewd statesmanship of Franklin, and on September 3rd,

The Early Settlers

1783, a general treaty of peace was signed by all parties. The signing of the general peace gave formal recognition to the terms agreed upon by England and America in their Treaty of November 3rd, 1782.

Points Gained Under Terms of Treaty.
1. Complete freedom from England and recognition of the United States as an independent nation.
2. All the land West of the Mississippi River and South from the Great Lakes to Spanish Florida.
3. The right to share in the Newfoundland fisheries.

GENERAL WASHINGTON, COMMANDER IN CHIEF OF THE AMERICAN FORCES, DISBANDS THE ARMY.

On April 19th, 1783, the eighth anniversary of the Battle of Lexington, General Washington issued a proclamation to his troops announcing the end of the war of the Revolution. After eight years of service the Continental army was disbanded, and the war-worn veterans set out for the homes they had fought so bravely to defend.

In the latter part of November, 1783, the British evacuated New York, which they had occupied for seven years. America was now a free nation. On November 25th, 1783, Washington entered New York, which had been occupied by the British since 1776. As the last of the British soldiers were embarking on transports in the river General Washington and Governor Clinton of New York led a triumphal procession down to the old Bowery.

After an affectionate farewell to his officers, Washington went to Annapolis to resign his office as Commander in Chief of the American Army. On December 23rd, 1783, the great leader resigned at the State House. In addressing Congress he closed his remarks by saying, "Having now finished this work assigned me I retire from the great theatre of action. I here offer my commission, and take my leave of the employments of public life." On Christmas Eve, 1783, Washington returned to Mt. Vernon, his estate on the Potomac; having served his country well, he now planned to devote his time to his family and management of his estate.

The Early Settlers.

THE BRITISH GOVERNMENT REGRETTED THE CONFLICT.

The British Government had now to look back regretfully on their failure to rule the American Colonies upon a different basis; but thanks to Providence no such feeling has ever since been invoked against her rule. Apparently she has striven to do justice to all mankind alike. Her subjects in a vast Empire, over which the sun never sets, can think of no other nation upon the earth that is quicker to show their dislike to iniquity and more ready to defend one's rights, even though it may be at the point of the bayonet. Her principles of freedom, politically, intellectually and socially, are without blemish, and as long as she continues to defend the Christian Faith she must conquer.

EULOGIES TO GENERAL WASHINGTON.

Lord Erskin, in writing to General Washington from London, said: "I have taken the liberty to introduce your august and immortal name in a short sentence which is to be found in a book I send you. I have a large acquaintance among the most valuable and exalted classes of men; but you are the only human being for whom I have ever felt an awful reverence. I sincerely pray God to grant you a long and serene evening to a life so gloriously devoted to the universal happiness of the world."

Charles James Fox, the British Premier, declared of Washington in the presence of Parliament: "How infinitely wiser must appear the spirit and principles manifested in his late address to Congress than the policy of modern European Courts! Illustrious man, deriving honour less from the splendour of his situation than from the dignity of his mind; before whom all borrowed greatness sinks into insignificance, and all the potentates of Europe—excepting the members of our Royal Family—become little and contemptible. I cannot indeed help admiring the wisdom and fortune of this great man. A character of virtues, so happily tempered by one another, and so wholly unalloyed by any vices. is hardly to be found on the pages of history. For him it has been reserved to run the race of glory without experiencing the smallest interruption to the brilliancy of his career."

EARLY HISTORY
of the
BAHAMAS.

A brief review of the Early History of the Bahamas, presents a good many features of interest in the Colony's varied development.

In 1670, the Bahamas was granted to six Lords Proprietors of Carolina, who were responsible for the good government of the Islands.

The inhabitants, after organizing the settlement of New Providence instituted an Elective Assembly and selected Captain John Wentworth as their Governor.

In 1671, John Wentworth was confirmed in office by the Lords Proprietors and a regular system of Government was established, including a Parliament and a Lower House which was also elective.

This system of Government continued until the Crown resumed the responsibility for the Government of the Islands.

The first instructions issued by the Lords Proprietors to the Governor and his Council at New Providence, were also accompanied by the Proprietors' Commission to the Governor.

The Early Settlers.

These Commissions were dated at Whitehall, London, 24th April, 1671, and contained the duties of the Assembly, to wit: That within 30 days after the instructions were received all the freeholders, inhabitants of New Providence and Eleuthera and the rest of the Islands, were to be summoned and required to elect 20 Representatives of the people, together with the Governor and 5 Representatives of the Lords Proprietors and 5 other Councillors "As Ye Nobility," constituted the Assembly, by, or with whose consent, or, the major part of them, such laws were to be made as should from time to time be found necessary.

That these laws when ratified under the hand and seal of the Governor, and the hands and seals of any three of the five Proprietors' Deputies, were to be in force for two years after such ratification, provided that the Proprietors' pleasure were declared to the contrary in the meantime.

Copies of all laws so enacted had to be sent to the Lords Proprietors, so that such of the laws as they approve of might be ratified by their hands and seals, and any act so ratified was to remain in force for sixty years, unless provision for its sooner determination was contained in the Act itself. The Assembly was required to choose five of the fittest Freeholders, who with five of the Proprietors' Deputies composed the Grand Council by and with whose consent, or, the consent of six of them, three of whom must always be the Proprietors' Deputies, would determine all controversies between the inhabitants, both civil and criminal causes and be adjudged by them, also, that all public concernments of the Islands were likewise to be directed and governed accordingly.

Members of the Assembly, as well as the Deputies and Councillors and other officers, were to swear allegiance to the King, and their fidelity and submission to the Lords Proprietors.

WOODES ROGERS, ESQ., FIRST ROYAL GOVERNOR.

The affairs of the Colony were not conducted on a satisfactory basis under the rule of the Lords Proprietors, and with the taunts of the Spaniards from time to time, the inhabitants became discontented, and, in order to settle

The Early Settlers

these unsatisfactory conditions, recommendations were made officially to the Crown to take the Islands under its protection.

Complaints were made as early as 1708, and after repeated representations to the same effect the question was ultimately brought up in the English Parliament, and finally, steps were taken toward the appointment of a Royal Governor of the Bahamas.

In 1717, the Lords Proprietors surrendered the government to the King, who, in February, 1718, issued his Commission to Woodes Rogers as Governor, and the Royal instructions were issued the next day.

The following are the reasons which led to the resumption of the Government of the Islands by the Crown:—

GEORGE, By the Grace of God, etc. To Our Trusty and Well-beloved Woodes Rogers, Esquire, Greeting: WHEREAS, by reason of the neglect of the Proprietors of the Bahamas Islands the government of the said Islands is fallen into great disorder and confusion by means Whereof not only the Public Peace has been disturbed but the Administration of Justice Whereby the properties of our subjects should have been preserved have entirely stopped and there has also been an utter want of Provisions for the Guard and Defence of the said Islands against the enemy insomuch that most of the inhabitants are fled from the same Whereby the said Islands are exposed to be plundered and ravaged by pirates and others and in danger of being lost from Our Crown of Great Britain AND WHEREAS four of the six Proprietors being sensible that the said Islands of our Good Subjects, the inhabitants thereof, cannot be defended and secured by any other means than by our taking the government of the same under our Royal Protection and Immediate Care, have executed and made a formal and entire surrender of their Right or pretended Right and Title to the Government thereof unto us, the other two proprietors being minors, and not capable as yet to join in such surrender which surrender we accepted and by these presents do accept.

The instructions to govern were to be given to the Governor from time to time " and according to such reasonable laws and statutes as hereafter shall be made and

The Early Settlers

agreed upon by him with the advice and consent of our Council and Assembly of our said Islands hereafter to be appointed."

The Council was to consist of twelve members.

The Royal Instructions were as follows:

INSTRUCTIONS for Our Trusty and Well-beloved Woodes, Rogers, Esquire, Our Captain General and Governor in Chief in and over Our Bahama Islands in America GIVEN at Our Court at St. James the 6th day of February, 1718, in the Fourth year of Our Reign.

With these Our Instructions you will receive Our Commission under Our Great Seal of Great Britain constituting you Our Captain General and Governor in Chief in and over Our Bahama Islands in America.

2. You are therefore to fit yourself with all convenient speed and to repair to Our said Islands, where being arrived, you are to take upon you the Execution of the Peace and Trust we have reposed in you, and as soon as may be, to call together the Persons We have empowered you by our Commission to appoint as Our Councillors there, and before them to publish Our said Commission, and to administer to Our said Councillors the Oaths therein mentioned.

3. You are to send us by one of Our Principal Secretaries of State and to Our Commissions for Trade and Plantations the names and characters of such persons as shall be appointed by you of the said Council and to permit them to have and enjoy freedom of debate and Vote in all the affairs of Public Concern that may be debated in Council.

4. And that We always be informed of the names and characters of persons fit to supply the vacancies which shall happen in Our Council, you are to transmit unto Us by one of Our Principal Secretaries of State and to Our Commissions for Trade and Plantations with all convenient speed, the names and characters of twelve persons, inhabitants of Our said Islands, whom you shall esteem the best qualified for that Trust and so from time to time, when any of them shall die or depart out of Our said Islands or become otherwise unfit, you are to nominate so many other persons to us in

The Early Settlers

their stead, that the List of Twelve Persons fit to supply vacancies in Our said Council may be always complete.

5. And the better to enable us to settle and establish a Civil Government in Our said Bahama Islands you are to give us and to Our Commissioners for Trade and Plantations as aforesaid by the first opportunity and afterward as soon as may be, a true state of the said Islands, particularly with respect to the numbers and qualifications of the people, that either are, or shall resort thither, what number it may be proper to constitute the Assembly, of what persons are proper and fit to be Judges, Justices or Sheriffs, and any other matter or thing, that may be of use to us in the establishing of a Civil Government as aforesaid.

6. In the meantime, till We shall have established such government, you will receive herewith a copy of several instructions by Us given to Our Governor of Jamaica which are to be as a Rule to you as near as the circumstances of the place will admit in such things as they can be applicable to, till our further pleasure be known. But you are not to take upon yourself to enact any laws, till We shall have appointed an Assembly and given you Directions for your further proceedings therein.

Neither are you to suspend any of the members of Our said Council without good and sufficient cause, which you are to signify to Us and to Our Commission for Trade and Plantations as aforesaid.

(Sgd.) G.R.

WOODES ROGERS SWORN IN AS GOVERNOR,
Together with 12 Members constituting a Council.
200 Pirates Pardoned.

On the 1st August, 1718, Woodes Rogers assembled the principal inhabitants to hear his Commission as Governor, Captain-General and Vice-Admiral, read.

Having chosen his Council of twelve and taken the Oaths in their presence, he administered the Oaths to them.

The Early Settlers

The Chief Justice and other principal officials were duly appointed. "There came before the Council about 200 of those who had been Pirates and surrendered themselves to the Governor in order to take the benefit of His Majesty's Proclamation relating to Piracy and took the Oaths of Allegiance to His Majesty King George as did also several inhabitants of these Islands."

Seventeen other pirates more turbulent than the rest were brought before Chief Justice Walker, and tried by the Court for murder on the high seas. They were condemned and sentenced to be hanged.

PUBLIC WORKS AND OTHER UTILITIES WERE IMMEDIATELY UNDERTAKEN BY WOODES ROGERS.

The Governor lost no time in setting in motion urgent works of a public nature.

The work of putting the settlement in order and to place it in a state of defence was undertaken first.

Work was commenced on the Fort which was in bad repair. Streets were laid out and other public works performed. Every male inhabitant between 18 years and 60 years was required to give so many days work weekly. The wages of all artisans working for the public received a "Dollar" a day. The prices of fresh meat were regulated in consequence of "Murmur amongst Many" because of the extortion of charging nine pence a pound for beef. Official Notice of these two ordinances was made by the Secretary General.

APPREHENSION OF A SPANISH INVASION.

On account of the apprehension of a Spanish invasion the Council lost no time in passing a resolution for the speedy dispatch of public business. Arrangements were quickly made for the said Council to meet and to sit every Sunday in the afternoon to consider of and order everything necessary for the good and welfare of the settlement.

By January, 1719, all public works were so advanced that the inhabitants were permitted by the Council to return to their occupations of cutting brazeletto wood and raking salt. In the meanwhile, England declared war against Spain, and was proclaimed in the Colony on the 31st March, 1719.

The Early Settlers

With great speed five privateers were fitted out to visit the Spanish Wrecks off Florida, with a view to capturing the Spaniards who might be exchanged for English prisoners in Havana. Two of the privateers soon returned with 75 prisoners who were put to work on the fortifications. The expenditure on public works was heavy, for Woodes Rogers, during the first ten months of office, spent on fortifications, etc., £11,344 2s. 3d., and these fortifications were none other than Forts Charlotte and Fincastle. News of an expedition of 1,500 men, two galleys, two brigantines and two sloops from Havana and Trinidad having been received, the Governor and Council kept all shipping in the harbour, and ordered assistance from Harbour Island and Eleuthera; but neither Harbour Island nor Eleuthera sent any assistance during the threatened Spanish invasion. However, the Council made an order that all able bodied men in those settlements —excepting ten who were to remain to keep guard—were to come to New Providence for guard duty. At length the Spaniards arrived and made several attempts to land on the Eastern part of the Island, but their efforts were frustrated by the guards. In the meanwhile, Woodes Rogers' health was so seriously impaired that he left the Colony about the end of November, 1720, for South Carolina, where he hoped to regain his health.

GEORGE PHENNY WAS THE NEXT GOVERNOR.

Within a fortnight of the arrival of George Phenny, Esquire, on the 12th November 1721, he, with the assistance of the Council, had selected from among the inhabitants of the Colony twenty-seven fit persons to be recommended to His Majesty to be elected by the public to make an Assembly.

The persons agreed on to be recommended were as follows:—

New Providence:

William Jones.
William Pinder.
John Thompson, junr.
Richard Thompson, junr.
Benjamin Bullock.
Francis Beasey.
Saltus Weatherly.
John Watkins.
Joseph Hall, senr.
Benjamin Saunders.
Thos. Saunders.
Samuel Frith.
Thomas Barnett.
Thomas Spence, senr.

The Early Settlers.

Harbour Island:
William Thompson, senr.
William Thompson, junr.
Nathaniel Coverly.
John Thompson.
John Albury.
John Griffin.

Eleuthera:
Joseph Ingraham.
John Beak.
Nathaniel Bullard.
Hall Newbold.
Peter Saunders.
Thomas Leary.

Phenny's Report on the Military Strength of the Colony was as follows:—

Providence, being garrisoned by His Majesty's Forces otherwise would be a Nest of Pirates and is a great security to the American Trade. There are 500 Whites which are formed into three companies of Militia, and about 250 Negroes.

Eleuthera, there are 200 Whites of which are formed two Companies, and about 40 Negroes.

Harbour Island, about 150 Whites which make one Company, and some Negroes.

We are proceeding on the works of fortifications at Providence with as much expedition as our ability will give us leave, and when completed will be impregnable to any ordinary Force; with the addition of one more independent Company of 100 men to supply the three Garrisons.

Soil in general is various, being white towards the North Shores, reddish and black in the Valleys, deep between the Rocks and produces very large sugar canes, the finest cotton in the world, fine Madera, Mahogany, Cedar and Pine fit for building of vessels; Manchineel, Prince Wood, Lignum Vitae, brown Ebony, great quantities of Brazeletto, Fustick and other dying woods, Senna, Gum-Elmi, Guiacum, Mastick and several other Gums and Medicinal Drugs.

The Palmetto Trees afford as good Platt as on Bermuda with which I have invited some people hither to make an Essay thereon. The land produces most sorts of provisions for families, various sorts of fine fruits, the Pineapple here being of the best kind in America.

On Exuma and several other Islands large quantities of salt are naturally made every year, sufficient to supply all of His Majesty's Plantations.

The Early Settlers.

Our present inhabitants are mostly sea-faring men.

The Trade chiefly consists in cutting the Dye Woods, which with the Salt, Turtle and Turtle Shell and Fruits n their seasons are exported to the neighbouring Colonies of America, for which sometimes, vessels belonging to North America, bring in barter several Commodities.

In summing up his report the Governor expressed the hope that the inhabitants would before long enjoy the privilege of an Elective Assembly, the absence of which was repeatedly given as the reason, or excuse for the many shortcomings of the government of the Colony.

WOODES ROGERS APPOINTED GOVERNOR A SECOND TIME.

Woodes Rogers was appointed Governor a second time on the 20th December, 1728.

The Royal Commission to him revoked Governor Phenny's Commission and removed him from office.

In due course the Governor arrived in the Colony on the 25th August, 1729, and two weeks later, on the 8th September, 1729, issued the following Proclamation after acquainting the Council to that effect.

The Proclamation read:—

WHEREAS I have thought fit pursuant to His Majesty's Instructions by and with the advice and consent of His Majesty's Council of the Bahama Islands, to call a General Assembly to consist of twenty-four persons who are to be the representatives of the freeholders, planters and inhabitants of the said Islands, WE do hereby order and direct the inhabitants of the Town of Nassau to meet on Monday next, being the 15th inst., at the house of Mr. Samuel Lawford to elect members for the said Town, the District Whereof is limited to extend from the house of William Spatches, Sr., Esqur., to the house of Thomas Barnett, Sr., Esqur., and the inhabitants of the Eastern District are hereby ordered to meet on the 18th instant at the house of Mr. Samuel Frith, and the inhabitants of the Western District, on Saturday, the 20th inst., at the house of Mr. John Watkins, to elect four members for each District. And the

The Early Settlers.

inhabitants of the Island of Eleuthera are hereby ordered to meet on the 20th inst. at the most convenient place. And that those of Harbour Island, to meet on the same day, to elect each of them, four members for each of the said Islands, and of which Members are hereby directed to assemble at the House of Mr. Samuel Lawford in the Town of Nassau, New Providence, on the 29th, of this instant being Michealmas Day.

Given at Nassau this 8th day of September, 1729.
Woodes Rogers.
BY ORDER of His Excellency the Governor and Council,
William Whelston Rogers,
Clerk to the Council.
GOD SAVE THE KING.

The House accordingly met on the 29th day of September, 1729, and proceeded with the responsibilities and duties of the newly created Assembly.

New Providence, seat of Government.

List of the persons chosen to be Representatives for the Bahama Islands at an Assembly held at Nassau, Monday, the 29th September, 1729.

For the Town of Nassau:—
- John Colebrooke, Esqr.
- Mr. Edward Elding.
- Mr. Peter Goudet.
- Mr. Benjamin Hall.
- Mr. Samuel Lawford.
- Mr. William Pinder.
- Roger Reading, Esqr.
- Mr. Moses Simms, Sr.

For the East:—
- Mr. John Bennet.
- Mr. Thomas Downham.
- Mr. Samuel Frith.
- Mr. Thomas Saunders.

For the West:—
- Mr. Jacob Jarroed.
- Mr. Cane Belou.
- Mr. Florentine Cox.
- Mr. Thomas Lory.

For Harbour Island.—
- Mr. John Thompson.
- Mr. John Roberts.
- Mr. Seabom Pinder.
- Mr. John Thompson, Jr.

For Eleuthera:—
- Mr. John Bethell.
- Mr. Joseph Ingraham.
- Mr. Paul Newbold.
- Mr. John Carey.

An Assembly was holden at Nassau on Monday, the 29th September, 1729, for the dispatch of business, after which, adjourned till the next day at 9 o'clock. This was the first proceedings of the first Elective Assembly.

The Early Settlers

Virginia and the Bahamas.

The History of the Colonization of the Bahamas is somewhat interwoven with the History of the United States of America and indeed is more pronounced to-day than ever.

Commercial intercourse between America and the Bahamas is what we may say—a sine qua non—to the existence of the latter country.

In referring to Virginia, it is a matter of History that the Bahamas was supplied with provisions and other commodities in the early days by the Virginians.

In this way the hardships and privations felt by the Colonists of the Bahamas were greatly alleviated. The Bahamas in turn supplied Virginia with salt and valuable dye woods. We are therefore proud of Virginia's early association with the Bahamas.

Another insoluble bond in the History of America and the Bahamas was the appointment of Lord Dunmore to the Governorship of the Bahamas.

On his arrival in the Colony his attention was drawn towards the strength of the fortifications, and he also urged upon the inhabitants, the necessity of developing the soil and to making their homes as happy and peaceful as possible.

After fortifying New Providence he built Forts at Exuma and Mayaguana, and also strengthened the defences at Harbour Island.

He also acquired 2,000 acres of land at Long Island and purchased a building site from the Crown at Harbour Island where he built his summer residence.

The Early Settlers

He built a palatial residence in New Providence called "Dunmore House," occupied it, and on his departure from the Colony leased it to the Government as a Governor's Residence, until the present Government House was built on the site known as "Mount Fitzwilliam." This property was finally sold to the Catholic Mission and is now the residence of His Lordship Bishop Bernard, D.D., O.S.B., and his Staff of Priests. The Rev. Father Bonaventure is Senior Priest.

Lord Dunmore also owned an estate known as the "Hermitage" which was purchased by the Catholic Mission in America and is the Winter Residence of Cardinal O'Connell, Archbishop of Boston.

ADMIRAL HOPKINS, OF THE AMERICAN NAVY, CAPTURED NASSAU, 1776.

The Spanish Invasion, 1781.

In 1776, during the Revolutionary War, Admiral Hopkins, of the American Navy, with a force of eight vessels, attacked and captured New Providence.

He sacked the Forts and left the following day for North America, carried off the Governor of the Colony as a hostage.

The Grand Union Flag was hoisted over Nassau for one day only.

In 1781, Don Juan de Cargigal, Governor General of Cuba, attacked and captured New Providence with a large force.

The Spaniards retained nominal possession of the Islands until the conclusion of the British-Spanish War. In the meantime, however, Andrew Deveaux, a Loyalist Colonel of the South Carolina Militia, before he heard of the conclusion of peace negotiations between England and Spain, fitted out an expedition at his own expense, and with a handful of men, many of whom had been recruited from Harbour Island and Eleuthera, retook New Providence and drove the Spaniards out of the Islands. At the Peace of Versailles in 1783, the Islands were again restored to the British.

The Early Settlers

INHABITANTS OF NEW PROVIDENCE, 1671.

The following is a list of the inhabitants of New Providence as shown by the census of 1671*:—

Albury, Joseph; Sarah his Wife;
    Mary and Sarah, Daughters;
    Joseph, Son.
Albury, Benjamin; Martha, his Wife;
    Benjamin, Son;
    Miriam, Mary, Martha, Daughters.
Anderson, Leah; Mary, Daughter;
    Peter, Son; 14 Slaves.
Barnett, Thomas; Samuel, Son; 5 Slaves.
Barnett, Thomas; Hannah, his Wife;
    Thomas, Son;
    Hannah, Daughter; 6 Slaves.
Bissey, Francis; Sarah, his Wife;
    John, Son; 8 Slaves.
Beck, William; Patience, his Wife;
    Richard, Son; Catherine, Daughter.
Bell, James; Ann, his Wife.
Bill, John; Hannah, his Wife;
    Mary, Hannah, Susannah, Daughters.
    Benjamin, John, Thomas, Sons; 7 Slaves.
Bisley, Timothy; Mary his Wife.
Blay, John; Rose, his Wife; John, Son;
    Phenny, Elizabeth, Mary, Daughters.
Bullock, Benjamin; Mary, his Wife;
    John, Man; Sarah, Girl; 22 Slaves.
Burrum, Edward; Mary, his Wife;
    James, William, Sons.
Brown, William; Martha, his Wife;
    Sarah, Child; Sarah, Sister to William.
Bower, Benjamin; Mary, his Wife;
    Martha, Ann, Daughters.
    Benjamin, John, Nathaniel, William, Sons.
Carter, Jane, Elizabeth and Peter.
Charles, William; Ann, his Wife.
Cimberlin, James; Mary, his Wife.

* For Reference Registra of Records Office Book C Pages 166—175.

The Early Settlers

Cox, James; Sarah, his Wife; 11 Slaves.
Coverley, Wm.; Jane, his Wife;
 Thomas, Mary and Nathaniel, Children.
Curtis, Neptune; Frances, his Wife;
 Charity, Daughter.
 Richard, Andrew and Faith, Children.
Curtis, Neptune; Elizabeth, his Wife; Neptune, Son.
Curtis, Henry; Susanna, Wife;
 Thomas, Henry, Sons.
Curry, John, Jr.; Martha, his Wife;
 Cosiah and Mary, Daughters.
Curry, Richard; Mary, his Wife.
Darvil, Zachaeus.
Darvil, Marmaduke; Mary, his Wife;
 Mary, Daughter; 9 Slaves.
Downham, Thomas; James, Son; 21 Slaves.
Driscoll, Lawrence; Mary, Wife;
 Thomas, Lawrence, Sons;
 Sarah, Child; 4 Slaves.
Duncome, Nehemiah; Susannah, his Wife;
 Samuel and William, Boys; 7 Slaves.
Elding, Reed; Anna, his Wife;
 Hannah, Daughter; 2 Slaves.
Evans, Ruth; 3 Slaves.
Fernando, William; Mary, his Wife; one Girl; two Boys.
Fife, John; Phenny, his Wife;
 John and Andrew, Sons.
Fisher, Abraham; Martha, his Wife;
 Abraham, John, Sons;; Elizabeth, Daughter;
 10 Slaves.
Fox, Joseph; Sarah, his Wife;
 Mary and Martha, Daughters;
 John, Son.
Fox, James; Mary, his Wife; Nancy, Child.
Fountaine, Julien La; Sarah, his Wife; 2 Slaves.
Fraser, William; Susannah, his Wife;
 John, Edward and Thomas, Sons;
 Eliza, Daughter; 7 Slaves.
Frith, John; Catherine, his Wife;
 Jasper, Son; 1 Slave.

The Early Settlers

Gascoigne, Moses; Frances, his Wife;
    Charles, his Son.
Gibbons, Samuel; Mary, his Wife;
    Jemmima, Mary, Girls.
Graham, Eliza;
    James, Nancy, Esther, Children; 1 Slave.
Griffin, John; Miriam, his Wife;
    William, John, Thomas, Benjamin, Sons.
    Mary, Hannah, Girls.
Griffin, Hannah;
    William and George, Sons;
    Hannah, Daughter.
Hall, John; Jane, his Wife.
Hall, Joseph; Catherine, his Wife; Mary, Daughter;
    Patience, Joseph, Son (Man);
    John and William, Boys; 12 Slaves.
Hale, Elizabeth; Matther, Son; Sarah, Daughter.
Harnott, Margarett.
Howell, John; Ann, his Wife;
    Susannah, Daughter; Moore Sanderson, Son.
    41 Slaves.
Hunter, Andrew; Elizabeth, his Wife;
    One Daughter; 5 Slaves.
Irving, James.
Jackson, Hannah; Calvin, Son; Mildred, Girl.
Jennings, John; Sarah, his Wife; Susannh, Daghter.
Johnson, Samuel; Catherine, his Wife.
    Nathaniel and Samuel, Sons;
    Sarah and Mary, Girls.
Johnson, Thomas; Sarah, his Wife;
    Thomas, Son; Mary, Daughter.
Kewin, John; Ruth, his Wife;
    Margaret and Mary, Daughters.
Knowles, Alexander; Sarah, his Wife;
    Ann, Daughter; 1 Slave.
Knight, Edward; 33 Slaves.
Knight, Ann; Jane, Daughter; 5 Slaves.
Lemon, Benjamin; Mary, his Wife;
    Richard, John and Rebecca, Children.
Lincoln, Ann; Martha, Child.
McKenzie, Alexander;
    Eliza and Thomas, Children; 2 Slaves.

The Early Settlers.

McKenzie, John; Hannah, his Wife;
   Mildred, Mary, Ann, Daughters; 3 Slaves.
McKenzie, Roderick; Elizabeth, his Wife;
   Joseph, John, Sons; 26 Slaves.
McKenzie, Anthony; Mary, his Wife;
   Hannah, one-year-old Child.
Marshall, David; Margery, his Wife; 2 Slaves.
Minos, Joseph; Martha, his Wife;
   Elizabeth, his Mother;
   William Pierce, Man.
Mitchael, John; Ruth, his Wife;
   William and John, Sons; Sarah, Daughter.
Morton, John; Sarah, his Wife;
   Warren and Howard, Sons.
Moter, Abednego; Joannah, his Wife;
   Shadrach, Abednego, Jeremiah, Sons;
   Ruth and Esther, Daughters.
Moreley, Samuel; Mary, his Wife;
   Susannah, Daughter;
   Samuel, Benjamin and John, Sons.
Mounsey, Thomas; Athanias, his Wife;
   Daniel and George, Sons; 8 Slaves.
Moxey, Jonathan; Mary, his Wife; Humphrey, Son;
   Mary and Sarah, Daughters.
Newman, Josiah; Hannah, his Wife;
   Elizabeth, Daughter;
   Samuel, Joseph and John, Sons.
Pinder, Salem; Elizabeth, his Wife;
   William and Timothy, Sons; 2 Slaves.
Pinder, John; Sarah, his Wife; Mary, Daughter;
   John, Thomas, William and Michael, Sons.
Pinder, John; Frances, his Wife;
   Mary, his Daughter; Susannah, Daughter;
   13 Slaves.
Pye, James; Sarah, his Wife;
   James, William and John, Sons.
   Mary, Sarah and Deborah, Daughters.
Roberts, John; Martha, his Wife; Mary, Girl;
   Benjamin, George and Merriham, Sons;
   Jane, Martha and Mary, Daughters.
Roberts, Ruth; John, Joseph, Benjamin, Sons.

The Early Settlers.

Roberts, Richard; Elizabeth, his Wife;
  Richard, Son; 2 Slaves.
Roberts, John; Martha, his Wife; Ruth, Girl;
  Mary, Girl; John, Joseph, Sons.
Ross, Wm.; Sarah Myers, Wife;
  Susannah Myers, Ruth Myers, Daughters.
Russell, Elizabeth; Daniel, Son.
Russell, Benjamin; Sarah, his Wife; Elizabeth, Girl;
  Benjamin, Son.
Saunders, John; Catherine, his Wife;
  John, Martha, Mary, Children; 2 Slaves.
Saunders, Benjamin; Jean, his Wife;
  Jane and Sarah, Daughters;
  Benjamin, Son; 2 Slaves.
Saunders, Martha; Eliza, Daughter;
  Samuel, Thos. and Henry, Sons.
Saunders, Jane.
Saunders, Thos.; Ruth, his Wife;
  Thos., Nathaniel and Benjamin, Sons.
Sears, Thos.; Martha, his Wife; Hannah, Daughter;
  24 Slaves.
Scott, James; Margaret, his Wife; 24 Slaves.
Simms, Moses; Aim, his Wife;
  James, Son; Mary, Daughter.
Simons, Nathaniel; Elizabeth, his Wife;
Smith, Mary; Samuel, Son; 3 Slaves.
Smith, Richard; Mary, his Wife; Mary, Child.
  Robert, Samuel, John, Boys.
Spatches, Anthony; Susannah, his Wife.
Spatches, Wm.; Eliza, his Wife; Mary Huggins, Woman;
  Mary, Daughter; John and Arthur, Sons;
  7 Slaves.
Stewart, Samuel; Mary, his Wife;
  Samuel and Wililam, Sons.
  Nancy, Icodan, Sarah, Daughters.
Stewart, William; Ann, his Wife; Rebecca, Daughter.
Stewart, Roderick; Margaret, his Daughter; 2 Slaves.
Stow, James; Mary, his Wife; John, Son; 16 Slaves.
Supple, John.
Sweeting, Thos.; Sarah, his Wife;
  Nathaniel, Son; Mary, Martha, Eliza, Daughters.
Sweeting, Thos., Jr.; Margery, his Wife.

The Early Settlers.

Sweeting, Letitia, Wife.
Sweeting, Benjamin; Martha, his Wife;
    Samuel, Thos., Sons; Sarah, Daughter; 3 Slaves.
Sweeting, William; Elizabeth, his Wife;
    Elizabeth, Daughter.
Thompson, Joseph; Ann, his Wife;
    William, John, Joseph and Richard, Sons;
    Mary, Martha, Catherine and Ann, Daughters.
    1 Negro Slave.
Thompson, John; Priscilla, his Wife·
Thompson, Joseph; Sarah, his Wife;
    Sarah (Child).
Thompson, John, Esq.; Sarah, his Wife;
    Sarah, Ann, Catherine, Girls;
    Joseph, John, Boys; 9 Slaves.
Thompson, John; Martha, his Wife;
    Joseph and John, his Sons; 4 Slaves.
Thompson, William, Snr.; Mary, his Wife;
    Martha, Catherine, Rebecca, Margery, Daughters;
    Richard and Thomas, his Sons; 1 Slave.
Thompson, William, Jun.; Sarah, his Wife;
    William, Son;
    Mary and Elizabeth, Daughters;
    2 Slaves.
Thompson, Richard; Mary, his Wife;
    Richard (a Man);
    William (a Man); Thos. D.,
    Catherine.
Thompson, James; Eliza, his Wife;
    Eliza, his Daughter;
    Ann, his Daughter;
    James, his Son.
Tedel, John; Mary, his Wife;
    Joseph and Mary, their Children·
Watkins, Benjamin; Sarah, his Wife;
    4 Slaves.
Watkins, Martha; Watkins, Sarah; unmarried.
Walker, Chas.; Ann, his Wife;
    Chas., John, Thomas, Sons;
    Alice, Elizabeth, Daughters·
Whitehead, Roland (a Man).

The Early Settlers

Wright, Wm.; Sarah, his Wife;
   William, his Son;
   Mary, his Daughter;
   Ann, his Daughter; 4 Slaves.
Young, Thos.; Kessiah, his Wife;
   William, his Son;
   Elizabeth, his Daughter.
Young, Richard, Brother to Thomas.
Yates, Jeremiah; Sarah, his Wife;
   Sarah (Child).

ELEUTHERA.

Eleuthera is a beautiful name to be given to an Island. Its derivation is from the Greek, meaning "Freedom." Andros is another Greek name given to one of the largest Islands in the Bahamas group.

We would like to have some determination as to the origin of these Greek names, but it is hardly possible to-day to trace the connection between English and Hellenistic names of Islands in these far off lands of the New World, though, in Bermuda, on the Ordnance Survey Maps, you will find five Islets in the Great Sound, named from four letters of the Greek Alphabet which are, Alpha, Beta, Gamma, Delta and Zeta.

The question then may be asked, who was that Greek Scholar who loved the Islands so much as to scatter these starry names to perpetually remain on these Western Seas?

In any case, if we can neither ascertain nor trace the link in this connection, surely one is to be found between Bermuda and Eleuthera.

As regards to Eleuthera, let us now say something about its history which is deeply interesting.

In 1650, Capt. John Forester, writing to the Honourable Company of Adventurers for the Somers Island, refers to Capt. Sayle as sailing with some adventurers to his new plantation in Eleuthera, but letters received from Eleuthera by the Company certified that the little Island they were upon was mostly barren rock, shallow earth, and not hopeful to provide food for the inhabitants.

Capt. Sayle had already visited Eleuthera, he had first gone there from Bermuda in 1646; taking with him a batch of settlers; so he really knew what the barren rock was.

The Early Settlers

It was not commercial profits that attracted him to the Island; what then might it be? It was that there, men would have intellectual and religious "freedom" such as they did not have elsewhere.

"Freedom," Eleutheros, the Greek word given to it perhaps by those who went to that barren Island originally named "Sagatos" in search for a freedom never made workable among men. But what was it after all that drove that little band of adventurers southward from Bermuda to take possession of the Isle of Freedom—their Eleuthera? It was the Political and Ecclesiastical struggle which beset England at the time.

The Monarch and Religion were two mighty seas of controversy, flooding England at this period, which spread out their waves till they reached "Eleuthera" there to break and be lost.

In 1646, Capt. William Sayle of Bermuda is alleged to have obtained from the Parliament of London a grant of the Island of Sagatos in the Bahamas which was to be named "Eleuthera," but no confirmation of such grant to the Island has been found in the Journals of the House of Commons, though it is a fact that Sayle and his son did exercise so far as they could, propriety rights over the Island.

Governor Wenthrop of Connecticut, states that Capt. Sayle had obtained of Parliament, some rights to the Island (see Lefroy Vol. II., page II.) to undertake the work of making a Colony and drew up a covenant and articles for all to enter into who would come into the business.

The first article Wenthrop contends was for liberty of conscience wherein was provided that the Civil Magistrate should not have cognizance of any matter which concerned religion, but that everyone might enjoy his own opinion on religion without control or question.

In 1646, Sayle, along with his party and the Rev. Patrick Copeland, with some of his Independents, sailed from Bermuda. There were in the ship 70 persons who bravely voyaged South for Eleuthera.

Before the ship reached "Eleuthera" a young man who came in the ship from England made use of his liberty, to disturb all the company on board. He could not endure any

The Early Settlers

ordinances or worship, etc., and when they arrived at one of the Islands and intended there to settle, the young man made such a faction as enforced Capt. Sayle to remove to another Island, and being near the harbour the ship struck the shoals and was lost; all lives were saved, but one.

In 1649, a second batch of settlers sailed from Bermuda for Eleuthera as a consequence of another religious disturbance in that Island, on the execution of Charles I., and the establishment by Oliver Cromwell of the Commonwealth of England.

The native Royalists in Bermuda, not only acknowledged Charles II. to be their sovereign, but rose in arms, and elected John Trimmingham to the office of Governor, and banished the more influential Independents, including Rev. Nathaniel White to the New Colony of Eleuthera.

But this additional strength to the Island of freedom brought no success to the venture. The banished Independents very soon began to be in want, but, being under the guidance of Divine Providence as it seemed, they were not left to perish.

Some account of this Island and its settlers had reached Boston where the Puritans would naturally be interested in any venture made for religious freedom.

According to the New England Chronicler, Edward Johnson of Woburn, reported that the Eleutherians were enduring "much hardships," from this news eight of the Puritan Churches in New England collected some Eighty pounds with a promise of provisions and other necessaries which were shipped at once (1650) in a small vessel chartered for that purpose.

In 1656, the banished Loyalists were recalled from Eleuthera.

Among the returned wanderers was the Rev. Nathaniel White whose zeal for independency seems to have abated, and after his return to Bermuda, became Parish Minister of Northampton, where he peacefully ended his days.

The people of Eleuthera receiving the gift of eighty pounds sent to them by the New England Churches, expressed their gratitude to God; and to "avoid that foul sin of ingratitude abhorred of God and so hateful to men," sent in return, ten tons of Brazeletto wood, a valuable dye

The Early Settlers

wood, the nett proceeds of which they desired to be given to Harvard College Endowment Fund.

The vessel sailed from Eleuthera on July 17th, 1650, and arrived at Boston August 6th, taking as passenger, Nathaniel White, son of Rev. Nathaniel White, who afterwards had taken his Master's Degree at Harvard College.

The records of Harvard College tell us the exact sum realized by the sale of Brazeletto Wood—£124.

The gift was a very generous one for that time, when £100 was the salary of the President of Harvard College. It was the largest single donation they had yet received, excepting the original grant from the General Court of £400 and John Harvard's legacy of £800.

So it came about that out of the sorrows of the search for freedom for the Elutherian Adventurers, the largest single sum (except John Harbard's bequest) received by Harvard College during the first thirty years of its History, was sent from Eleuthera, Bahamas.

Note.—We hope that the day is not far distant when a memorial will be erected at Eleuthera in honour of the acquaintance of Harvard's Ancient University, America, with Eleuthera.

FIRST LIST OF INHABITANTS.

The following is a list of persons comprising the first enumeration of the inhabitants of Eleuthera:—

Bethell, John; Sarah, is Wife;
    John, Son (man);
    Elizabeth, Sarah, Daughters (women);
    Noah, Winer, Prenza Jonathan (boys);
    Joannah, Daughter (girl).
Bethell, Nathaniel; Ann, his Wife;
    Nathaniel, Son (boy);
    Mary, Bethia, Sarah, Daughters (girls).
Been, Andrew; Elizabeth, his Wife;
Bradwell, Jacob; Mary, his Wife;
Bullard, Solomon; Ann, his Wife;
    Nathaniel, Charles, Sons (men);
    Ann, Eliza, Esther, Daughters (women).
Carey, William; Mary, his Wife;
    Sarah, Daughter;
    William, Son (boy).

The Early Settlers.

Carey, John;
    Richard (man);
    Mark, Abraham, Sons.
Carey, Mark (single man).
Charlow, John; Martha, his Wife.
Charlow, Joseph; Martha, his Wife.
    Thomas, Son (boy).
Culmer, Daniel; Mary, his Wife;
    Thomas, Son.
Culmer, Thomas; Judith, his Wife.
Dickenson, John; Mary, his Wife.
Dorsett, Mary (single woman).
Evans, William; Amelia, his Wife;
    John, Son; 8 Slaves.
Evans, Elizabeth;
    John, Joseph, Sons; 2 Slaves.
Ingraham, Joseph; Mary, his Wife;
    Duke (boy);
    Sarah, Mary, Ann, Bethia, Catherine, Daughters.
Ingraham, Benjamin; Rebecca, his Wife;
    Benjamin, Son (man).
Ingraham, William; Miriam, his Wife.
Knowles, Robert; Martha, his Wife;
    Eliza, Ann, Mary (girls);
    Thomas, Daniel, Sons (boys).
Knowles, Elizabeth, Widow;
    John, Samuel (boys).
Knowles, John; Ann, his Wife;
    Hannah, Judith, Sarah, Daughters.
Kemp, Benjamin;
    Jane, Mary (women).
    Martha, Girl (Daughter).
Kemp, Anthony;
    John, Anthony, Sons (men);
    Benjamin (boy).
Low, Gideon, Martha, his Wife;
    Eliza, Martha, Daughters (girls).
Low, Matthew; Sarah, his Wife;
    Thomas (man);
    Mary, Frances, Daughters (girls).

The Early Settlers.

Low, John; Elizabeth, his Wife.
Newbold, Sarah (single woman).
Newbold, Samuel; Mary, his Wife;
    Eliza, his Daughter.
Oliver, Charles;
    Thomas, Charles, John, Benjamin (Sons);
    Mary, Daughter (girl).
Penshaw, John; Sarah, his Wife;
    Mary, Sarah, Susannah, Daughters (children).
Pinder, Richard.
Ronland, Charles; Elizabeth, his Wife;
    Chas., Jr.;
    Mary Coverley, Daughter-in-law);
    11 Slaves.
Spencer, Moses; Mary, his Wife;
    Thomas, Son;
    Mary, Daughter.
Sands, Samuel; Sarah, his Wife;
    William, Samuel, (boys).
Sands, Peter, Snr.; Sarah, his Wife;
    John, Charles (boys).
Sands, Peter, Jnr.; Mary, his Wife;
    John (boy); Mary (girl).
Sawyer, Richard; Ann, his Wife;
    Wm. (man); John (boy);
    Mary and Sarah (girls).
Watkins, Wm.;
    Hodon;
    Mary, William's Mother;
    Mary Susannah;
    4 Slaves.
Watkins, Benjamin; Mary, his Wife;
    Hannah, his Sister (woman);
    5 Slaves.
Weatherly, Wm.; Mary, his Wife;
    Martha, May (girls). *

---

* For Reference Registra of Records Office Book C, Page 175—177.

The Early Settlers.

JOHN BETHELL.

The Bethells were among the English adventurers who settled at Eleuthera in 1646. The original two brothers, John and Nathaniel, gave each of their sons the name of John, which has been retained in every generation that followed. About the end of the first hundred years of their colonization they began to branch off to the other Islands in the group. In the year 1785 John, the son of Noah Bethell, left Eleuthera to live in the Island of New Providence. Benjamin and Nathaniel, two other sons of Noah Bethell, made their homes in New Providence. In 1790 John, the son of Nathaniel, left Eleuthera, and went to Harbour Island, where he purchased lot No. 46 in the Township which was being laid out by the Earl of Dunmore, Governor of the Bahamas. From Harbour Island went another John and Winer Bethell to Abaco, where they settled. David, son of Thomas Bethell, went to the Caicos Island. After a while Winer, the son of Winer, went to Key West, Florida. Thomas, the son of Charles Alexander, went to Jacksonville, Florida. In 1728 one of the sons of John Bethell, senior, of Eleuthera, was elected a member of the first Colonial Parliament. In 1838 William Bethell built the first Anglican Church at Governor's Harbour at his own expense; and in his will he gave his mansion house on the hill top at Governor's Harbour to St. Patrick's Church after the death of a certain Mary Bullard.

The Last Will and Testament of John Bethell,
of Eleuthera.
Bahama Islands, Eleuthera.
In the name of God, Amen.

I, John Bethell, of Eleuthera, being of sound mind, memory, etc.:

First, I give, devise and bequeath to my beloved wife, Anne Bethell, three negro slaves and 70 pieces of eight in cash and all houses and lands, together with furniture belonging to my houses.

Secondly, I give, devise and bequeath to my eldest son John, by my former beloved wife Sarah, twenty pieces of eight in cash and his equal part of my clothing and one pistol.

The Early Settlers

Thirdly, I give, devise and bequeath to my son Noah twenty pieces of eight in cash, and his equal part of my clothing and one pistol.

Fourthly, I give, devise and bequeath to my son Winer twenty pieces of eight in cash and his equal part of my clothing and one small arm.

Fifthly, I give, devise and bequeath to my son Jonathan twenty pieces of eight in cash and one negro wench named Lucy and one pair of gold buttons and one silk waistcoat and one small arm.

Sixthly, I give to my daughter Sarah twenty pieces of eight in cash.

Seventh, I give to my daughter Joanna twenty pieces of eight in cash.

Eight, I give, devise and bequeath to my son Jeremiah twenty pieces of eight in cash and one negro man named Jack.

And I do hereby appoint my two eldest sons, John and Noah, executors to this my last Will and Testament.

(Signed) JOHN BETHELL.

In Witness, etc.,
Dated 1722.

John, the son of John Bethell, senior (wife Elizabeth), dies in 1783, and leaves six children, namely: John, Noah, Sarah, Ann, Patience and Catherine.

Noah, the son of John, senior, dies 1757, and leaves eight children, namely: Noah, Nathaniel, Charles, Benjamin, Jonathan Winer, Sarah and Ann.

Nathaniel, the son of John, senior, dies 1761, and leaves four children, namely: Noah, John, Thomas and Susannah.

The Wills of Winer, Jonathan and Jeremiah are missing.

The late Charles E. Bethell, the wealthy real estate owner, and Herbert Bruce and Bruce Stanley are the grandsons of Charles Samuel George Bethell, who was the son of Charles Bethell, whose last Will and Testament is herewith given in part:

The Early Settlers

In the name of God, Amen·

I, Charles Bethell, gentleman, of the Island of Eleuthera, being of sound and disposing mind, etc., etc., etc.:

I give, devise and bequeath unto my youngest son, Charles Samuel George, a tract of land situate at Governor's Harbour, Eleuthera, containing 300 acres to be enjoyed by him, his heirs and assigns for ever. Other bequests were made in the Will to his daughters, namely, Catherine Elizabeth Steward and Ann Thompson.

(Signed) Charles Bethell.
Date of Will 1817.

The testator, namely, Charles Bethell's father, was one of the six sons of Noah Bethell, who died at Eleuthera in 1757·

(The Author of this book is the grandson of John Edward Bethell, who was a lineal descendant of John, senior, of Eleuthera.

The Early Settlers

The Arrival of Governor Woodes Rogers.

THE ESCAPE OF VANE, THE PIRATE.

About the 20th July, 1718, Mr. Woodes Rogers, Governor and Vice-Admiral of the Bahama Islands, being sent from England with the King's proclamation and pardon for all pirates who had surrendered by a time specified in the said proclamation, arrived at Providence.

It was evening when the fleet came off the town f Nassau in the said Island, when the pilot did not judge it safe to venture over the bar that night, wherefore it was resolved to lay by until morning.

In the meantime, there came some men on board the fleet from a little Island called Harbour Island. The advice they brought was that there were near a thousand pirates on shore upon the Island of Providence waiting for the King's Pardon, which had been long expected; that their commanders, Benjamin Hornygold, Arthur Davis, Joseph Burgess and Thomas Carter, were all in and about the town of Nassau.

That the fort was extremely out of repair, there being only one gun mounted, a nine-pounder, and no accommodation for men, but one little hut, which was inhabited by an old fellow, whom pirates in derision called Governor Sawney.

Captain Charles Vane, a famous pirate, had no design of surrendering; but fitted out his ship with a resolution of

The Early Settlers

attempting new adventures. He took the advantage of the night to make his escape. The Harbour was blocked up, and his ship drew too much water to get out by the East passage; whereupon he shifted his hands and things of most value into a lighter vessel and charging all the guns of the ship he quitted, leaving her on fire.

Those in the fleet saw the light, and heard the guns, but fancied that the pirates on shore were making bonfires and firing guns for joy that the King's free pardon had arrived.

Captain Whitney, commander of the "Rose," man-o'-war, sent his boat with a lieutenant and boat's crew on shore. They were intercepted by the Pirate Vane, who carried the boat with crew to his vessel and took all stores they had in his boat. He kept them until he got under sail, which was until daybreak, when there was light enough for him to see how to steer his way through the East passage. As soon as he got under weigh he fired a gun and hoisted a black flag, leaving the lieutenant and boat's crew to join their fleet.

When the fleet got into the harbour, and as soon as the lieutenant arrived on board and related what had happened, the sloop "Buck" was ordered to chase Vane. She made what sail she could through the East passage after him, having a recruit of men well armed sent to her from other ships; but being heavily laden with rich goods, Vane got away, which the Commodore observing, made a signal for the sloop to give up the chase and return, which she did accordingly.

The next morning the Governor went on shore, being received at his landing by the principal people in the government of the place, viz.: Thomas Walker, Esq., Chief Justice, and Thomas Taylor, Esq., President of the Council.

The pirate captains and others drew up their crews in two lines, reaching from the water side to the fort, the Governor and officers marching between them; they fired a continuous salute until he reached the fort. His commission was opened and read and he was then and there sworn in Governor of the Island, according to form.

The next day the Governor made out a commission to Richard Turnley, the chief pilot, and some others to go on board and examine all suspected ships and vessels in the

The Early Settlers

harbour, to take an inventory of their several ladings, and to secure both ships and cargoes for the use of the King and Company, until such time as a Court of Admiralty could be called, that they might be cleared or condemned by proving which belonged to pirates, and which to lawful traders.

The day following a court-martial was held, in which a military discipline was settled in order to prevent surprises from Spaniards and pirates, until such time as the fort could be repaired, and put into a condition of defence.

He next formed a Civil Government appointing some of the principal officers Justices of Peace others of an inferior degree he appointed Constables and Overseers of the ways and roads, which were overgrown with bushes and underwood, all about the town of Nassau.

The Governor with some soldiers guarded the fort, and the inhabitants, who were formed into trained bands, took care of the town; but as there was no sort of accommodation to lodge such a number of people, they were forced to unbend the sails, and bring them on shore in order to make tents until they had time to build houses, which was done with all possible expedition, by a kind of architecture altogether new.

Those that were built in the fort were done by making six little holes in the rock, at convenient distances, in each of which was stuck a forked pole. On these, from one to the other, were placed cross poles or rafters, which were lathed at the top and sides with small sticks and were then covered with Palmetto leaves, and thus the house was finished.

In the meantime the repairs of the fort were carried on, and the streets were ordered to be kept clean, both for health and convenience, so that it began to have the appearance of a civilized place.

A proclamation was published for the encouragement of all persons as should be willing to settle upon the Island of New Providence, by which every person was to have a plot of ground one hundred and twenty feet square in or about the town of Nassau, that was not before in the possession of others provided they should clear the said ground and build a house tenantable, by a certain time therein limited, which might be easily done, as they might have

The Early Settlers.

timber for nothing. This had the effect proposed, and a great many immediately fell to work to comply with the conditions, in order to settle themselves there.

Many of the pirates were employed in the woods cutting down sticks to make palisades, and all the people belonging to the ships, officers excepted, were obliged to work four days in the week on the fortifications, so that in a short time a strong entrenchment was cast round the fort, and being well palisaded, was rendered tolerably strong. But it did not much suit the inclinations of the pirates to be set to work; and though they had provision sufficiently, and also a good allowance of wine and brandy to each man, yet they began to have such a hankering after their old trade, that many of them took opportunities of seizing boats in the night, made their escape, so that in a few months there were not many left. However, when the Spanish war was proclaimed, several of them returned of their own accord, tempted with the hopes of being employed upon privateering, as Nassau, lying so near the coast of Spanish America and not far from the Gulf of Florida, seemed to be a good station for intercepting the Spanish vessels going to old Spain. They were not mistaken in their supposition, for the Governor, according to the power vested in him, did grant commissions for privateering, and made choice of some of the principal pirates who had continued upon the Island, in obedience to pardon, for commanders.

About this time a fishing vessel belonging to the Island of Providence brought in the master of a ship in a canoe. —the said master was called Captain King—and a few sailors, whom she had picked up at sea and who sailed in the ship " Neptune," belonging to South Carolina, laden with rice, pitch, tar and other merchandise bound for London.

The account he gave of himself was that he was met with by Charles Vane, the pirate, who carried him into Green Turtle Bay, one of the Bahama Islands, by whom he was plundered of a great part of his cargo, which consisted chiefly of stores that were of great use to them; that afterwards they cut away part of one of the masts of the ship and fired a gun down her hold, with intent to sink her; that they took some of his men into their service, and when

The Early Settlers.

they were sailing off gave him and the rest a canoe to save themselves; that with this canoe they got from one island to another, until they had the good luck to meet the fishing boat which took them up; and that he believed Charles Vane might still be cruising thereabouts.

Upon this intelligence the Governor fitted out a ship, which was named the "Willing Mind," manned with forty stout hands, well armed, and also a sloop with thirty hands, well armed, which he sent to cruise among those islands, in search of Vane, the pirate, giving them orders also to endeavour to find the ship "Neptune," which Captain King told them had still goods of considerable value left in her. However, they found the "Neptune," which was not sunk as the pirates intended, for the ball they fired into her stuck in the ballast, without passing through. They returned with her about the 10th of November, but an unlucky accident happened to the "Willing Mind," occasioned either by the ignorance or carelessness of the pilot, which bilged in going over the bar.

In the meantime Vane made towards the coast of Hispaniola, living riotously on board, having an abundance of liquor and plenty of provisions. They cruised to about February, when, near the windward passage of Cape Mase, they met with a large rich ship of London called the "Kingston," laden with bale goods and other rich merchandise, and having several passengers on board, some English, and some Jews, besides two women.

Towards the north end of Jamaica they also met with a turtle sloop bound for that island, on board of which they put the captain of the "Kingston," some of his men, and all the passengers except two women, whom they detained, contrary to their usual practice.

The "Kingston" they kept for their own use; for now their company being strengthened by a great many recruits, some volunteers and some forced men out of the "Neptune" and "Kingston," they thought they had hands enough for two ships. Accordingly they shifted several of their hands on board the "Kingston," and John Rackman, alias Jack Calico (so called because his jackets and pants were always made of calico), quarter-master to Vane, was uanimously chosen captain of the "Kingston."

The Early Settlers.

The empire of these pirates had not been long divided before they had like to have fallen into a civil war among themselves, which must have ended in the destruction of one of them.

The fatal occasion of the difference between these two brother adventurers was this: It happened that Vane's liquor was all out, who sending to his brother captain for a supply, Rackman accordingly spared him what he thought fit; but it falling short of Vane's expectation, as to quantity, he went on board of Rackman's ship to expostulate with him, so that, words arising, Rackman threatened to shoot him through the head if he did not immediately return to his own ship, and told him likewise that if he did not sheer off and part company he would sink him. Vane thought it best to take his advice, for he thought Rackman was bold enough to be as good as his word, for he had it in his power to do so, his ship being the largest and strongest of the two.

Accordingly they parted, and Rackman made for the Island of Princes, and having great quantities of rich goods on board taken in the late prizes, they were divided into lots, and he and his crew shared them by throwing dice, the highest cast being to choose first. When done, they packed up their goods in cask, that they might have room for fresh booty. In the meantime, it happening that a turtle sloop, belonging to Jamaica, came in there, Rackman sent his boat and brought the master on board to him, and asking him several questions, the master informed him that the war with Spain had been proclaimed in Jamaica, and that the time appointed for the general pardon for pirates to surrender, in order to receive the benefits thereof, had not expired. Upon this intelligence Rackman and his crew suddenly changed their minds, and were resolved to take the benefit of the pardon by a speedy surrender; wherefore, instead of using the master ill, as the poor man expected, they made him several presents, desiring him to sail back to Jamaica, and acquaint the Governor they were willing to surrender, provided he would give his word and honour they should have the benefit of the pardon, which, extensive as it was, they apprehended they were not entitled to because they had run away in defiance of it at Provi-

The Early Settlers

dence. They desired the master also to return with the Governor's answer, assuring him he should be no loser by the voyage.

The master very unwillingly undertook the commission, and arriving at Jamaica delivered his message to the Governor according to his instructions; but it happened that the master of the "Kingston," with his passengers, having arrived at Jamaica, had acquainted the Governor with the piracies of Vane and Rackman, before the turtler got thither, who was actually fitting out two sloops, which were now just ready, in pursuit of them, so that the Governor was very glad to discover by the turtler's message where Rackman was to be found.

The two sloops, well manned accordingly, sailed out, and found Rackman in the station where the turtler had described him, but altogether in disorder, and quite unprepared either for sailing or fighting, most of his sails being on shore erected into tents and his decks lumbered with goods. He happened to be on board himself, though most of his men were ashore, and seeing the two sloops at a distance bearing towards him, he observed them with his glass, and fancied he saw on board something like preparations for fighting. This was what he did not expect, for he looked for no enemy, and while he was in doubt and suspense about them, they came so near that they began to fire.

He had neither time nor means to prepare for defence, so that there was nothing to be done but to run into his boat and escape to the shore, which he did accordingly with the few hands he had with him, leaving the two women on board to be taken by the enemy. The sloops seized the "Kingston," manned her, and brought her into Jamaica, having still a great part of her cargo left. When she arrived the master of her fell to examining what part of the cargo was lost and what left. He searched also for his bills of lading, but they were all destroyed by Rackman, so that the ship, being freighted by several owners, the master could not tell whose property was saved and whose lost until he had fresh bills of parcels of each owner from England. There was one remarkable piece of good luck which happened in this affair. There were, amongst other goods, sixty gold watches on board, and thirty silver. The pirates

The Early Settlers

divided the silver, but the gold being packed up among some bales of goods were never discovered by them, and the master, in searching, found them all safe.

In the meantime Rackman and his crew lived in the woods, in very great suspense what to do with themselves. They had with them ammunition and small arms, and also some of the goods, such as bales of silk stockings, and laced hats, with which, it is supposed, they intended to make themselves fine. They had also two boats and a canoe.

Being divided in their resolution, Rackman, with six more, determined to take one of the boats, and make the best of their way for the Island of Providence, and there claim the benefit of the King's pardon, which they fancied they might be entitled to, by representing that they were carried away by Vane against their wills. Accordingly they put some arms, ammunition and provision into the best boat, and also some of the goods, and set sail.

They first made the Island of Pines, from thence got over to the North side of Cuba, where they destroyed several Spanish boats and launches. One they took, which, being a stout sea boat, they shifted themselves and their cargo into her, and sunk their own. They they stretched over to the Island of Providence, where they landed safely about the middle of May, 1719, where, demanding the King's pardon, the Governor thought fit to allow, and certificates were granted to them accordingly. Here they sold their goods and spent the money merrily.

THE ACCOUNT
of the
LOYALISTS

Who fled from East Florida shortly after the American Revolution and came to the Bahamas.

Refugees on board the Transport Ship "Spring."
From St. Mary's, East Florida, arrived at New Providence, 1784.
John Martin, Esq., and 29 slaves.
    also
Lieutenant Generals Grant and Yates, and 32 slaves.

On the 29th September, 1784, the Transport Brigantine "Clementine" arrived with a cargo of building material.
Arrived on board the Transport
"Countess of Darlington"
From St. Mary's East Florida, 4th April, 1784, 72 slaves and building material.

Return of Refugees arriving at New Providence from St. Mary's, East Florida, on board the Transport "Charlotte," 23rd June, 1784.

White Families:—
    John Mills.
    Sarah Hewitt.

The Early Settlers

Mrs. Simmery and family.
Samuel Dames.
Diana Moore and Child.
Jonah Rooker, wife and 2 children.
John Muir, wife and 4 childrtn.
Thomas Muir and wife.
William Simmery and child.
William Brockley (3 in family).
Charles Cox.
Mary Rush and 2 children.
Lawrence Dorkins.
Samuel McCarthy, wife and child.
Mark Carey, wife and 2 children.
Randall Wilson.
Elizabeth Carey, wife and 3 children.
James Shirley and wife.
Samuel Pheemer and 16 slaves.

Return of Refugees from St. Mary's, East Florida, on board Schooner "Elizabeth," 1784.
60 Negro Slaves owned by Mr. Huosne.
52 ,, ,, Mr. Lewis.
13 ,, ,, Different Owners.
And Messrs. Johnstone and John Woodside.

Arrived at New Providence on board the Transport "Nancy," 1784.
128 Negro Slaves; 4 Whites, among whom was Mr. John Moss and James Darvil.

Arrived at New Providence on board the Transport "Ann," 1784.
34 Negro Slaves and a Cargo of Lumber and Shingles from St. Mary's, East Florida, and about 1,500 other arrivals.

       Capt. Touyn,
       Governor General,
        Nassau.

In the following list of Loyalists, are found a few names of the Bahamian Early Settlers. This is accounted for from the fact that the Early Settlers of the Bahamas moved about not only within their own borders, but made frequent visits to the neighbouring Colonists along the Atlantic Coast of

The Early Settlers

East Florida, carrying on trade which was indispensable for their existence, and, no doubt some remained, but returned to the Bahamas on account of the results of the Revolutionary War.

The coming of the Loyalists to the Bahamas presents a picture of the unhappy results of War.

Their property was confiscated by an Act of Confiscation passed by the several States of America.

Great Britain's claim on behalf of the refugees for the restitution or compensation of all Confiscated Estates were met with a blunt refusal from America, upon the ground that the Loyalists were the principal cause of the War and were instrumental in aggravating its worst horrors.

In 1782, they were given twelve months to leave the country, and in 1783, one thousand five hundred or more, together with their slaves, landed on the shores of the Bahamas. They endured many privations, and passed through many trials.

However, they were determined to face life anew, in spite of privations and discomforts, which naturally would follow them. But their wanderings were only a minor result and a slight picture of War, so then, when we hear of it, let us think what it means, horrors, from which we should shudder.

Alexander Ross.
Wm. Henry Hamilton, Esq.
John Morris, Esq.
Archibald MacArthur, Esq.
Thos. North.
Peter Dean, Esq.
Robert Moodie, Esq.
Rt. Hon. Earl of Dunmore
  (250 acres at Long Island)
Wm. Lyford, Esq.
Wm. Carr.
Robert Spence.
Hon. John Boyd.
Hon. Josiah Tatnell.
Ann Bigland Hodgson.
Hon. Robert Hunt.
John Buckley.
Lieut.-Col. John Hamilton.

Joseph Stout.
Andrew Deveaux.
Robert Johnstone, Esq.
George Gray.
Thomas Shirley.
Hon. Alexander Murray.
Hon. John Miller.
John McKenzie, Esq.
Charles Dames.
James Stevens.
Dugald Forbes.
Dennis Rolle.
Geo. Campbell Parks.
  (Island of Eleuthera)
John Moultrie.
Robert Rumer, Esq.
Walter Brown.
Geo. Gray.

The Early Settlers.

Bromfield Bonamy.
Frederick Stage.
Wm. Wilson, Jr.
Wm. Wilson, Esq.
Thos. Boon, Esq.
George Johnson
  (500 acres at Long Island)
Hon. Geo. Barry.
Alexander Harrold.
Thomas Roker, Esq.
Abraham Adderley
  (700 acres at Long Island)
Wm. Moss.
William Simmery.
Isaac Balliou.
Thomas Simpson.
James Hume.
Robert Curry.
Alexander Todd.
Amelia Smith.
Robert Halliday.
  (700 acres, Long Island)
Luke Augustus Chilcott.
John Cornish.
William Charlton.
Richard Micklithwait.
William Pritchard.
Alexander McKay.
Christopher Neilly.
John Douglass, Esq.
Thomas Smith.
  (300 acres, Long Island)
John Crosskill.
Ridley Pinder.
Martin Jollie.
Samuel Mackey.
Thomas Howe.
William Wells.
Thomas Thompson.
Alexander Gibson.
Jesse Goldsmith.
Alexander Grayham.

Ann Wilkins.
Chas. Fox Taylor.
Richard Pearis.
James O'Neal.
John Fox.
John Stephens.
Robert Cunningham.
Malcolm McKay.
Doctor John Allen.
Margaret Pearis.
Daniel McKay.
William Talfair, Esq.
Andrew Skinner, Esq.
William Fair.
Donald Cameron.
James Kelly
  (500 acres, Eleuthera).
Catherine Davis.
Wade Stubbs.
Nicholas Martin.
John Morris.
Richard Stubbs.
James Braynen
  (120 acres, Exuma).
Edward Lowe.
Samuel Higgs
  (300 acres, Eleuthera).
George Weech.
William Clarke.
Matthew Petty.
Capt. Alexander Campbell
  Wylly (Royal Militia).
William Johnstone.
Ann Thompson.
Joseph Hunter.
O'Lof Paterson.
John Brice.
John Ferguson.
John Wood, Esq.
Margaret Rearden
  (Later Margaret Jones)

The Early Settlers.

Lieut.-Col. Andrew Deveaux
(Land 4 miles to the West of the Town of Nassau)·
Lewis Johnstone.
Peter Dean.
Nathaniel Hall·
Johh Nulywn Tatnall, Esq.
James Howe.
Hugh Dean.
Philip Moore, Esq.
(1,180 acres, Exuma)·
Elenor Gambier.
Samuel Gambier.
Nat· Hall.
Thomas Bird.
Rebecca Cuthbert.
Peter Wemyss.
William Bowe·
Roger Bowe.
John Dennestone.
Daniel McKenzie.
John Ragala·
Alexander Drysdale.
John McIntosh.
Mary Minns.
Philip Shears·
Abraham Martinanget.
Abraham Adderley.
Nicholas Burrows.
Walter Turnbull·
Lieut.-Col. Thomas Brown.
William Panton.
Roger Kelsall, Esq.
(40 acres, Exuma).
William Armstrong·
John Wells.
Henry Williams·
Samuel Williams.
James Samson.
John Valentine.
Dennis Rolle
(200 acres, Exuma).
John Russel
(1,460 acres, Abaco).
William Burrows
(200 acres, Long Island)--
Thomas Williamson.
John McDonald·
Conrade Pennybaker.
Robert Humber.
William Morley.
Anthony Stenffort.
John Mackay.
Burton Williams·
Samuel Wilson.
John Hogan·
Anthony Roxburgh.
James Shirley.
John Simpson.
John Mowbray.
William Moss.
William Scott·
Joshua Nixon.
John Martin·
John Wells.
Robert Basden.
Philip Bullard.
Oswell Eve.
Alexander Taylor.
Alexander Begbie·
John Gibson.
John McDonald·
Joseph Eve.
James Hepburn.
Thomas Hodgson, Sr.
William Williams
(120 acres, Watlings)-
Alexander Johnson.
Wilson Williams·
John Douglas.
Charles Dames·
Mary Robinson.
Jane Davis.
Benjamin McKiney.

The Early Settlers.

Isabella Barrow.
John Wallace Barclay.
Augustus Underwood.
Henry Smith.
Michael Malcom
  (160 acres, Crooked Island).
Daniel Culmer
  (57 acres, Long Island).
Margaret McAllister.
John Rowland.
John Burnett.
James Marks.
William Gamble.
Margaret McNeil.
James Clements.
Isaac Dubois.
Alexander McLean.
James Wallace.
John Rhaming.
Henry Sweeting.
James Knowles
  (150 acres, Long Island).
William McLeod.
Richard Colby.
William Butler.
George Flowers.
Randall Wilson.
John Jones.
Helena Tubley.
John Joachin Tubley.
Elizabeth Tubley.
David Tubley.
Edward Gibbons.
Robert Thompson Henzell.
James Johnstone.
Mary Robertson.
Hector McAlister.
Henry Glinton, Esq.
Charles Daniels.
John Harrison.
Robert Wilson.
Magdalene Baldwin.
Patrick Mullins.
Richard Curry.
David Anderson.
Abraham Pratt.
Elizabeth Smith.
John Kerr.
Henry Rae.
James Pringle.
Daniel McCann.
Gilbert Grant.
Abraham Greenage.
Samuel McKinen.
William Wylly.
John Watson.
William Rigby.
John Ferguson.
Kenneth Ferguson.
John Braddock.
William Matthews.
Nancy Maddocks.
Elizabeth Christian.
John Horn.
Abraham Culver.
Anthony Holmes.
James Baird.
Mary Johnstone.
John Benzie.
James Mitchelson.
Timothy Berry.
Ernest Reister.
Hugh Kelly.
James Baird.
John Monbray.
Donald McDonald.
James Rose.
Thomas Foster.
William Curtis.
Joseph Smith
Alexander Stewart.
Daniel Sutherland.
John McKee.

The Early Settlers

Michael McKee.
Alexander McKee.
John McFarlane.
John Martin Struder.
Duncan Taylor
(180 acres, Watlings Island).
John McCowan.
Michael Brown.
Alexander Harrold.
John Hanna
(1,000 acres, Acklins).
Donald Ferguson.
Archibald Taylor
(400 acres, Long Island).
Thomas Armstrong.
Thomas Brown.
William Garrard.
Thomas Williamson.
John Storr.
Thomas Ellorby.
Thomas Smith.
Joseph Morris Moore.
Thomas Waters.
William Lockhart.
William James.
James Misick.
Charles Pasteur.
John McIntosh.
James Oniel.
John Philips.
David McKins.
John Rainger.
Benedict Plenis.
John Cooke.
Hugh Dean.
George Smith.
John Marks.
Salvadore Mucadell.
John Edwards.
Andrew Blanchard.
William Gilchrist.
Sweeting Maycock.
Ancel Ferguson.
Silvester Crispin.
John Cochran.
William Moxey.
Hannah Short.
Dennis Flyns.
Edmund Rush Wigg, Esq.
John Lovell.
Seth Yeoman.
Ann Mary Cargill.
James Pringle.
Patrick Miller.
John Jordan.
James Ridley.
Anthony Fryar.
William Haynes.
Samuel Fox.
Thomas Wood Gillet.
Thomas Stevens.
Alexander Campbell.
John Weir.
Edward Haynes.
Solomon Glass.
Eleoner Stevens.
William Wilcox.
George Loveck.
Joseph Taylor
Margaret McNeil.
Lawrence McCarthy.
William Keinhart.
Mary Major.
John Cornish.
Josiah Vallean.
Alexander Lorinner.
John Russell
(200 acres, Abaco).
Judith Lesvis.
Robert Linton.
Samuel Knowles.
Charles Zannical.
Samuel Roworth.

The Early Settlers

Elizabeth Mullins.
Joseph McKenzie.
Robert Craimel.
Mark Kersey.
Robert Curry
 (85 acres, New Providence).
John Penn.
Daniel Dalby.
Christian McMeyers.
Philip Dumaresque.
Duncan Taylor.
Louisa Waldron.
Martin Weatherford
 (110 acres, Abaco).
Nathaniel Hall.
John Johnstone.
William Pritchard
 (80 acres, Long Island).
Setts Freeman.
John Bromhall.
Elizabeth Green.
John Stewart.
John Wallace.
James Cadwell.
John Hall.
William Queen.
George Harkness.
Henry Wells.
Peter Cartes.
George Miller.
Carles Farquharson.
Charles Richter.
James Pringle.
Joseph Young.
Peter Selon.
Marmaduke Wright.
Jeremiah Stewart.
Mary Cruden.
Major Alexander Mair
 (100 acres, Watling).
Hannah Motte.
James Brisbane, Esq.
Thomas Manuel.
John Griffith.
John Roberts
 (80 acres, Long Island).
George Beaker.
John Evelyn.
James Armbrister.
 (40 acres, Long Island).
Joseph Fox.
Alexander Loriner.
William Rees.
Amelia Smith.
Sarah Powell.
George Outlaw.
Samuel Wilkins.
Sophia Forbes.
Susannah Brown.
James Rose.
Richard Young.
George Harkness.
Samuel Sweeting.
John Ferguson.
John Drudge.
John Petty, Esq.
Sophia Darville.
William Wilson.
John Alexander.
Thomas Cockshis.
John Fox.
Sarah Chavers.
Robert Weir.
Ann Murphy.
Sarah Fish.
Robert Hunt, Esq.
Thomas Brown
 (20 acres, Abaco).
Thomas Ross, Esq.
William Lyford.
Joseph Shoemaker.
John Wallace Barclay.
Alexander Spiers.

The Early Settlers

Richard Curtis.
Neptune Curtis.
Rosanna Newman.
George Davis.
Anthony Friar.
Henrietta Nicklethwaite.
Sett Yeoman.
Alexander McDonald.
James Ford.
Rebecca Darling.
Francis Kirk.
Benjamin Newton.
Henry Hall.
William Thomson.
George Farquharson
 (1040 acres, Crooked
 Island).
Christopher Neilly.
John Armstrong.
James Lane.
John Longley.
James Pemberton.
William Eve.
John and Ann Kelsall
 (60 acres, Exuma).
George Augustus Gamble.
Robert Grant.
Jacob Kiercher.
Peter Edwards.
William Alexander.
John Anderson.
John Coakley.
George Nodlings.
Seth Dowd.
John Clarke.
Phebe Ray.
Stephen Haven.
Bainhear Miller.
Miles McInnes.
Joseph Curry
 (220 acres, Eleuthera).
Griffin Jenkins.
John Kersey.
Alexander McQueen.
Jonathan Belton.
John Benzie.
Richard Hayman.
Henry Duncan.
Thomas Johnson.
Kersey Sturrup.
Margaret Bell.
William Haskey.
Alexander Campbell Wylly.
Martin McEvoy.
Michael Rodgers.
Rush Tucker.
Maria Dans.
James Burns.
John Lewis.
Robert Holliday.
Thomas Tyack.
James Gray.
John Poor.
Stephen Holdsworth.
Jeremiah Tinker.
Thomas Carrier.
George Loveck.
Charles Fox Taylor.
Thomas Carroll.
Thomas Forbes.
Jane Davis.
Alexander Collie
 (1000 acres, Crooked
 Island).
John Crosskill.
Philip Fry.
Ambrose Lee.
Rose McLeod.
Benjamin McKinney.
Winer Bethell
 (100 acres, Eleuthera).
Frederick Frosback.
John Cruden.
Solomon Glass.

The Early Settlers

Thomas Roker.
John Petty.
Susannah Townson.
John Hendricks.
Jeremiah Cushing.
John C. Kemp.
Hon. Stephen Delancy.
Gerhart Raab.
Benjamin Saunders.
William Cash.
William Mina Chrystie.
William Moss.
James Lane.
Alexander Todd.
William Barton.
Mary Hardy.
Abraham Pratt.
Peter Pyfrom.
James Wolfe.
John Harrison.
Thomas Bill.
Susannah Leary.
Sarah Hudson.
Timothy Cox.
Peter Bethune.
Benjamin Lord.
William Stipper.
Michael Samuel DeBruhl.
Isaac Bunting.
John Falconer, Esq.
John Bramhall.
Susannah Hawkins.
Peter Edwards, Esq.
Edward Gibbony.
Samuel Clutsam.
Peter Southall.
Thomas Water, Esq.
Elisha Swain.
Eleanor Parker.
William Middleton.
John K. Reckley.
Charles Marshall.

John Outten.
Ebenezer Love.
George Gray.
Philip Moore, Esq.
Joseph Evans
Elizabeth Mason.
James Armbrister.
James Burns.
George Weech.
James Mysick.
Elizabeth Shears.
Mary Mathilda Payne.
John Jacob Payne.
Mary Bell Payne.
William Middleton.
Frederick Fine.
Hon. Robert Sterling.
Rose Minors.
Thomas Minors.
Drover Minors.
James Minors.
Juba Baldwin.
Robert Duncombe.
Robert Scott.
James Stevens.
James Braynen.
Grace Rhoden.
Chas. Culmer.
Constant Culmer.
Charlotte Christie.
John McIntosh
Samuel Knowles.
James White.
John Dunn.
Amos Williams.
Honor Conolly.
Sarah McKelvey.
Lawrence Perch.
Moody Pinder.
Judith Conolly.
Sarah McKelvey.
Lawrence Perch.

The Early Settlers

Moody Pinder.
Thomas North.
Edward Barton.
John French.
Thomas Young.
Kersey Sturrup.
Anna Beak.
Noah Bethell
(400 acres, Eleuthera).
Robert Cumming.
John Deveaux.
Elizabeth Bowles.
William Bunch.
Hon. George McKenzie.
Edward Morley.
Richard Pearis.
John Lewis Frazer.
Paul Lightbourn, Esq.
James Baird.
Dennis Fowler.
Martin Mackarthy.
Andrew Deveaux.
Reuben Holmes.
William Newman.
Elizabeth Fisher.
James Samson.
Hon. Alexander Murray.
James Kelly.
Richard Thompson.
John Dickson.
Paul Lightbourn, Esq.
(1000 acres, New Providence).
John Multryne.
William Bradford.
Edward Murray.
Gilbert Grant.
Thomas Bowles.
Charley Sanders.
Richard Sweeting.
Richard Barnett.
Venus Watkins.
William Simms.
Thomas Neeks.
Paul Dromgoole.
Samuel Moxey.
Benjamin Moxey.
William Smith.
Joseph Pinder.

PUBLIC SERVICES
and
GENERAL INFORMATION
(Present and Past).

Officers of the Government, Etc.

Appointment.
    Governor and Commander-in-Chief in and over the Bahama Islands, Vice-Admiral and Ordinary.

1937   His Excellency the Governor,
THE HON. CHARLES DUNDAS, C.M.G., O.B.E., Governor Elect.
Administrator during the absence of the Governor,
The Hon. J. H. Jarret, K.C., Colonial Secretary.
Private Secretary and Clerk of Executive Council,
Captain Clement Holland.

The Early Settlers.

MEMBERS OF HIS MAJESTY'S EXECUTIVE COUNCIL.

Appointment.
1st and 2nd.

1933, 1935	Hon. James Henry Jarrett, K.C., Colonial Secretary.
1910, 1928	Hon. Charles P. Bethell, Asst. Colonial Secretary.
1936	Hon. J. Bowes Griffin, LL.D., M.A., Attorney General.
1936	Hon. R. W. Taylor, C.M.G., C.B.E., Receiver General and Treasurer.
1936	Hon. O. H. Curry.
1926	Hon. A. K. Solomon, K.C.
1933	Hon. Ralph Collins.

MEMBERS OF HIS MAJESTY'S LEGISLATIVE ASSEMBLY.

1933	Hon. W. K. Moore, C.B.E., President.
1916	Hon. P. W. D. Armbrister, O.B.E.
1935	Hon. Dr. J. Baird Albury.
1923	Nigel Burnside, I.S.O.
1924	C. O. Anderson.
1931	A. K. Cole.

CIVIL SERVICE OF THE BAHAMAS.

Colonial Secretary's Department.

1933, 1935	Hon. James Henry Jarrett, K.C., Colonial Secretary.
	Charles Percival Bethell, I.S.O., Asst. Colonial Secretary.
1920, 1928	Sybil Burnside.
1928, 1932	Newton Clyde Roberts.
1934	Lois Chipman.

Receiver General's Department.

1936	Hon. R. W. Taylor, C.M.G., C.B.E., Receiver General and Treasurer.
1929	Charles S. Thompson, Cashier.
1913, 1928	S. A. Eldon.
1931	Thomas I. Kemp.

The Early Settlers.

1927, 1931   Doris R. Lowe.
1927, 1929   R. B. Haxton.
1927, 1929   E. S. Wells.
1925, 1934   Frederick A. Taylor.
1927, 1931   William A. Sweeting.

Attorney General's Department.

1936   Hon. J. Bowes Griffin, Attorney General.

Registrar General's Department.

1911, 1923   R. J. A. P. G. de Glanville, Registrar General.
1937   Mervyn Johnson, Asst. Registrar General.
1903, 1931   F. A. C. Duncombe, Acting Registrar.
1929   Edith S. Clarke.

Audit Department.

1936   E. A. Stoodley, Auditor.
1910, 1927   J. L. Lightbourn.
1919, 1928   E. H. Stuart.
1936   G. D. Gamblin.
1932   W. P. Bethell.

Post Office Department.

1904, 1908   James Herbert Peet, Postmaster General.
1921, 1927   C. A. Bowen.
1920, 1931   Alfred Eldon.
1926, 1929   Mary V. Dupuch.
1927, 1929   Emerald E. Nicolls.
1929, 1931   Emily E. Dupuch.
1926, 1931   Viola T. Knowles.

Customs Department.

1907, 1928   A. K. Cole, Comptroller of Customs.
1924, 1931   N. E. Lightbourn, Asst. Comptroller of Customs.
1921, 1927   James H. Wallace.
1927   H. R. Cooper.
1927   Timothy McCartney.
1927   Edward Seymour Mitchell.
1928   Vivian N. Pinder.
1927, 1931   Alice Smith.
1921, 1927   Margaret Malcolm.

The Early Settlers

Harbour Master.

1921 — George Campbell Roberts.

Judicial Department.

1932 — Sir Richard Clifford Tute, K.C.M.G., Chief Justice.
1926 — J. F. Greenidge, Crier.
1936 — Major R. A. Erskine Lindop, Commandant.
1937 — O. L. Bancroft, M.A., Stipendary and Circuit Magistrate.
1926, 1927 — Jerome F. Greenidge, Magistrate's Court.
1927 — H. Pemberton, Inspector of Police.
1928, 1929 — Capt. R. M. Millar, Gaoler.
1928 — F. G. Lancaster, M.C., Detective Inspector.
1908, 1927 — C. H. King, Sergeant Major of Police.

Education Department.

1909, 1917 — Wilton G. Albury, Inspector and General Supt.
1912, 1928 — Cleveland H. Reeves, Secretary.
1909, 1917 — Thomas A. Thompson, Principal Instructor (Western Central School).
1917, 1924 — Mary B. Albury.
1917, 1931 — E. P. Roberts.
1924 — P. E. Smith.
1908, 1931 — Charles I. Gibson, Principal Instrctor (Eastern Central School).
Mary A. Sands.

Medical Establishment.

1928, 1931 — John M. Cruikshank, Chief Medical Officer (Bahamas General Hospital).
1920, 1931 — Dr. Fitzmaurice, Medical Officer and Bacteriologist.
1932 — Dr. Soyons, Assistant Medical Officer.
1927 — Henry L. Sumner, Superintendent, Hospital.
1927, 1933 — H. F. Knowles, Sanitary Inspector.
1930 — G. B. Strachan, Dispenser.
1933 — A. S. Wallace, Relieving Officer.
1928, 1934 — Annie Baines, Matron.
1933 — Sarah G. Raine, Sister.
1932 — Lilly Sutton, Sister.
1928, 1931 — L. B. Albury, Supervisor, Market.

The Early Settlers

The Surveyor General's Department.

His Excellency the Governor, Er-Officio Chairman.
1918   William N. Aranha, Deputy Surveyor.
1926   I. V. Cox, Assistant Surveyor.
1926   George E. Johnson.
1921   Gwendolin Cash.

Public Works Department.

1925, 1928   Frederick C. VanZeylen, Director of Public Works.
1927   John F. G. Holmes, First Asst. Engineer.

Electrical Department.

1934   Henry H. Manson, Director.
1909, 1923   Edward L. Moore, Supt. and Chief Engineer.
1923, 1931   Frederick R. Moultrie, Engineer.
1923, 1927   George Pierce, Engineer.
1927   William Lightbourn, Engineer.
1927   Dudley A. W. Taylor, Linesman.
1927   Henry V. Brown, Engineer.

Telegraph Department.

1921, 1932   David Salter, Superintendent.
1932   Lionel S. Hughes, Asst. Superintendent.
1928   Paul Albury.
1922, 1935   E. H. McKinney.
1922, 1925   Robert H. Sands.
1924, 1935   Kenneth R. Ingraham.
1923   George L. Bethel.
1923   Stafford Symonette.
1926   John L. Saunders.
1926   Ronald G. Sands.
1927   Willard Dorsett Parkinson.
1928   John P. Culmer.
1931   Theodora S. Roberts.
1931   Howard W. Russell.
1931   Henry Milton Clear.
1935   Eric P. Pinder.
1931   Basil Albury.

The Early Settlers

Telephones.

1925, 1928	Hattie J. E. Moore, Supervisor of Telephones.
1917, 1925	Kathleen Bannister.
1921, 1925	Lillian Bode.
1921, 1926	Elsie G. Gignac.
1924, 1935	Edith Rode.
1926	Madge K. Roberts.
1926	Florence Smith.
1927	Leonora McKinney.
1927	Doris M. Smith.
1929	Constance M. Bedford.
1932	Joyce McKinney.

MEMBERS OF THE HOUSE OF ASSEMBLY.

Elected.
1914-35	W. C. B. Johnson, Speaker.
1935	G. W. Higgs, Deputy Speaker.
1935	Arthur H. Sands, City.
1937	Stafford Sands, City.
1935	A. K. Solomon, K.C., Southern District.
1935	Dr. C. R. Walker, Southern District.
1935	R. T. Symonette, Eastern District.
1935	L. W. Young, Eastern District.
1935	A. F. Adderley, Western District.
1935	Percy E. Christie, Western District.
1935	W. C. B. Johnson, Harbour Island.
1935	Reginald Farrington, Harbour Island.
1935	H. N. Chipman, Harbour Island.
1935	R. W. Sawyer, Eleuthera.
1935	G. W. K. Roberts, Eleuthera.
1935	O. H. Curry, Eleuthera.
1935	B. R. Russell, Abaco.
1935	J. W. Roberts, Abaco.
1937	Frank Christie, Abaco.
1935	A. E. J. Dupuch, Inagua.
1937	J. K. A. Kelly, Grand Bahama and Bimini.
1935	R. H. Curry, Andros and Berry Islands.
1935	B. H. McKinney, Andros and Berry Islands.
1935	A. R. Braynen, Cat Island.
1935	Harold G. Christie, Cat Island.

The Early Settlers

1935	L. C. Brice, Long Island.
1935	L. G. Dupuch, Long Island.
1935	George Murphy, Exuma.
1935	E. V. Solomon, Exuma.
1935	G. W. Higgs, Rum Cay and Watlings.
1935	Hon. R. G. Collins, Crooked Island.

THE IMPERIAL LIGHTHOUSE SERVICE.

Commander Langton-Jones, Inspector, Imperial Lighthouses.

Staff.

J. G. Palfrey, Chief Clerk.
F. Pool, Chief Engineer of Lighthouse Tender "Firebird."
W. Moxeley, Captain.
H. Pinder, Second Officer.
P. G. Rogers, Store-keeper.

CHURCHES.

Cathedral.—The site on which the present building now stands was an old parish Church known as "Christ Church" facing a sand bank to the North of its present location. Between this bank and the Church was the street known as "Bay Street" some distance from the Church.

It was the only Church in New Providence in 1723, where the inhabitants could meet together for Divine Worship.

The records which are still kept in Christ Church Cathedral show all the marriages performed, and births, baptisms and deaths are entered in the Register from 1723 to the present day.

This building was pulled down some time after the advent of the Loyalists from East Florida and the present Christ Church Cathedral constructed on the same foundation in 1837. The new Church was opened in 1840.

It is a fine specimen of a County Church in England and has sittings for about 1,200. It has withstood the most devastating hurricanes for 100 years, in fact, stood, while scores of other Churches and buildings had been carried away by storms.

The Early Settlers

In 1861, the See of Nassau was founded, in Her Majesty's Reign, by Letters Patent, when Christ Church was designated the Cathedral of the Diocese.

At an early date the Vestry of Christ Church exercised the Authority of issuing Licences instead of the Government and this practise was carried on until the Act of Disendowment became law.

St. Matthew's Church.—The foundation of St. Matthew's Church was laid in the year 1800, and was opened for Divine Service in 1802.

The Church can accommodate 550 persons and unlike other Churches in the Colony has an extensive Burial Ground which surrounds the Church and is sufficiently large enough to take care of all the members of the Church as well as a great many others.

In this Churchyard are found, tombs, monuments and graves of the most distinguished citizens who came here after the American Revolution.

St. Agnes' Church.—St. Agnes' Church was consecrated in 1868 and can accommodate 600 persons. It is the only Church in the Diocese that one cannot find sitting space during the Sunday services. Such popularity is wholly due to the good work performed in the Parish by the present Rector, the Rev. Canon George Pyfrom, O.B.E.

St. Mary's Church.—St. Mary's Church stands upon the site formerly known as "Brays School House."

The original Church was destroyed by the hurricane of 1866. It can accommodate about 300 persons. The corner stone was again laid in 1868. The consecration took place the following year. The Churchyard contains the Tomb of The Right Rev. C. C. Caufield, D.D., 1st Bishop of the Diocese who died 1862

St. Francis Xavier's Church.—The foundation of St. Francis Xavier's Church was laid in 1885, and is the first Roman Catholic Church in the Bahamas, (although there is some tradition that a Roman Catholic Church was built on Long Island by refugees from Haiti about 200 years ago).

The late Very Rev. Father Chrysostom Schreiner did much to build up a Church on a strong foundation. He was an exceptional Priest with great ability. He paved the way for the Lord Bishop Bernard and Father Bonaventure and

The Early Settlers.

Staff in the course of a few years to establish one high school and seven free schools containing about 3,000 children in all.

It would be fitting to erect a Memorial to the memory of the late Fr. Chrysostom Schreiner, O.S.B., whose life work leaves the impression of his most exemplary efforts to establish a great Roman Catholic Mission in the Bahamas, and, we also hope, that in the course of events it might fall to the lot of the Right Rev. Bishop Bernard to erect the first Roman Catholic Cathedral in the Island of New Providence.

Zion Baptist Church.—Zion Baptist Church stands on the corner of Shirley and East Streets. The former building was erected in 1835 and accommodated 800 persons.

It was destroyed by the hurricane of 1929 and is now being rebuilt.

Bethel Chapel.—Bethel Chapel was built in the year 1801 by coloured men from St. Augustine, Florida. The building was blown down by the hurricane of 1866 and was rebuilt by the congregation and aided by the grant of £200 from the Legislature.

The Church accommodates about 500 persons.

The Presbyterian Church.—The stately Presbyterian Church is the finest edifice in the Colony. It was built about 1803 by wealthy Loyalists (Scotch Settlers). The Rev. John Rae was its first Minister. It has sittings for more than 600 persons. Its Sunday School attracts children from all denominations and the care and instructions given the children by the Superintendents are admirable.

Trinity Church.—Trinity Church was rebuilt after the hurricane of 1866, which destroyed the old building. The present one is a grand edifice and the music and singing in this Church during the Sunday services is very inspiring to the mind. The building is in the Gothic style of Architecture.

THE GOVERNMENT HIGH SCHOOL.

The building which is now known as the Government High School was formerly the Boys' Central School.

This movement for a higher and broader Education for boys and girls is to supply a long felt want of a secondary

The Early Settlers.

education in the Island by the Government, and there is every reason for the Colony to be proud of having inaugurated this forward movement which will doubtless involve important consequence to Education.

Students enter this institution after having attended the elementary schools and provision is made for scholars to reach a standard by which they would be able to pass the Oxford and Cambridge examinations in all stages.

THE ROMAN CATHOLIC SCHOOLS.

The first high school conducted by the Roman Catholics was situated on West Hill Street and opened November, 1889, under the charge of the Sisters of Charity of Mt. St. Vincent on Hudson.

This School was recently removed to West Bay Street where it sits on a hill-top in very spacious grounds adjoining the historic Fort Charlotte.

The course of instruction embraces all the high branches of a finished education.

The founder of the High School was the late Father Chrysostom Schreiner, O.S.B., whose life work is a living monument to this Colony.

The schools are under the control of His Lordship, The Most Rev. Bishop Bernard, O.S.B., and include 7 free schools which are operated on much the same lines as the public schools. The children are well looked after and enjoy the privileges of sports and festivities in common with the Board Schools.

QUEEN'S COLLEGE.

This School was originally called The Nassau Collegiate School. Was opened by Rev. Terry Bain, 1871.

In 1890, the School was renamed Queen's College. It has three departments, one for boys, one for girls and one a Kindergarten. The curriculum of this School embraces all the subjects taught in an English High School and is a Centre for the Examination of the Cambridge Certificates and the London College of Preceptors.

The School can boast of a very efficient clerical Staff and is managed by the direction of the Superintendent of the Wesleyan Circuit and under the Headmastership of the Rev. R. P. Dyer.

The Early Settlers.

THE NASSAU GRAMMAR SCHOOL.

The old Nassau Grammar School for boys was an excellent institution, once a flourishing centre of Education in the Bahamas.

This School was conducted in the Church Hall which is within speaking distance to Government House.

It was flourishing in the year 1850, but about ten years later began to fall off in attendance.

In 1864, was reorganized by Bishop Venebales, and again placed on a sound footing.

Its staff of Masters possessed Classical and Mathematical Degrees from the English Universities.

The Lord Bishop of Nassau was its Patron, and religious instructions formed a part of the School's curriculum.

In those days it was the only school conducted on the same line of the English Public Schools—that is Educationally—and did excellent work in training the best classes of boys in the Colony.

Some may ask the question, why did this school close its doors some twenty years ago? Well, it might be answered that during this period the congregation of Christ Church fell off almost to a minimum attendance on account of not having a popular man in charge of the parish, from which two-thirds of the number of its Pupils were drawn and this naturally resulted in the closing down of the school.

As the Cathedral is now regaining its original foothold by the work of its present Dean, the Rev. Canon Streatfield, this School may yet reopen its doors.

The Early Settlers

Geology.

Geologically the Bahama Islands, like other parts of the globe, are made of rock and rocky substances. The rock in the Island of New Providence is soft and porous, but in the adjacent Islands is stronger in substance and more uniform in composition. Its formation is in beds or layers of coral limestone in regular order, one above another.

Fossils are found embedded almost in any depth of rock, and such marvellous and natural arrangements of the earth prove that at one time the whole area over which this stratified formation is formed was entirely under water, and would necessarily be subject to animal accumulations.

The coral reefs, sandbanks and shoals are things which contribute largely to the natural formation of the Bahama Islands. The reefs in these transparent waters are lineal and generally run along the coast line. In certain places they extend many miles from land and are exceedingly dangerous to navigation.

Many writers have said much about the nature of these islands. Professor Agassiz in his researches has laid it down that the Bahamas are simply wind-blown piles of shells and coral, and some time previously were more extensive than they are now. He also holds that there has been a general subsidence of some of 300 feet from the total area. The Chronology of such events is uncertain, but we know that changes in the physical condition of the globe have been continual and to a greater extent in some localities than in others.

The Early Settlers

The Bahamas undoubtedly bear relation to the Continent of America, also to fifteen other groups of the West Indian Archipelago. It is believed that they are merely the exposed tips of a great submerged ridge closely connected to Cuba, and the trend and character of the Islands are such as to suggest that they might possibly represent one of the lost Antilles.

You might rightly call the Bahamas the Peninsular of Florida, because the islands project South-easterly from the coast, and are almost contiguous to the narrow submerged shell of the Atlantic Coast, and could be no other than a submarine extension of Florida. There have been geological surveys in the past, which have shown that before the tertiary period the Gulf Stream crossed the Northern part of Florida completely severing the West Indies from North America, and that Southern Florida was at one time a West Indian Island, while the Bahama Banks to the Northward made a long peninsular projecting out from Florida.

GEOGRAPHICAL SUMMARY.

Lying off the East Coast of Florida, about 20 miles across the Gulf Stream, lies Grand Bahama, the nearest Island of the Bahama group to the mainland of Southern Florida. The great chain of Islands are lying between 21° 42′ and 27° 34′ North latitude and 72° 40′ and 79° 3′ West longitude. They are composed of twenty inhabited Islands and several thousand Islets and rocks, with a range of reefs and shoals practically fencing in every one of the Islands, either on one side or the other.

The whole group of Islands may be divided into three divisions, the first of which are those Islands lying off the coast of Florida, viz.: Grand Bahama, Bimini, Abaco, the Berry Islands and the North-western part of Andros. The second or central division is composed of New Providence, the capital of the Bahamas, Harbour Island, Eleuthera, a part of Andros, Exuma, Long Island and Cat Island. The third division is composed of Watlings Island, Rum Cay, Long Cay, Mayaguana, Acklins, Ragged Island and Inauga. The latter Island brings the end of the chain to within 30 miles of the Eastern part of Cuba, and within a hundred miles of the Northern part of Haiti.

The Early Settlers

THE LENGTH, BREADTH AND AREA OF THE LARGEST ISLANDS IN THE GROUP, AND THE NUMBER OF INHABITANTS OF EACH ISLAND AS ARE GIVEN IN THE CENSUS OF 1920, AND WHEN SETTLED.

Grand Bahama.

Length 83 miles. Breadth 4 miles. Area 430 square miles. First settled by a few Loyalists in 1787, viz.: The Hields, Feasters, Grants and the Wilchcomes. The present inhabitants are Creoles.

Biminis.

Length 7 miles. Breadth $1\frac{1}{4}$ miles. Area 8 square miles. Population 476. This island has never attracted enterprising settlers on account of its small area of land. A few families went there from the neighbouring islands of Great Bahama. It was on this island that the great explorer Ponce-de-Leon is supposed to have discovered the "Fountain of Youth."

Abaco and Cays.

Length 100 miles. Breadth $6\frac{1}{4}$ miles. Area 776 square miles. Population 4463. First settled by a large number of Loyalists in 1786. Many of the older Bahamian families branched off from Harbour Island, New Providence and Eleuthera, and joined the Loyalists in settling on most of the Northern islands of Abaco.

Acklins Island.

Length 45 miles. Breadth 3 miles. Area 120 square miles. Population 1733. Settled by Loyalists in 1787, who have all died out, leaving descendants of Creole slaves as the permanent inhabitants of the island. A valuable grade of sponge is found in the waters surrounding this island and the valuable Lignum Vitae, which is exported to England in large quantities, grows luxuriantly.

Eleuthera.

Length 100 miles. Breadth 8 miles. Area 164 square miles. Population 11599. The oldest settled island in the whole group.

Berry Islands.

Area 14 square miles. Population 487. The descendants of a few white settlers remain on the island. The rest of the inhabitants are Creoles. The soil is extremely fer-

The Early Settlers

tile, in fact the richest in these islands. The inhabitants are not as progressive as they might be, and are more restful and quietly disposed than in any of the other islands.

Andros.

Length 99 miles. Breadth 40 miles. Area 1600 square miles. Population 4545. The Neimos, McNeals, Scotch merchants, and several Loyalists settled on this island in 1790, and more recently the late Mr. Joseph Chamberlain a member of the English Parliament, owned a very extensive sisal plantation on the island. The present inhabitants are Creoles, the descendants of former slaves, upon whom the life of the sponge industry of the Bahamas greatly depends.

Crooked Island.

Length 30 miles. Breadth 7 miles. Area 76 square miles. Population 1541. The descendants of former slaves constitute the entire population. Great quantities of Lignum Vitae are exported from this island. The Crooked Island passage is well known to mariners, and is in the roadstead of steamships going southward to Mexican ports, Haiti and the West Indian Islands.

Exuma and Cays.

Length 50 miles. Breadth 5 miles. Area 100 square miles. Population 3465. This island is exceedingly attractive and has played an important part in the history of the Colony. It was one of the most favourite islands of the Loyalist settlers. Lord Rolle and Lord Wright settled on the island during the time of the American Revolution. The Earl of Dunmore, Governor, laid out several townships on the island, and appointed a company of Militia for the protection of the Loyalist settlers. The Rev. William Twing, S.P.G., looked after the spiritual welfare of the new settlers. The present population is composed of Creoles and a few descendants of Loyalists.

Inagua.

Length 45 miles. Breadth 18 miles. Area 5600 square miles. Population 1343, composed of Creoles and descendants of a few white settlers. Though one of the largest islands in the whole group, it does not appear to have had any attraction for the Loyalist settlers nor for the earlier settlers of the Bahama Islands. It is noted for its large salt ponds and wild animals. Previous to the war of 1914 the

The Early Settlers

inhabitants were exceptionally prosperous, and the island was the centre of the agencies for steamers calling for labourers on their way to Central American ports.

Long Cay.
Length 15 miles. Breadth 2 miles. Population 376, composed of Creoles and descendants of white settlers. Like Inagua, Long Cay was a somewhat prosperous island before the war of 1914. An agency for steamers going to Central American ports taking labourers as employees for handling ships' cargoes was also established on this island.

Long Island.
Length 98 miles. Breadth 7 miles. Area 130 square miles. Population 2150. Five hundred Loyalists settled on this island, and it has a greater number of their living descendants than any other island in the group. Before the coming of the Loyalists this island was peopled by a few of the old settlers, who at first lived in the Island of New Providence and some time later moved off to Long Island. For instance, the Simms, the Darvills and the Foxs have been living on Long Island for the last 200 years. The settlement called Simms' is where they first built their homes. The Loyalists settled on Long Island in 1788, during the time when the Right Honourable the Earl of Dunmore was Governor of the Colony. They built up the island, laid out townships, and owned most extensive cotton and sugar plantations, also large cattle ranches. Some of their palatial residences, which are scattered here and there on the island, have fallen into ruins.

Mayaguana.
Area 96 square miles. Population 358 are all Creoles. The island is more noted as a pirates' haunt. The famous Blackbeard's well is located on this island.

Rum Cay.
Length 8 miles. Breadth $3\frac{1}{4}$ miles. Area 29 square miles. Population 430. Robert Rumer, Esq., a Loyalist, settled on this island. One thousand two hundred acres of land was granted to him by the Right Honourable The Earl of Dunmore. The name Rumer is very common among the Creole population, which means that he had a very large number of slaves on his plantation. Rum Cay is the birth-

The Early Settlers.

place of the late Rear-Admiral Forsyth, of the United States Navy. It is a salt making centre, tons of which are exported to the United States annually.

Ragged Island and Cays.

Length 4 miles. Breadth 1¼ miles. Area 5 square miles. Population 343. Settled by a few Loyalists in 1788. William Lockhart, a Loyalist, owned the principal part of the island, whose property has since been inherited by his descendants. This island is by far the greatest salt making centre in the Bahamas. It not only supplies the whole colony, but exports hundreds of tons to the United States, Cuba and Jamaica.

Cat Island.

Length 45 miles. Breadth 4 miles. Area 160 square miles. Population 5,072. First settled by a great number of Loyalists. Colonel Andrew Deveaux, John McDonald, Esq., James Hepburn, Esq., David Tulby, Esq., John Mulyne, Esq., John Cornish, Esq., and James Howe, Esq., made their homes in this island shortly after the American Revolution. The island is extremely fertile, and in bygone days contained very large cotton estates. Horned cattle always did well on the island. The present population, with few exceptions, is composed of Creoles or descendants of the slaves of former Loyalists.

San Salvador or Watlings Island.

Length 12 miles. Breadth 5 miles. Area 60 square miles. Population 646. Major Henry Williams, Archibald Campbell, Esq., John Pennybaker, Esq., William Wilson, Esq., Margaret McAlister, Loyalists, made their homes on this island after the close of the American Revolution. The present population are the descendants of the slaves of former Loyalists. The Roman Catholic Church has recently been established on the island. Watlings Island is the rock upon which the Catholic "Te Deum" was first sung in the New World. After a lapse of 400 years a Catholic Mission is now being conducted on the island by the Rev. Chrysostom Schreiner, O.S.B., and late Vicar of Foraine of the Roman Catholic Church in the Bahamas.

Harbour Island.

Area 1½ square miles. Population 1072. The inhabitants consist partly of the old New Providence and Eleuthera families. These are the Russels, Sweetings, Saunders, Roberts, Pinders, Thompsons, Currys, Barnetts, Alburys and

The Early Settlers.

Johnsons from New Providence. The Ingrahams and Bethells were from Eleuthera. The Loyalist settlers were the Weatherfords, Prudens, Cashes, Pettees, Munroes and Higgs. The Creoles or descendants of the Africans number about one-half the population. On this island was built the summer residence of the Right Honourable the Earl of Dunmore.

New Providence.

Length 23 miles. Breadth 7 miles. Area 58 square miles. Population 13,554. Permanently settled after 1666. Many Loyalists settled in New Providence in 1788. Nassau, the capital, is the seat of Government. On Mount FitzWilliam is built the Governor's residence. The Priory was built and occupied by the Right Hon. Earl of Dunmore as his official residence in 1789. The Executive Government is conducted under Letters Patent by the Governor, aided by an Executive Council of nine members. The Legislative authority resides in the Governor, a Legislative of nine members, nominated by the Crown, and a representative assembly of twenty-nine members elected for fifteen districts, by persons owning land of the value of five pounds, or occupying houses of the rental of two pounds eight shillings in New Providence or one pound four shillings in the outlying islands. The qualification of election are full age, a residence of twelve months with land value five pounds or being a home holder of premises valued two pounds eight shillings in New Providence or one pound four shillings elsewhere for six months. The qualification of members is possession of an estate of real or peronal property of the value of two hundred pounds. The Executive Council is composed partly of official and partly of unofficial members, who have a seat in one of the branches of the Legislative. Higher education is provided at the Queen's College; the Rev. Georges' Grammar School; a Secondary Government School, and St. Hilda's School, all in Nassau. No regular system of Government was set up until 1728, when an elective assembly was established and has remained the only form of Government to this day. New Providence was laid waste by the Spaniards in 1680, or 1682. In 1703 the French and Spaniards combined, and practically annihilated the settlement. The pirates were finally extirpated in 1718 by the English, under Capt. Woodes Rogers.

The Early Settlers.

A Land Sale.

LAYING OUT THE TOWNSHIP OF HARBOUR ISLAND, AND SALE OF THE FOLLOWING LOTS:—

These lots were sold on the 5th October, 1791, at a yearly rent of 2/6, to be paid 14 days after the first day of St. John the Baptist:—

Bahama Islands, George III., Etc., etc., etc.

Know ye, that We, of Our Special Grace, certain knowledge and motion have given and granted by these presents, for Us, Our Heirs, and Successors. Do give, and grant, unto the several persons hereinafter particularly named, All those lots of land in the Township of Dunmore on Harbour Island, one of the Bahama Islands:—

To Wit:

Jones, Wm., Esq.,	His Heirs and assigns for ever	Lot No.	22
Frank Moses, Esq.	do.	do.	23
Saunders, Nathaniel, Jn.	do.	do.	25
Curry, Richard	do.	do.	36
Russell, Nathaniel	do.	do.	37
Bethell, John	do.	do.	46
Roberts, James	do.	do.	47
Holmes, Mary	do.	do.	48
Brooks, Peter	do.	do.	49
Lowe, Gideon	do.	do.	50
Roberts, John	do.	do.	51
Curry, John	do.	do.	52
Russell, Daniel	do.	do.	53
Saunders, John	do.	do.	54
Curry, John, Sn.	do.	do.	56
Curry, Thomas	do.	do.	58

The Early Settlers

Saunders, Nathaniel	do.	do.	59
Curry, John	do.	do.	60
Johnson, Samuel, Jr.	do.	do.	61
Roberts, Richard	do.	do.	62
Cleare, John	do.	do.	63
Roberts, John	do.	do.	64
Russell, Thomas	do.	do.	65
Roberts, Richard	do.	do.	66
Albury, Joseph	do.	do.	68
Pearce, Thomas	do.	do.	70
Ranger, John	do.	do.	71
Roberts, Joseph	do.	do.	72
Higgs, Samuel	do.	do.	73
Roberts, Wm.	do.	do.	74
Roberts, Martha	do.	do.	75
Albury, Sarah	do.	do.	76
Roberts, John	do.	do.	77
Albury, Joseph	do.	do.	78
Johnstone, Nathaniel	do.	do.	79
Patrick, Samuel (Free Mullatto)	do.	do.	80
Curry, Joseph, His heirs and assigns	do.	do.	81
Ingraham, John	do.	do.	82
Tedder, Joseph	do.	do.	83
Albury, Wm.	do.	do.	84
Roberts, Benjamin	do.	do.	85
Russell, Joseph	do.	do.	86
Sweeting, Samuel	do.	do.	87
Sawyer, Daniel	do.	do.	88
Thompson, Richard	do.	do.	89
Saunders, Thomas, Sn., His heirs, etc.	do.	do.	90
Saunders, Benjamin	do.	do.	91
Roberts, John	do.	do.	92
Cleare, Thomas	do.	do.	93
Pearce, Joseph.	do.	do.	94
Tedder, Joseph, Jr.	do.	do.	95
Tedder, John	do.	do.	96
Cash, Thomas	do.	do.	97
Ferguson, Anne	do.	do.	98

The Early Settlers

Parks, Mark	do.	do.	99
To public for schoolhouse	do.	do.	100
Kemp, Benjamin	do.	do.	101
Robertson, Rev. Thomas	do.	do.	102
Cash, Thomas, Sr.	do.	do.	103
Cash, Robert	do.	do.	104
Lightbourn, Thos. (Free Mulatto)	do.	do.	105
Cash, Wm.	do.	do.	106
Saunders, John	do.	do.	107
do.	do.	do.	109
Tatnall, Hon. Josiah, Esq.	do.	do.	110
Roberts, George	do.	do.	111
Russell, Benjamin	do.	do.	112
Albury, Joseph	do.	do.	113
Sweeting, Wm.	do.	do.	114
Saunders, James	do.	do.	115
Roberts, John	do.	do.	116
Lightbourn, Henry	do.	do.	117
Albury, Matthew	do.	do.	118
Russell, Wm.	do.	do.	119
Russell, Benjamin, Jr.	do.	do.	121
Thompson, F.	do.	do.	122
Albury, John	do.	do.	123
Albury, Benjamin, His heirs, etc.	do.	do.	124
Sawyer, Samuel	do.	do.	125
Sweeting, Samuel	do.	do.	126
Curry, Benjamin	do.	do.	127
Curry, Richard	do.	do.	128
Sweeting, Rebecca (Free Black)	do.	do.	129
Johnstone, Thomas	do.	do.	130
Saunders, Benjamin	do.	do.	131
Sawyer, John	do.	do.	132
Roberts, Benjamin	do.	do.	133
Simms, Wm. (Free Black)	do.	do.	134
Thompson, Florence	do.	do.	135
Christie, Hon. Adam	do.	do.	181
Robertsone, Rev. Thos.	do.	do.	189
Moore, John, Rt. Hon. John, Earl of Dunmore	do.	do.	190
Dumaresque, Philip, and others	do.	do.	21

The Early Settlers

Appointment of J.P.'s.

BY AN ORDER IN COUNCIL.

Bahama Islands.

George III. By the Grace of God of Great Britain, France and Ireland, King Defender of the Faith and so forth:

To our Trusty and well beloved John Brown, Robert Hunt, Robert Sterling, George McKenzie, Josiah Tatnall, John Boyd, John Miller, Wm. Gamble, Alexander Murray and Adam Christie, Esquires.

Members of Our Council of said Islands, and Thomas Roker, Thomas Ross, John O'Halloran, Michail Grant, Thomas Smith, John Martin, Wm. Jones, John Douglass, Esquires.

The Rev. John Richards (Clerk), the Rev. Thomas Robertson (Clerk), the Rev. Wm. Gordon (Clerk), Alexander Campbell Whylly, Samuel Higgs, Abraham Pratt, Nicholas Martin, George Bunch, James Baird, Richard Sweeting, Richard Curry, Charles Culmer, Wm. Wilson, Joseph Morris Moore, Joseph Smith, Phillip Dumoresque, James Brisbaine, James Menzies, Wm. Moss, Peter Wemyss, John Ferguson, Wm. Miller, Nathaniel Hall, Wm. Telfair, Peter Edwards, John Goodie, George Gibbs, Oswald Eve, George Gray, George Leitch, Joseph Eve, John Carmichael, Robert Ramer, George Augustus Gamble, James Kelly, John Lorrimore, John Bell, Wade Stubbs, James Kerr, Martin Weatherford, John Crosskill, Alexander Ross, Peter Dean, James Stevens, Archibald Taylor, Lieut.-Col. Walter Turnbull, John Styles, Edward Murray, Goerge Farquharson, Alexander Callie, Andrew Deveaux, Sr., William Rhodes, Col. James Armbrister, Robert Holliday, and Thomas Hunloke, Esquires.

The Early Settlers

Greeting:—
Know ye that we have assigned you, and every one of you jointly and generally and every one of you, Our Justices to keep the Peace, Our Peace, in Our Bahamas Islands during pleasure, etc., etc., etc.

Dated 17th October, 1791.

(Sg.) John, Earl of Dunmore.

AN ECCLESIASTICAL APPOINTMENT.

The Rev. William Gordon, appointed Clerk to St. John's Church, Harbour Island, by the Right Hon. the Earl of Dunmore.

Bahama Islands.

George III. By the Grace of God of Great Britain, France and Ireland, King Defender of the Faith.

To all to whom these presents shall come. Know ye that we, having received a good report of the loyalty, abilities, prudent conduct, and sober conversations of Our Trusty and well beloved William Gordon, Clerk to the Church and Parish of St. John's, Harbour Island, in our Bahama Islands in the room of Philip Dixon, Clerk, deceased.

To have and to hold and enjoy the same unto him, the said Wm. Gordon during his natural life.

In testimony Whereof, We have caused these, our Letters Patent under the seal of Our Said Islands.

Witness our Right Trusty and Well beloved cousin John, Earl of Dunmore, Our Lieut. Governor of Our Said Islands, etc., at Nassau, the 15th day of March, in the year of Our Lord 1796 and the 36th year of our reign.

(Sd.) John, Earl of Dunmore.

In these early days ecclesiastical appointments were made solely by the Governors of the Colony, and, singularly, the Wardens of Christ Church were a body vested with certain civil powers, and were practically in the same position as a Town Council. The Clergy, in those days, were termed as Clerks of a parish; thus, on the death of the Rev. Philip Dixon, of the Parish of St. John's, Harbour Island, the Earl of Dunmore appointed the Rev. Wm. Gordon, Clerk, to fill up the vacancy.

The Early Settlers

Freeing of Slaves.

MANUMISSIONS OF CERTAIN SLAVES BEFORE FREEDOM HAD BEEN GIVEN.

Lord Rolle, of the Island of Exuma, frees two girl slaves. Bahama Islands.

Know all men by these presents, that I, John, Lord Rolle of the United Kingdom of Great Britain and Ireland and owner of a number of slaves on the Island of Exuma, one of the said Bahama Islands, for and in consideration of services, and other good causes have manumitted, enfranchised, absolved, and set free from every tie of slavery, and servitude whatsoever, my two mulatto girl slaves named Ann and Elizabeth. The former about 11 years of age, and the latter about 7.

Witness my hand and seal at Exuma aforesaid the 30th day of October, 1821.

(Sg.) John, Lord Rolle,
Per Thomas Lampin, Attorney.

Signed, sealed and delivered in the presence of Henderson Ferguson,
John, Lord Rolle.

The Early Settlers.

The Hon. James Moss frees one negro woman.

Bahama Island.

Know all men by these presents that I, the Honourable James Moss, at present of the Island of New Providence, Esquire, for good and sufficient causes and considerations, me hereunto moving, have manumitted and made free, and from all obligations of involuntary servitude forever and discharge and release my negro woman slave named Sally, age twenty-eight, and the said negro woman is hereby forever manumitted and made free accordingly.

In witness I have set my hand and seal, etc.
28th May, 1823.
(Signed) James Moss.

Annotte Cunningham, a woman of colour, releases her female slave.

Bahama Islands.

I, Annotte Cunningham, of the Island of New Providence, free my black woman, for divers good causes, and considerations, me hereunto moving, do hereby manumit and make free my female slave called and known by the name of Harriet, together with her future issue and increase.

In witness I have set my hand and seal, etc.
17th August, 1821.

               her
(Sd.) Annotte X Cunningham.
              mark

George I. Brook releases a slave for the sum of £100.

Bahama Islands.

Know all men by these present that I, George Brook, of the Island of New Providence, gentleman, for and in consideration of the sum of one hundred pounds lawful money of these Islands, to me in hand well and truly paid by my negro woman slave named Bell for and on account of herself the receipt whereof and of every part thereof, I do hereby acknowledge, having manumitted, made free and released from bondage, and by these presents do manumit, make free and release from bondage, and all servitude, the said negro woman slave named Bell and her issue.

Witness my hand, etc., Jan. 3rd. 1823.
(Sg.) George I. Brook.

The Early Settlers.

Bahama Islands.

Stephen Dillet frees a negro male slave from bondage for £180.

To all to whom these presents shall come be seen or made known. I, Stephen Dillet, of the Island of New Providence, send greeting. Know ye, that I, the said Stephen Dillet, for divers good causes, me thereunto moving, and for and in consideration of the sum of one hundred and eighty pounds lawful money of these Islands aforesaid, to me in hand well and truly paid by William Bain, a slave to me belonging, before the sealing and delivery of these presents, the receipt whereof I do hereby acknowledge, have manumitted, enfranchised, made free from every tie of slavery and servitude, absolved, and by these presents to all intents and purposes do manumit, enfranchise, make free from every tie of slavery or servitude. And the said William Bain shall from henceforth and forever be as free to all intents, constructions and purposes whatsoever as any other subject of the realm of Great Britain.

In witness whereof, etc., dated 2nd May, 1826.

(Sd.) Stephen Dillet.

There are five hundred of such manumissions recorded, fifteen or twenty years before the abolition of slavery in the West Indies.

The importance of such manumissions, is, that they embodied the principles laid down by the Wilberforce Party in England, who clamoured for the liberty and freedom of the down-trodden slaves in His Majesty's Dominions. Furthermore, Abraham Lincoln undertook to wage a war from the same force of reason, and so hated was the idea of slavery to him that he drew the sword for the freedom of millions of those who were held in bondage on the American Continent. When, therefore, we imagine the agonies associated with slavery, the names of those foremost liberators should be held in as great a veneration as the names of those Saints and martyrs who laid down their lives for what they felt to be a righteous cause. And those slave owners who left on record these manumissions are worthy enough to be placed on a roll of honour.

The Early Settlers.

THE CAUSE OF EMANCIPATION CHAMPIONED BY DANIEL O'CONNELL, AN EMMINENT LAWYER.

Speaking before a a large gathering of members of the Catholic Association, Daniel O'Connell said: "No man can more sincerely abhor, detest, and abjure slavery than I do. I hold it in utter detestation, however men may attempt to palliate or excuse it by differences of colour, creed or clime. In all its gradations, and in every form I am its mortal foe. The speech of an opponent on this question has filled me with indignation. 'What,' said this party, 'would you come in between a man and his freehold!' I started as if something unholy had trampled on my father's grave, and I exclaimed with horror, 'A freehold in a human being!' I know nothing of this individual. I give him credit for being a gentleman of humanity; but, if he be so, it only makes the case stronger; for the circumstances of such a man upholding such a system shows the horrors of that system in itself and its effect in deceiving the minds of those who are connected with it, wherever it exists. We are told that the slave is not fit to receive his freedom—that he could not endure freedom without revolting. Why does he not endure slavery without revolting? With all that he has to bear he does not revolt now; and will he be more ready to revolt when you take away the lash? Foolish argument! But I will take them upon their own ground—the ground of gradual preparation. Well; are not eight years of education sufficient to prepare a man for anything? Seven years are accounted quite sufficient for an apprenticeship to any profession, or for any art or science; and are not eight years enough for the negro? If eight years have passed away without preparation, so would eighty if we were to allow them so many. There is a time for everything, but it would seem there is no time for the emancipation of the slave!

"Mr. Buxton most ably and unanswerably stated to the House of Commons the awful decrease in population. That in 14 Colonies, in the course of 10 years, there had been a decrease in the population of 145,801 human beings—that is in other words, 145,801 human beings had been murdered by this system—their bodies gone to the grave—their spirits before their God. In the eight years that they have had to educate their slaves for liberty, but which have been useless to

The Early Settlers

them—in those years one-twelfth have gone into the grave —murdered! Every day ten victims are thus despatched! While we are speaking, they are sinking; while we are debating, they are dying! As human, as accountable beings, why should we suffer this any longer? Let every man take his own share in this business. I am resolved if sent back to Parliament that I will bear my part. I purpose fully to divide the House on the motion that every negro child born after the first of January, 1832, shall be free. They say 'Oh, do not emancipate the slave suddenly; they are not prepared, they will revolt!' Are they afraid of the insurrection of the infants? Oh, no! there can be no such pretence. I will carry with me to my own country the recollection of this splendid scene. Where is the man that can resist the argument of this day? I go to my native land under its influence; and let me remind you that land has its glory that no slave ship was ever launched from any of its numerous ports. I will gladly join any party to do good to the poor negro slaves. Let each extend to them the arm of his compassion; let each aim to deliver his fellow-man from distress. I shall go and tell my countrymen that they must be first in the race of humanity."

The Early Settlers

Slavery Abolished in the Bahamas.

In the year 1834 the King's procamation for the abolition of slavery was read by Lieut. Governor Colebrook, who himself was glad to announce the joyful news to 13,000 human beings previously bound with the chains and fetters of slavery; and the end of a conflict between despotism and liberty. Such blessings having been brought about by the hand of Almighty God under the influence of Christianity was the signal of great peace of mind and happiness to those who originally were brought captives from the shores of Africa, and sold as cattle upon an open market.

So great was the joy that public demonstrations and other exercises of rejoicings were carried on almost indefinitely by the liberated slaves. Hundreds of cattle were slaughtered and roasted, and hundreds of gallons of molasses and water with a full supply of bread were given them by the townsfolk and Government.

"Massa," said an old woman to Governor Colebrooke, "I have had 20 children. My Massa and Missus sole 'em all off. One of my gals was sole to buy young Missus a piano, and whenever I heard her play on it, I used to stop my ears; I thought I heard my child crying out dat it was bought with her blood. Dey was all sole off. I have not got one left to bury me but now me see freedom! Ah! and my old heart is glad because I will go happily to my grave."

SLAVE POPULATION IN THE BAHAMAS IN 1819.

	Under 13 years.	From 13 to 60.	From 60.	Total.
Creole Male	1954	2122	72	4148
Creole Female	1998	2370	73	4441
African Male	18	1375	155	1548
African Female	15	906	97	1013
	3985	6773	397	11155

The Early Settlers

Graveyards and Monuments.

Prior to an Act of the House of Assembly for authorising the Churchwardens and Vestry of Christ Church Parish to enclose Eastern and Western burying grounds, all dead bodies were interred: (1) In the old burying ground, north of St. Matthew's Churchyard; (2) In Potter's field; (3) Along the Western beach or Esplanade; (4) In the old burying grounds, Charlotte and Shirley Streets; (5) In private yards.

The vaults in some of these burying grounds are in bad repair; a few have tumbled in, due to age and neglect. The tablets on many graves cannot easily be deciphered, age has shown its mark of destruction on those that were not of a good quality; while good marble and slate slabs hold inscriptions as good as the day they were inscribed upon.

In the Old Burying Ground to the North of St. Matthew's Churchyard many headstones are lying about the ground in broken pieces; a very dreadful sight of negligence, indeed. Most of the historic sights are neglected in this Colony; and one hundred years ago would not have been too early to take steps to preserve historic monuments in the Bahama Islands.

Along the Western beach several tablets and skulls have been unearthed while trenches were being dug for a concrete sea-wall; and thirty years ago many marble slabs opposite Fort Charlotte were to be seen lying on graves; to-day, they have disappeared.

In churches the tablets in the side walls present a good appearance. Those which have been set in the concrete floors in churches have suffered from being trampled upon for over one hundred years, and important inscriptions on one or two are difficult to decipher.

The Early Settlers

THE FOLLOWING ARE INSCRIPTIONS ON TOMBSTONES AND TABLETS IN GRAVEYARDS AND CHURCHES.

In the Old Burying Ground, North of St. Matthew's Churchyard.
In Memory of
John Wells, Esq.,
Late Editor of the "Bahamas Gazette," which he conducted 15 years with approbation.

In him, the public have lost a respectable and useful member of society, and his family have sustained an irreparable loss.
He departed this life Oct. 29th, 1799, aged 47.
And
beneath this tombstone lie the remains of Mary Hamilton Wells, eldest daughter of John and Frances, who departed this life 5th Jan., 1807, in the 18th year of her age.
To soothe,
by her tender care the pangs of disease, she accompanied a sick friend from Charleston, South Carolina, to this Island, and fell a martyr to her philanthropy the day following her arrival.
As
a mark of respect due to a loving and dutiful daughter this tomb is erected by
E. Wells.

In Loving Memory
of
John Whippo,
of a respectable family, in Connecticut, North America, who died on this Island, Jan. 30th, 1799, in the 17th year of his age.

In Loving Memory of
Charles Davis, Esq.,
who departed this life on the 28th Nov., 1819, age 69.

In Memory of
William Thomas,
son of William and Ann Gould, who departed this life Aug. 30th, 1801, aged 13 months and 20 days.

The Early Settlers

Sacred to the Memory of George Johnson, Junior, son of George Johnson, Esq., of this Island, who departed this life July 4, MDCC. (Other portions of inscription broken off).

Here lieth the body of Thomas Pinckney, late M. and S. of the sloops "Adventurer," of Charleston, South Carolina, who, living justly, obtained the character of a man of strict honour, and is now as justly lamented by all he knew.

He departed this life the 6th May, A.D. 1733, in the 31st year of his age.

This stone is gratefully dedicated by his most affectionate brother, Charles Pinckney, of Charleston, S.C., as a monument sacred to the friendship which ever subsisted between them.

Vivat Post funera Virtus.

Here lies the body of William Thompson, Esq., one of his Majesty's Council of the Bahama Islands. He was born in the year 1725 and died Oct. 31st, 1756.

Here lies interred the body of Mrs. Deborah Gambier, who was an affectionate wife, a tender mother, sincere friend, and charitable to the poor. She departed this life the 21st Oct., 1761, age 33.

MONUMENTS IN CHRIST CHURCH CATHEDRAL.

Sacred to the Memory of William Moss, Esq., born at Huyton, in the County of Lancaster and Kingdom of Great Britain, but he passed the greatest portion of the last 24 years of his life in Georgia, East Florida, and these Islands, where he died on the 9th day of Dec., 1796, age 45. His probity and public spirit commended general esteem and respect, while his hospitable, sincere and benevolent deportment in private life conciliated the good-will and friendship of all who knew him.

Here lieth the body of the Hon. James Moss, who departed this life on the 20th October, 1820, age 61.

The Early Settlers.

Here lies the body of Elizabeth Dixon, late of Philadelphia, who departed this life on the 18th Sept., 1779, age 54.

In Memory of John Falconer, Loyalist and Merchant, who died at Nassau, in New Providence, on the 3rd day of Nov., 1793, age 51.

Here lieth interred the body of His Excellency John Tinker, Esq., who for 18 years, Governor and Commander in Chief in and over the Bahama Islands. He died the 10th July, 1743, aged 58.

Sacred to the memory of Stanley Byng Hornby, Esq., late 1st Lieut. of H.M. Royal Regiment of Artillery, who departed this life on the 2nd day of Nov., 1865, in the 29th year of his age, leaving a wife and two children to mourn his loss.

Lieut. Hornby entered the service in 1852. In 1854 he came to this Island in command of a detachment of his regiment. In 1859 he was appointed a Lieut.-Magistrate for the Bahamas and filled this post until 1861, when from extreme ill-health he was obliged to return to England, and eventually to retire from the service. Lieut. Hornby, who married the second daughter of Joseph Thompson, Esq., Merchant, of this town, was the third son of the Rev. Geoffry Hornby, Rector of Bury, in Lancaster, England, and was related to the present Lord Stanley. His remains are interred in Potter's Field. A tablet marks the spot.

Sacred to the Memory of Captain Henry Harvey, of H.M.S. Eclipse, and senior officer of the Bahamas Division, who died at Nassau, N.P., on the 19th day of July, 1869, of yellow fever. Age 45.

This tablet is erected by the officers and ship's company of H.M.S. Eclipse as a token of their esteem.

Sacred to the Memory of Charles M. Bode, Esq., who departed this life on the 20th Dec., 1859 age 59. The deceased was a native of these Islands, and for upwards of forty years was attached to the Nassau Field Artillery Company of Militia, and at his death was in the distinguished position of Lieut.-Colonel Commanding that corps.

The Early Settlers.

He was the last surviving son of the late Dr. Charles Bode, who during the whole period of the American Revolution was surgeon of the Hessian Grenadiers, and afterwards practised medicine in the Colony for nearly half a century.

In Memory of
The Right Rev. Charles Caufield, D.D., First Bishop of Nassau, consecrated 24th Nov., 1861, died Sept. 4th, 1862, age 59.

Sacred to the Memory of
The Right Rev. Addington R. Venerables, D.D., Bishop of Nassau, consecrated Nov. 30th, 1863, died Oct. 8th, 1876, at Hartford, Conn., U.S.A., age 49.

MONUMENT IN ST. MATTHEW'S CHURCHYARD.

Here lies the body of the Hon. John Storr, a native of St. Augustine, Fla., and during many years an upright and useful member of Her Majesty's Council for these Islands. He was born 1783, and died at Nassau, July 2nd, 1845. As a Merchant was largely connected with the commerce of this Colony, and as a philanthropist always the first to identify himself with any movement to advance the happiness of his adopted country.

MONUMENTS IN THE WESTERN CEMETERY.

Sacred to the Memory of Ann,
the wife of William Brown, late of Philadelphia, North America, who departed this life Feb. 15th, 1811, age 29.

Sacred to the Memory of Daniel Doley, Jr., M.D.
of Charleston, S.C., who died of consumption in this Island on Feb. 14th, 1816, age 51.

Sacred to the Memory of
James Thayer, Esq., of Providence, Rhode Island, U.S.A., who died in this Island, Aug. 21st, 1817.

Sacred to the Memory of
John Conyers Dean, a native of Bermuda, who departed this life Feb. 22nd, 1815. Age 32 years.

The Early Settlers.

Beneath this stone are deposited the remains of William Farrington, a native of Aberdeen, N.B., and an inhabitant of this Island, who departed this life Oct. 7, 1809. Age 51 years.

Also

Mrs. Sarah Anderson Farrington, the wife of William Farrington, who died Jan. 17, 1798. Age 30.

Sacred to the Memory of
Alexander Nimmo, Merchant, a native of Falkirk, in Stirlingshire, who died 1822.

Sacred to the Memory of
Peter Nimmo, who was born in Stirlingshire, April 29th, 1785, and died in this Island, 1831. Age 46.

Here lieth the body of Sir Henry Marr, Knight, late Major in His Majesty's 47th Regiment of Foot, who during a service of — years in that regiment, behaved with such exemplary honours, loyalty and integrity as endeared him to his brother officers, and made him an object of respect and love of his inferiors. Age 38. Died Nov. 29th, 1793.

IN SCOTS BURYING GROUND, CHARLOTTE AND SHIRLEY STS.

In Memory of Capt. James Burnside, who was born Sept. 22, 1758, and drowned in the hurricane of Oct. 3, 1795. Age 38 years and 11 days.

Here lies the body of
Henrietta Gould, the wife of William Gould, who died May 17, 1797. Age 22 years.

In Memory of Elizabeth Patton, wife of George Patton, who departed this life Aug. 13, 1796. Age 32 years.

The Early Settlers

The Cholera.

Amongs the monuments in graveyards there may be seen rows of black headstones, marking the graves of those who had died from that most direful scourge of cholera, a plague, which was brought to these Islands in the year 1852, by one Samuel Evas from St. Augustine, Fla. On the report of the first fatal case the inhabitants became terror-stricken, and fled by hundreds from Island to Island, endeavouring to escape the dreadful disease.

It was reported in the month of October, and became an epidemic in December. It continued throughout the summer of the following year, and played havoc amongst the poorer classes, who fell ready and easy subjects of its power. Many of the rich were carried to their graves before the situation was held in check. The dread of this contagion is said to have driven parents from their children, and wives from their husbands. At the sight of a hearse coming people would turn in any gateway till the corpse had passed. Friends and acquaintances avoided each other in the streets, and only by a cold nod did they signify their acquaintance.

The old custom of shaking hands as a friendly greeting was strictly avoided. Any person wearing crape or having any appeaance of mourning was shunned like a viper and made their way to windward of every person they saw approaching. Hundreds of people who could procure no attendance died without a human being to hand them a drink of water. A man and his wife in comfortable circumstances were found lying dead in bed, and between them was their infant child sucking its mother's breast. In many cases an

The Early Settlers

entire family would be carried off within a few hours. The township showed a spectacle of mournful gloom. Empty streets, their silence broken only by the rumbling of the dead-carts, and the driver's loud cry, " Bring out your dead!" Many a house was left open—fully furnished, but the inmates gone—they fled.

Ships at anchor in the harbour were all deserted. On the masts of some of these vessels hung the unfurled sails. On the wharves you would see merchandise, which terror had left there. No danger of it being stolen. There was only one thing uppermost in men's minds—death!

The clergy, generally speaking, during this calamity, showed great self-sacrifice and devotedness; many of them fell on the road while carrying the Blessed Sacrament to the sick. There was, however, an occasional exception. An anecdote related by one of the Wardens of the Church is as follows: " While the plague was raging I had occasion to go a short distance from the town. I took a hack to make the journey as quickly as possible. It was not long before I was breathing the pure air in the open country, and just as I was about to return towards the town I met a clergyman, the father of a numerous family. He, like many others, had fled from the fatal contagion; yet still, he was a pious soul, of a very exemplary character and an all-round good Christian to his flock. He preached to them with sincerity and eloquence, but in spite of all, in the hour of danger, he fled— not so much for himself—his family were alarmed by the panic and he felt he must go with them. ' What is going on in the town, John?' asked the reverend gentleman. ' We are taking care of the sick,' was the reply. ' The doctors are discharging most nobly their glorious mission, but what can we do for " Men's Souls "? Nothing is wanted but the " Bread of the Word." Those wretched creatures are calling for your consolations; which alone can rob death of its terrors. Well! reverend, what do you say? There is room on my hack for you: come on." The clergyman simply pressed John's hands with gentleness, and pointed to his wife and family who were standing a little way off, and walked away in silence.

Another clergyman, more like the good Samaritan, was visiting the sick from house to house. At noon one day, during the epidemic, he was attracted to a number of work-

The Early Settlers

ing men collected around some object. Forcing his way through the crowd, he found a poor man lying on the ground, violently sick with the prevailing disease, exposed to the sun and suffering extremely. The crowd, though pitying his condition, appeared to be either too much frightened to render him any aid or too ignorant how they could relieve him. The clergyman did not long consider his duty on such an occasion. Seizing a wheelbarrow near by, he rolled it alongside the sick man, and laying him gently in, wheeled the poor man to the nearest place where he might be taken care of, and sent him immediate medical aid, which finally led to the poor man's recovery.

The mortality was greater among men than women, and greater among the middle-aged and robust than the old and infirm. Men and women of wild life were rendered an easy prey to the epidemic. Homes debarred of a free circulation of air were death-traps to their occupants. The remedies used for this disease were garlic, tobacco smoking, vinegar sprinkled about the house, and camphor bags tied round the neck. Tarred rope was carried in the hands and pockets, and " drink plenty of water " was advised by doctors. When the cholera disappeared it was found that seven-eighths of deaths from the disease were among the poor.

The Early Settlers

Running the Blockade.

BETWEEN THE SOUTHERN PORTS AND NASSAU DURING THE AMERICAN CIVIL WAR.

During the Civil War between the Northern and Southern States of America Nassau played a popular game in contraband of war intended for the armies of the Confederate States, then in arms against the Federal Government. The blockade was proclaimed on the 19th of April, 1861, when twelve ships were sent at once to the most important harbours in the South. The number of ships grew steadily until three hundred were on the blockading line. They were divided into three squadrons, namely, the North Atlantic, the East Gulf line, and the West Gulf line.

The first blockade runner to arrive at the Port of Nassau was the steamship "Kate." She came from Charleston, S.C., with a full cargo of cotton, tobacco and turpentine, and an enormous quantity of gold to be deposited in the Bank of Nassau, as a precautionary measure against war risks. She returned with ammunition imported from foreign countries for the Southern forces. Captain Lockwood was in command of the "Kate," who on his arrival reported to have had an uneventful voyage from Charleston to the Bahamas. His return cargo consisted of ammunition.

The s.s. "Eagle" was the second blockade runner to arrive from Charleston. She brought twelve thousand bales of cotton and tobacco and a stowaway negro slave, who concealed himself between two bales of cotton, where he remained without food until the "Eagle" came into port. In

The Early Settlers

finding himself in a country where former slaves were then enjoying their liberty, and realising that he was now a free man he fell on his knees before leaving the dock, and gave thanks to God for his deliverance from the yoke of bondage. He was welcomed among members of his race, who placed him in care of the Bahamas Friendly Society. The "Eagle" returned to Wilmington, South Carolina, with a cargo of contraband of war.

A ship which could make two or three successful voyages netted a handsome return to her owner, even if she was captured afterwards. In the event of a blockade runner being captured that ship would be taken into the port of Key West, Florida, which was held by the Federal Government. Occasionally, usually at night, a luckless blockade runner was seized as she tried to dart through the opening. Sometimes she stole through so cautiously as to elude the blockading ships. After getting through it was an easy matter for the goods to be landed, and immediately the cargo was discharged the ship would reload with cotton, tobacco and turpentine for the account of the Confederate States.

The blockading ships generally covered a radius of 40 miles off the harbour during the day, and closing in to anchor during the night, like sentinels on each side of the harbour's entrance. When an opportunity offered to chase a blockade runner every effort would be made to make a capture, and to allow a ship to escape was felt to be an unpardonable sin by the blockader. To chase a ship near her port of entry was one of the most exciting phases of the game.

The following is an account of the narrow escape of a blockade runner being chased within an hour's steam to the entrance of the harbour. It was early in the morning when the captain of the s.s. "Antinego" saw the gunboat "Adriondike" approaching in his wake. He was not more than seven miles from the entrance to the harbour, and had luckily taken his pilot on board a few minutes before, which enabled him to drive his ship for the harbour with all possible speed. In the meantime the pilot boat was running in, behind the "Antinego," not being more than one mile away. Feeling anxious for the safety of the "Antinego," the pilot boat made rapid signals to her to push on as the gunboat was gaining on her. At this moment shots from the gunboat were falling on all sides of the "Antinego," and as she was

The Early Settlers.

about to cross the bar at the entrance of the harbour a well-directed shot struck her on the side, doing slight damage. The next moment the "Antinego" was safe within the land-locked harbour of Nassau, and much to the disappointment of the "Adriondike."

While shipping was fraught with a considerable amount of danger foreign merchants, who came to Nassau to do business in the interests of the Southern States, were stocking large warehouses with contraband goods and co-operating with local merchants on behalf of those whom it concerned. They gave their attention chiefly to the re-export of the goods which were brought to the Bahamas for foreign countries for the use of the Confederate States.

There was a vast amount of United States gold then in circulation in the Bahamas, and fortunes were made by many local business men. Among those who became wealthy were Henry Adderley, R. W. Sawyer, Menendez and Company, Sweeting and Bethell (partners), John M. Meadows and Company, Count Johnson, William Weech, I. Harris, and Alexander Bain. At the close of the war quite a number of these Bahamians left the Colony to live in England, where they could derive more pleasure from their riches. Apart from individual wealth the Government accumulated large surplus amounts during the war, but, unfortunately, on account of the short-sighted policy in its expenditure, the large funds in the Treasury were depleted in an uncommonly short time.

During the second and third year of the war the monthly average of steamers arriving at the port of Nassau was 45. Shipping activities were then at their height. Wharfs, baylots and warehouses were always congested, while the vigilance of blockading ships was a handicap to steamers ready to sail with cargoes for Charleston or Wilmington. These conditions did not change until the turning point of the war in favour of the Northern States, when a sharp decline in business followed and the pendulum ceased to swing. Then the mind of the people, which was so quick to develop into the lust for all they could get by handling contraband of war, began to assume sobriety when the ugliness of their actions weighed heavily on their conscience.

The fact that the Northern States were waging a righteous war against the Southern States with no object

The Early Settlers.

but to force them to discontinue the diabolical slave traffic, and that thousands of lives were being sacrified, and millions of pounds spent to relieve a suffering humanity from such inhuman conditions, should have influenced all right-thinking people to support its noble efforts. And here let me say that the Bahamas did not go unpunished, for in the year 1866, only one year after the cessation of hostilities between the North and the South, the memorable '66 hurricane swept over the Bahamas, and destroyed houses, churches, wharfs and shipping, doing damage to property far in excess of what the Colony gained by lending aid to the slave belt of the Southern States of America.

The Early Settlers.

Piracies and Protests.

LAWFORD'S PROTEST.*

Be it known to all whom these Presents may concern, that on the Eighteenth day of August in the year of Our Lord one thousand seven hundred and thirty-five came personally before me Richard Fitzwilliam, Esq., Captain General and Governor-in-Chief in and over the Bahama Islands, Samuel Lawford, late master of the sloop Mercury, of New Providence, John Grimes and William Young, late mariners of the said sloop, make oath on the Holy Evangelists of Almighty God that about the middle of June last there was loaded and put on board the said sloop at the Island of Jamaica by Messrs. Peter and Organ Furnell, Merchants, three hundred and fifty barrels of beef, ten barrels of pork, one hundred and two firkins of butter, fifty barrels of flour, fourteen casks of beer and cider in bottles, which said goods and merchandize were consigned to Mr. Maduras, merchant, in the Island of Curacao, to which place the sloop was bound, that on the 17th June aforesaid. After the said sloop had been registered and cleared at the offices at Jamaica the deponent did proceed with the said vessel on their intended voyage to Curacao, that in their passage having had strong easterly winds, they were obliged on the second of July following to stretch southwards in hopes cf getting up to the Island of Arruba, but the current running so strong to the westward the said sloop fell in on the South of July aforesaid with some rocks commonly called the Monkeys, whereupon the deponent continued on a south-

*Book C Page 262—265.

The Early Settlers

ward course until they made the Continent of America, and stood in thereto until six o'clock the same evening, at which time they tacked the sloop and steered northward until 12 o'clock at night, and then stretching southward again until 6 o'clock in the morning, which was the seventh. The weather became quite calm. Deponent being then about four leagues distance from that part of the mainland known by the name of "The Bush," which bore south by east, at which time they discovered near the land a small vessel assisted by a fresh land breeze bore down upon the deponent in the said sloop Mercury until she was within pistol shot of the deponent, when the Captain or Commander of the said unknown vessel ordered the deponent and his crew to strike the sails of the said sloop Mercury, and soon after sent his boat on board with armed men, who, in a hostile manner, carried the said Samuel Lawford and six of his crew on board the vessel, which proved to be a Spanish sloop belonging to Maracaybo, under the command of Don Pedro de Castro, who afterwards took possession of the said sloop Mercury and carried her about eight leagues to leeward to a place called the Salinas, where the aforesaid Don Pedro de Castro ordered the said Samuel Lawford back again on board the sloop Mercury, and having searched and rummaged her took from him the said Samuel Lawford all his papers and ordered the said sloop Mercury's sails be unbended, and leaving the said Samuel on board under guard of a Lieutenant and six men. The next morning being the eighth of July aforesaid the said Pedro de Castro came on board the sloop Mercury and ordered the said Samuel Lawford on board the Spanish sloop and told him that he would carry the sloop Mercury to Maracaybo, and thereupon sent the deponent and four others of the Mercury's crew, namely, Joseph Cash, William Pearce and the two passengers aforementioned, on shore to the Salinas, notwithstanding the earnest entreaty of him the said Samuel Lawford to the contrary by reason he was unacquainted with the country which seemed to be and proved uninhabited by other than savages. Besides he was desirous to go to Maracaybo with his sloop to make his case known to the Governor, and the deponents further say that after they were put on shore they were almost famished for want of water and other substance before reaching Macumbas. From whence they

The Early Settlers

travelled to Ariculo, where they were obliged to be very quiet for seventeen days, being informed by the inhabitants that if they were seen by the party of soldiers appointed to guard the coast they would be taken and sent to Cora, where they would certainly be imprisoned until an opportunity offered of sending them to Puerto Cavallo, at which place they would be obliged to carry stones, and work at the fortifications which were being erected. And the deponents further say that they have used all lawful and possible means to get to Maracaybo in pursuit of the said Pedro de Castro and to claim the said sloop Mercury, which have proved ineffectual by reason of the great distance from the place where they were put on shore. The want of necessary substance and many other difficulties in travelling through a desert country added to their misfortunes.

Therefore the said Samuel Lawford, John Grimes and William Young do hereby on behalf of themselves, the owners, freighters and all other persons whatsoever concerned in the said sloop Mercury and cargo, in the most solemn manner protest against the said winds and currents which they were driven to the westward of their intended Port, and up against the said Pedro de Castro and all and every other person whatsoever concerned in the unjust and illegal capture of the sloop Mercury and for all the damages, losses, costs, and charges that are already, or shall hereafter be sustained by the said Samuel Lawford, Peter Furnell and all other persons whatever concerned in the said sloop Mercury and cargo.

(Signed) JOHN GRIMES.
WM. JONES.

Sworn to before
RICHARD FITZWILLIAMS,
Governor.

SEYMOUR'S PROTEST.

By this public instrument of protest of November the Eleventh in the Year of Our Lord One thousand seven hundred and sixty-three; before James Bradford, Secretary of the said Islands, and Notary and Tabellion public, by Royal Authority admitted and sworn, dwelling and practising in

The Early Settlers

New Providence aforesaid, personally appeared Andrew Seymour, who being duly sworn declares that on the twenty-eighth or twenty-ninth day of October last deponent being on board the brigantine "Hannah," William Buddon, Master, and belonging to Philadelphia, which vessel this deponent had then partly loaded and being chartered on his and his brother's account to load in the Island of Hispanola.

The brigantine was boarded (being at that time in Monto Christo Bay in the said Island) by a Spanish boat full of hands, who after being on board for a little time, took possession of her by force and carried deponent on shore to the house of the Royal Officer, who examined him, and asked how he dared stay above twenty-four hours in their harbonr without permission and was he not informed that no foreign vessel whatever was allowed to come upon their coast without first obtaining permission. Deponent answered that the brigantine was leaking and as the two Crowns of Great Britain and Spain were at peace, he imagined that he had a right to come into any port belonging to the King of Spain in order to get the necessary repairs. The officer in reply said that they had a right to make a prize of all vessels which either came into their harbour or upon their coast. Some hours afterwards the interpreter told the deponent that the Royal Officer and Governor were willing to let him go with his brig and cargo on condition he made them a present of twelve hundred pieces of eight in cash, otherwise they would detain and confiscate his vessel and cargo. The deponent, knowing full well into whose hands he had fallen, consulted his friends, who advised him to accept the offer, otherwise his vessel would probably have sunk in a few days if kept in their hands. He went on board several vessels then lying in the harbour and borrowed the money at the rate of 28 per cent. interest in order to redeem his brig. Having first paid into the hands of the Royal Officer in Portugal money the sum of twelve hundred pieces of eight he signed several papers written in Spanish, which the deponent did not understand. The brig sustained damage by the unjust seizers to the amount of fifteen hundred pieces of eight, besides what was stolen and wasted on board the said brig whilst in possession of the Spaniards, whereupon this deponent hath requested of me the said Notary to Protest.

(Signed) ANDREW SEYMOUR.

The Early Settlers

PAYNE'S PROTEST.

Thomas Payne, late of Nassau, in the Island of New Providence, one of the Bahama Islands, and now of Liverpool, in the county of Lancashire and Kingdom of Great Britain, Mariner, maketh oath that in or about the year one thousand seven hundred and seventy-four, this deponent sailed in the Snow Chance, William Booth master, from the Proponges River on the Coast of Africa to Savannah, Georgia. That after the said Snow Chance was full slaved and all the people were on board ready to leave the coast a schooner came to anchor near the said Snow Chance, having on board some gentlemen who came to visit Capt. Booth who, on seeing them, sent his boat out and brought them on board the Snow Chance; that when the boat returned the said Captain Booth sent an officer with the boat's crew armed with pistols and cutlasses to the schooner, and ordered them to bring the Patroon or Master of the schooner on board the Snow Chance. That such Patroon or Master was called Cymbello and is the negro man who accompanied Messrs. William and James Moss on the voyage from the Bahama Islands to Liverpool aforesaid, and who is now present before the Worshipful Mayor, and this deponent said that the crew who went in the boat brought him accordingly, and as soon as Cymbello came on board Capt. Booth ordered him to be stripped, put in irons, and turned amongst the slaves, which was done. That after Capt. Booth had taken Cymbello on board an offer was made by some of Cymbello's friends that if the Captain would release him they would deliver to him slaves. Whereupon the said Booth declared he would not send him ashore on any consideration, but would rather cut off his head and send that ashore. That Booth aferwards became apprehensive that the natives might come down and attack the vessel, and therefore got away with as much expedition as possible and sailed within two days afterwards, many days sooner than he would otherwise have done, in the meantime, ordering the crew to keep a strict watch lest the vessel should be attacked. And this deponent saith that he hath been informed and from his conversation with Booth hath reason to believe that his motive for carrying off Cymbello was from an apprehension that he was too familiar with a black woman

The Early Settlers

called Domingo, by whom the said Booth was reputed to have had two children and not with any design of selling him as a slave, as also appeared by his subsequent conduct. And this deponent further saith that the said Capt. Booth set sail and proceeded from Rioponges to the Isles de Los and afterwards to Savannah, Georgia. That Cymbello was confined in irons amongst other slaves until they got into a colder climate, when he was set at liberty, being able to sew and make clothes for the slaves on board. That after their arrival at Savanah, Ga., the cargo of slaves was sold by William Moss, but this deponent had heard and believed that Cymbello was not sold, but was left with Mr. Moss, with whom he had continued ever since in the capacity of a mariner and for some time past as the master of a vessel in the employ of the said Wm. Moss and his partners. That during the time aforesaid Cymbello had never worked as a slave in the plantation, but hath always as far as this deponent hath observed been at liberty and to absent himself as often as he thought proper, and was not looked upon nor accounted as a slave; that at times he had accompanied the deponent on short passages amongst the Island, but was never compelled to do so, but several times refused to go on account of his health, and that this deponent is fully satisfied that Cymbello is a free man and was not purchased by the said Capt. Booth, but was carried off from the coast of Africa wrongfully and illegally, and that no person whatsoever hath any property in him or right to his service.

(Signed) THOMAS PAYNE.

Sworn to at Liverpool
in the year of Our Lord
one thousand seven hundred
and eighty-seven.

Before me JAMES GILDERT, JNR.,
Mayor of Liverpool.

WILLIAM HESTER'S PROTEST.

Bahama Islands.

By this public instrument of attestation and protest be it known and made manifest to all to whom these presents shall come or may in any wise concern, that on the 16th

The Early Settlers.

day of December in the year of Our Lord one thousand eight hundred and twenty-five and in the fifth year of his Majesty's reign before me, Charles Rogers Nesbit, Notary Public, by lawful authority duly admitted and sworn, residing in the Town of Nassau, in the Island of New Providence, personally came William Hester, Master of the schooner Ballona, of the port of Nassau, in the Island aforesaid and being sworn on the Holy Evangelists of Almighty God, did depose and say that on the fourteenth day of October last he sailed on the said schooner, and having on board a cargo of salt provisions from the said Port of Nassau on a voyage to Honduras, with instructions to stop at Cape Catocke or the neighbouring Cays for Turtle; that nothing material occurred until the schooner arrived off Glover's Reef, about 30 miles southward from Belize. On the 27th day of November last at 10 o'clock past Meridian, the schooner was boarded by a piratical brig called the Amazon, commanded by one Hutcheson, who detained the schooner that night, but released her at daylight next morning, on discovering His Majesty's ship Icarus to windward. The Deponent arrived at Honduras the following day, and learnt that the said brig had been captured by the Icarus, but that the crew had escaped. The Deponent, after discharging the schooner's outward cargo, with the exception of ten barrels of beef, three bales of turtle twine, five pieces of cotton handkerchiefs, took on board eighteen and a half tons of logwood and four hundred and fifty dollars in cash. The Deponent left Honduras on the sixteenth day of November last in the said schooner, having one passenger on board for Nassau, Videlicet William Coffin, and made sail for the neighbouring Cape Catocke. He proceeded and came to anchor there on the twenty-seventh November at about 10 o'clock in the forenoon, when the Deponent forthwith went in his boat with three of his crew for the shore, and where there were plenty of turtle for sale. Shortly after the Deponent landed he observed a canoe put off from the shore and his schooner observed six men rise in the canoe and fired the muskets at the schooner. On the arrival of the Deponent on board his schooner he found twenty armed men from the canoe with a brace of pistols and cutlasses each, who confined the vessel's crew, consisting of negroes in the schooner's hold, placing a sentinel over the hatchway

The Early Settlers.

from the cabin on deck and took 450 dollars in cash. They threw overboard a quantity of logwood to get at the beef in the hold, two barrels of which they put on board the canoe, together with the said three bales of turtle twine and five pieces of handkerchief and three bags of bread and every other article they found in the cabin. They unbended the mainsail flying jib, main gaff and topsail, and after calling up and beating the crew of the schooner with their cutlasses, compelled them to load the schooner's boat with the aforesaid sails, masts, and oars belonging to the said boat, and also a quantity of the schooner's running rigging. They plundered the Deponent, his crew, and the said William Coffin, passenger, of all their wearing apparel and left them only with what clothes they had on. That the crew of the said canoe spoke chiefly Spanish and threatened with others to put the Deponent and all on board to death should they find another dollar concealed. The Deponent recognised the aforesaid Hutcheson to be one of the pirates and verily believed his companions also were part of the crew of the Amazon aforesaid at about five o'clock in the afternoon. On the same day the pirates left the schooner in their canoe and the schooner's boat laden as aforesaid with a threat that if the Deponent was not off by daylight next morning they would return and sink the schooner with her crew. The Deponent, after bending the foresail as a mainsail in lieu of the one they had been robbed, got under weigh without obtaining any turtle, and after clearing the said Island of Leontsy the Deponent made the best of his way to Havana in order to refit and get provisions, the pirates having left them with barely twenty pounds of flour for himself and crew to subsist on. The Deponent arrived at Havana aforesaid on the sixth December inst., from which port, after refitting, the Deponent sailed in the said schooner on the 8th December and arrived at the Port of Nassau on the 15th without any further material occurrence.

(Signed) WILLIAM HESTER.

Sworn to before me,
    C. R. NESBITT,
        Notary Public.

The Early Settlers.

MUTINY ON BOARD THE BRITISH SHIP KATE.

The crew, eight in number, of the ship Kate, Captain Purdy, landed in the island of Guadaloupe, on the 24th of January, 1821. They slept on the beach that night, and next morning a planter in the neighbourhood came to them, and brought them to his house. Their story was uniform, all said they belonged to the American ship Retrieve, Capt. Jacob Hawes, belonging to Messrs. Suydam and Wyckoff, merchants, of New York; that after six weeks' boisterous weather not being able to keep the ship free, she being very leaky, the Captain had given orders to get the boat in readiness, and that they were doing it, and getting into the boat about ten o'clock, when the Captain's son, about ten years old, fell overboard in trying to get into the boat, and that the Captain threw himself into the sea to save him, but both perished, and the ship went down; that after one night and two days in the boat, they reached the beach near the Mole, with great hazard of their lives.

They were afterwards escorted to Point Petre, where they were examined by the Judge, and persisted in the same story; except one French lad, who privately disclosed the truth to the Attorney General.

They had with them all their baggage, and considerable money. Among the baggage was a Bible, with the label, "Presented by the Merchants' Seamen Auxiliary Bible Society, to the ship Kate, of London—Gravesend, 11th May, 1818." This, the mate, Thomas Murdock, said was given to him by a fellow lodger in New York. The Judge, however, availed himself of this circumstance to interrogate them a second time. Calling on Murdock, he said: "There is the Bible belonging to the ship Kate, of London, Capt. George Purdy, and upon that very same Bible you swear to tell the truth, and nothing but the truth." Murdock, much embarrassed, said, in broken words, that he was not accustomed to swear on the Bible, and resisted some time, when the Judge observed to him, that if he would not answer to the questions, he would pronounce him guilty immediately; for to refuse answering the questions of the Court was declaring himself guilty. Murdock then kissed the Bible. "Since I have taken an oath (said he) on the Bible, I will speak the truth," and related the real story, in substance:—

The Early Settlers

"That they belonged to the ship Kate, of London, Capt. George Purdy, which ship had been chartered in August last, at Halifax, for a voyage to Berbice and back to Halifax. The ship took a cargo of fish, beef, and some lumber. They reached Berbice where the cargo was sold for cash. The proceeds were put on board in two boxes iron hooped, containing 5.600 dollars. The ship sailed for Halifax in ballast. The mate had been discharged at Berbice, after having some quarrel with the Captain. Six weeks after sailing, finding constant head winds, and in want of provisions, the water nearly consumed, the crew asked the Captain what he intended to to do. The Captain told them he had still some coffee which he would give them for their support, and that he would try to get to Bermuda; but after 24 hours, the winds against them, they tried for New York, but without success. On the morning of the 8th of January three of the crew went and seized the Captain as he was walking on the deck, and tied him. They said that he and those that lived in the cabin must either jump overboard, or go into the jolly boat alongside. They then embarked the Captain, who wished and asked to go into the cabin for his cloak and boots, but he was not allowed. They begged earnestly for a compass; his lady also went on her knees and begged for a compass, but this was refused also. His lady, with their two children, one a boy two years old, the other a girl four years old, Mr. Robert Meredith, a passenger, and a mulatto boy named William, steward in the cabin, were then forced into the boat, with 20lbs. of bread, two trunks of the Captain's and Mr. Meredith's trunks and two oars, and sent adrift. The crew were ignorant of their then latitude. After ten days' sailing for the West Indies, Deseada was the first land he made. They had rigged the long boat as a sloop, put in their baggage and money, which had been equally divided among them, excepting the two lads, who had a share between them, when two of the crew went below and scuttled the ship."

Afterwards the rest of the crew confessed their crime. About 1,400 dollars were found and lodged at the Register's office. Murdock said he buried in the yard of the tavern at the Mole 450 dollars, but the money could not be found. He had an American protection, said he was born in New Brunswick (N.J.), and had papers from the grand and private

The Early Settlers

lodges of New York. The cook was a negro, from Philadelphia, from whence he went in a schooner to Halifax; his name was Philip Fisher; he stuttered. One was a French lad; one a London boy, one Welshman, an Irishman, and two Scotchmen.

LIST OF ATROCIOUS PIRACIES AND ROBBERIES.

Boston, Nov. 6, 1821.

The brig Cobbessecontee, Capt. Jackson, arrived yesterday from the Havana, sailed thence on the morning of the 8th ult., and on the evening of the same day, about four miles from the Moro, was brought to by a piratical sloop, containing about 30 men. A boat from her, with ten men, came alongside, and soon after they got on board commenced plundering. They took nearly all the clothing from the Captain and mate—all the cooking utensils and spare rigging—unrove part of the running rigging—cut the small cable—broke the compasses—cut the mast's coats to pieces—took from the Captain his watch and four boxes of cigars—and from the cargo three bales cochineal and six boxes of cigars. They beat the mate unmercifully and hung him up by the neck under the maintop. They also beat the Captain severely—broke a large broad sword across his back, and ran a long knife through his thigh so that he almost bled to death. Capt. Jackson saw the sloop at Regla the day before.

Capt. Jackson informs us, and we have also been informed by other persons from the Havana, that this system of Piracy is openly countenanced by some of the inhabitants of that place—who say that it is a retaliation on the Americans for interfering against the Slave Trade, and for allowing Patriot privateers to refit in their ports. The Pirates, therefore, receiving such countenance, grow more daring—and increase in number from the success which has attended this new mode of filling their pockets.

Capt. Bugnon, who arrived yesterday from Charleston, spoke on the 2nd inst., off the S. Shoal of Nantucket, the brig Three Partners, from Jamaica for St. John—had been robbed, off Cape Antonio, by a piratical vessel, of about 35 tons, and 17 men, of clothing, watches, etc., and the captain was hung up by the neck to the fore yard-arm, till he was almost dead.

The Early Settlers

Capt. Bourn, who arrived yesterday, from Cape Haytein, spoke on the 26th ult., lat. 33, lon. 78, brig Sea Lion, 36 days from Cape Haytein for Belfast, Ireland, which had been plundered by a pirate in the Gulf.

The brig Harriet, Capt. Dimond, from St. Jago de Cuba, for Baltimore, arrived at Havana on the 16th ult., having been robbed of all her cargo of sugar, and 4,000 dollars in specie, off Cape Antonio, by a boat with 15 men, having two schooners in company. Capt. Dimond was hung up by the neck and remained senseless for some time after he was taken down.

The Dutch brig Mercury, 77 days from Marseilles, arrived at Havana on the 16th ult., after having been robbed of 10,000 dollars worth of her cargo, by a piratical schooner and boat, off Cape Antonio.

Fortunately a U.S. vessel has arrived at the scene of these daring robberies, and has already protected two fleets. It is to be hoped some of the villains who have so long preyed with impunity on mercantile property, and been guilty of the most savage acts, will speedily be caught and brought to justice.

U.S. BRIG SPARK.

A letter from a gentleman belonging to this vessel, dated St. Barts, Nov. 3rd, 1821, says:—

"We arrived here, after a rough passage, in eighteen days from Boston, all well. We found here the piratical ship which robbed the Orleans Packet. She is now in possession of the Swedish Government. She came into her possession in the following manner. The crew landed her cargo on a small island near this, from whence it was taken by a schooner to St. Thomas;—they then ran the ship into Five Island Harbour, where all the crew, except two men, deserted her. The Government, hearing of her being there, sent a guard and took possession of her, brought her into this harbour, and confined the two men found in her as pirates. It is said that Capt. Elton has requested the Governor to allow him to take them to the United States for

The Early Settlers

trial. This piratical ship was originally the U.S. brig Prometheus, which was condemned two years since, and was then sold."

A letter from on board the Hornet, dated at Cape Maise, 31st October, says:—" The pirate which we took yesterday mounted two long four pounders, and her crew consisted of twenty gallows-looking scoundrels." After the capture of the Hornet, spoke three merchant brigs, which probably would have fallen into the hands of the pirates;—and were very happy at their escape.

Piratical Forts.—Captain Sisson from Havana reports that seventy of the pirates belonging to the vessels captured and destroyed by the Enterprize have erected two forts on Cape Antonio for their defence.

A TERRIBLE EXPERIENCE.

In the early part of June I sailed from Philadelphia in the schooner Mary on a voyage to New Orleans. My principal object in going round by sea was the restoration of my health, which had been for many months declining. Having some friends in New Orleans whose commercial operations were conducted on an extensive scale, I was charged with the care of several sums of money in gold and silver, amounting altogether to nearly eighteen thousand dollars. This I communicated to the captain and we concluded to secure it in the best manner our circumstances would permit. A plank was accordingly taken off the ribs of the schooner in my own cabin, and the money being deposited in the vacancy, the plank was nailed down in its original place, and the seams filled and tarred over. Being thus relieved from any apprehension that the money would be found upon us in cast of an attack from pirates, my mind was somewhat easier. What other articles of value I could conveniently carry about me I did so. I had also brought a quantity of bank-notes to the amount of fifteen thousand dollars. Part of these I caused to be carefully sewn in the left lapel of my coat, supposing that in case of my being lost at sea, my coat, should my body be found, would still contain the most valuable of my effects. The balance was carefully quilted into my black silk cravat.

The Early Settlers

Our crew consisted of the Captain and four men, with a supply of live stock for the voyage, and a Newfoundland dog, valuable for his fidelity and sagacity. He had once saved his master from a watery grave when he had been stunned and knocked overboard by the sudden shifting of the boom. I was the only passenger on board. Our voyage at first was prosperous, and time went on rapidly. I felt my strength increase the longer I was at sea, and when we arrived off the southern coast of Florida my feelings were like those of another man.

It was towards the evening of the fourteenth day, two hours before sunset, that we espied a sail astern of us. As twilight came, it neared us with astonishing rapidity. Night closed, and all around was impenetrable darkness. Now and then a gentle wave would break against our bow and sparkle for a moment, and at a distance behind us we could see the uneven glow of light, occasioned by the foaming of the strange vessel. The breeze that filled our canvas was gentle, though it was fresh.

We coursed our way steadily through the night; though once or twice the roaring of the waves increased so suddenly as to make us believe we had passed a breaker. At the time it was unaccountable to me, but I now believe it to be occasioned by the bark behind us coming rather near in the darkness of the night. At midnight I went on deck. Nothing but an occasional sparkle was to be seen, and the ocean was undisturbed. Still it was a fearful and appalling darkness, and in spite of my endeavours I could not compose myself. At the windlass, on the forecastle, three of the sailors, like myself, unable to sleep, had collected for conversation. On joining them I found our fears were mutual. They all kept their eyes steadily fixed upon the unknown vessel, as if anticipating some dreadful event. They informed me that they had put their arms in order and were determined to stand or die.

At this moment a flash of light, perhaps a musket burning priming, proceeded from the vessel in pursuit, and we saw distinctly that her deck was covered with men. My heart almost failed me. I had never been in battle, and I knew not what it was. Day at length dawned, and setting all her canvas, our pursuer gained alarmingly upon us. It was evident that she had followed us the whole night, being

The Early Settlers.

unwilling to attack up in the dark. In a few minutes she fired a swivel and came along-side. She was a pirate. Her boat was lowered, and about a dozen hideous looking objects jumped in, with a commander at their head. The boat pushed off, and was nearing us fast, as we arranged ourselves for giving her a broadside. Our whole stock of arms consisted of six muskets and an old swivel used as a signal gun, belonging to the Mary, and a pair of pistols of my own, which I carried in my belt. The pirate boat's crew were armed with muskets, pistols, swords, cutlasses and knives; and when she came within her own length of us, we fired five of our muskets and the swivel into her. Her fire was scarcely half given, when she filled and went down with all her crew. At this success we were inclined to rejoice, but looking over the pirate schooner we observed her deck still swarming with the same description of horrid looking wretches. A second boat's crew pushed off, with their muskets pointed directly at us the whole time. When they came within the same distance as the other we fired, but with little, if any, effect. The pirate immediately returned the fire, and with horrid cries jumped aboard f us. Two of our brave crew were lying dead upon the deck, and the rest of us expected nothing better. French, Spanish and English were spoken indiscriminately, and all at once. The most horrid imprecations were uttered against us, and threats that fancy cannot imagine.

A wretch, whose black, shaggy yhiskers covered nearly his whole face, whose eyes were only seen at intervals from beneath his bushy eyebrows, and whose whole appearance was more that of a hell-hound than of a human being, approached me with a drawn cutlass in his hand. I drew one of my pistols and snapped it in his face; but it flashed in the pan, and before I could draw the other the pirate, with a brutality that would have disgraced a cannibal, struck me over the face with his cutlass, and knocked me down. I was too much wounded by the blow to resist, and the blood ran in torrents from my forehead. In this situation the wretch seized me by the scalp, and thrusting his cutlass in my cravat, cut it through completely. I felt the cold iron glide along my throat, and even now the very thought makes me shudder. The worst idea I had ever formed of human cruelty seemed now realised, and I could see death stare me

The Early Settlers.

in the face. Without stopping to examine the cravat, he put it in his pocket, and in a voice of thunder exclaimed. "Levez vous!" I accordingly rose on my feet, and he pinioned my hands behind my back, led me to the gunwale of the vessel, and asked another of the gang, in French, whether he should throw me overboard. At the recollection of that scene I am still staggered. I endeavoured to call the prospects of Eternity before me, but could think of nothing except the cold and quiverless apathy of the tomb. His infamous companion replied, "Il est trop bonne hetire l'envoyager au diable," and led me to the foremast, where he tied me with my face to the stern of the vessel. The cords were drawn so tight around my arms and legs that my agony was excruciating. In this situation he left me.

On looking around I found them all employed in plundering and ransacking everything we had. Over my left shoulder one of our sailors was strung up to the yardarm, and apparently in the last agonies of death; while before me our gallant Captain was on his knees and begging for his life. The wretches were endeavouring to extort from him the secret of our money; but for a while he was firm and dauntless. Provoked at his obstinacy, they extended his arms and cut them off at the elbows. At this human nature gave way, and the injured man confessed the spot where we had concealed our specie. In a few moments it was aboard their own vessel. To revenge themselves on our unhappy captain, when they had satisfied themselves that nothing else was hidden, they spread a bed of oakum on the deck, and after soaking it through with turpentine, tied the captain on it, filled his mouth with the same combustibles, and set the whole on fire. The cries of the unfortunate man were heart-rendering, and his agonies must have been unutterable; but they were soon over. All this I was compelled to witness. Heart-sick with the sight, I once shut my eyes, but a musket discharged close to my ear, was a warning sufficient to keep them open.

On casting my eyes to the stern of the vessel I discovered that the boatswain had been nailed to the deck through his feet, and the body spiked through to the tiller. He was writhing in the last agonies of crucifixion. Our fifth comrade was out of sight during all this tragedy. In a few minutes, however, he was brought upon the deck blindfolded.

The Early Settlers.

He was then conducted to the muzzle of the swivel, and commanded to kneel. The swivel was then fired off, and his head dreadfully wounded by the discharge. In a moment after it was agonizing to behold his torments and convulsions—language is too feeble to describe them. I have seen men hung upon the gibbet, but their death was like sinking in slumber when compared with his.

Excited with the scene of human butchery, one of those wretches fired his pistol at the captain's dog. The ball struck his shoulder and disabled him; he finished him by shooting him again, and at last by cutting out his tongue! At this last hell-engendered act my blood boiled with indignation at such savage brutality on a helpless, inoffensive dog! But I was unable to give utterance or action to my feelings.

Seeing that the crew had been every one despatched, I began to think more of myself. My old enemy, who seemed to forget me, once more approached me; but shockingly besmeared with blood and brains. He had stood by the side of the unfortunate sailor who suffered before the swivel, and supported him with the point of his bayonet. He drew a stiletto from his side, placed its point upon my heart and gave it a heavy thrust. I felt its point touch my skin; but the quilting of my bank bills prevented its further entrance. This savage monster then ran it up my breast, as if intending to divide my lungs, and in doing so the bank bills fell upon the deck. He snatched them up greedily, and exclaimed, "Ah! laissez mois voir ce que reste." My dress in a few moments was ripped to pieces at the peril of my life. He frequently came so near as to tear my skin and deluge me with blood; but by the mercy of Providence I escaped from every danger. At this moment, a heavy flaw struck the schooner, and I heard one of the pirates say, "Voila un vaisseau!" They all retreated precipitately, and, gaining their own vessel, was soon out of sight.

Helpless as I now was, I had the satisfaction of knowing that the pirates had been frightened by the appearance of a sail, but it was impossible for me to see it. Still tied to the foremast, I knew not what was my prospect of release. An hour or two had elapsed after they left me, and it was now noon. The sun played violently upon my head, and I felt a langour and debility that indicated ap-

The Early Settlers

proaching fever. My head gradually sunk upon my breast, when I was shocked by hearing the water pouring into the cabin windows. The wretches had scuttled the vessel, and, quarrelling on the question of putting all to death, left me pinioned to go down with her. I commended my spirit to my Maker, and gave myself up for lost. I felt myself gradually dying away, and the last thing I remembered was the foaming noise of the waves. This was occasioned by a ship passing by me. I was taken in, restored to health, and I am now a poor, ruined, helpless man.

The ship Liverpool packet, Ricker, of Portsmouth, N.H. was boarded on the 16th off Cape St. Antonio, Cuba, by two piratical schooners—two barges containing thirty or forty men. They robbed the vessel of everything movable, even to her flags, rigging, one boat which happened to be afloat, and having a boy in it which belonged to the ship. They held a consultation whether they should murder the crew, as they had done before, or not—in the meantime taking the ship into anchoring ground. On bringing her to anchor, the crew saw a brig close alongside, burnt to the water's edge, and three dead bodies floating near her. The pirates said they had burnt the brig the day before, and murdered all the crew!—and intended doing the same with them. They said "Look at the turtles (meaning the dead bodies), you will soon be the same." They said the vessel was a Baltimore brig, which they had robbed and burnt, and murdered the crew as before stated, of which they had little doubt. Capt. Ricker was most shockingly bruised by them. The mate was hung till he was supposed to be dead, but came to, and is now alive. They told the captain that they belonged to Regla, and should kill them to prevent discovery.

BRIG DOVER.

Extract from the Log-Book of the Brig Dover, Capt. Sabins, from Mantanzas for Charleston.

Jan. 16th, 1822, sea account, at 1 p.m.—Pan of Matanzas, bearing S., saw a boat coming to us from a small drogher, which came out of Matanzas the night before us,

The Early Settlers

with five Spaniards, armed with long knives, pistols, cutlasses, etc. When they got within hail, they fired a musket at us, cheered, and came on board. They were the most villainous looking rascals that anyone had probably ever behled. They immediately drew their weapons, and after beating us severely with their cutlasses, drove us below. Then they robbed us of all our clothes except what we had on. our watches, and everything of value. We were afterwards called up singly. Four men with drawn knives stood over the captain, and threatened him, if he did not give up his money, they would kill all hands and burn the vessel. After robbing the people they commenced plundering the brig. They broke open the hatches, made us get out our boat and carry their plunder to their vessel. They took from us one compass, five bags coffee, one barrel sugar, nearly all our provisions, our colours, rigging, and cooking utensils. Then they ordered us to stand to the north, or they would overhaul us, murder the crew and burn the vessel. We made sail, and shortly after were brought to by another boat of the same character, which fired into us, but left us upon being informed that we had been already robbed.

The Porpoise, Capt. Ramage, arrived at Charleston from his successful cruise against the pirates, having recaptured a Baltimore schooner which had been in their possession three days, destroyed three of their establishments on shore, 12 of their vessels, besides two on the stocks, and brought in four prisoners, against whom it is supposed there is strong evidence.

It is stated that a pirate captain and his mate quarrelled on the question of putting to death all captives. They fought a duel with muskets, the Captain being killed, and the mate (who was the advocate of mercy) succeeded to the command.

The schooner Jane, of Boston, was taken the 24th January by a pirate schooner. They were carried into a place where were three more of the same trade. The captain and crew were threatened, beat, and the vessel plundered of much property; after which they were released.

The Early Settlers

If the Spanish Government is unable to drive the pirates from their strongholds in Cuba, the "Baltimore Chronicle" suggests the necessity of occupying the island with American forces for that purpose, as robbers and pirates have a right to enjoy no protection whatever, and in this case all civilised powers are warranted in carrying the war into the enemy's territory.

PIRATES CAPTURED.

Charleston, Feb. 12.—The four pirates brought into this port by the United States Porpoise were landed yesterday from that vessel, and committed to prison. Three of them are Spaniards, the other a Portugese; two of the former, father and son, the son being only about 18 years of age.

Charleston, Feb. 14th, 1824.—The United States schooner Grampus, Lieut. Gregory, from a cruise of four months in the West Indies and along the Spanish Main, arrived at our port yesterday morning, last from Santa Martha. She has brought in three pirates, viz., James Maxfield, one of the crew that robbed the Orleans, of Philadelphia, and Charles Owens and James Ross, who robbed a Portsmouth schooner of 2.600 dollars in the Bight of Leogane. One of these daring freebooters was delivered up to Lieut. Gregory by the Governor of St. Barts, and the other two by the President of Hayti, for trial by the United States. The Grampus has boarded several privateers during her cruise, and traversed a space of 9,000 miles, spreading terror among those wretches whose impotence is equal to their atrocity, and who only require active pursuit to frighten them out of visible existence.

Mobile, June 1st, 1822.—Capt. Carter, of the schooner Swan, arrived yesterday from Havana, reports that on his outward passage from this port, on the 27th ult., at 8 o'clock a.m., being then within 30 miles from Havana, he was boarded by an open boat from the shore, manned with nine men, who all appeared to be Spanish armed with muskets, pistols, cutlasses, and knives, who plundered the vessel of everything they could carry off. They also robbed the captain and crew of their clothing, even stripping the jackets from their backs, and the shoes from their feet.

The Early Settlers

The villains would not even spare the property of a Spanish priest, passenger on board, but they robbed him also of his clothes, money, and plate, the value of 800 dollars; they, however, afterwards returned his gown.

A sail heaving in sight, they left the schooner with orders to steer E.N.E., and not go over three leagues from shore, under pain of death. From their conversation while on board it appeared that they intended to board the schooner again in the evening, run her ashore and burn her, but she escaped by the darkness of night.

LIEUT. ALLEN'S VICTORY AND DEATH.

Extract of a letter from Mantanzas, dated November 11th, 1822.

"The gallant ALLEN is no more! You witnessed the promptitude with which he hastened to relieve the vessels which I informed him had been captured off this port. He arrived just in time to save five sails of vessels which he found in possession of a gang of pirates, 300 strong, established in the Bay of Lejuapo, about 15 leagues east of this. He fell, pierced by two musket balls, in the van of a division of boats, attacking their principal vessel, a fine schooner of about eighty tons, with a long eighteen pounder on a pivot, and four smaller guns, with the bloody flag nailed to the mast. Himself, Capt. Freeman of Marines, and twelve men, were in the boat, much in advance of his other boats, and even took possession of the schooner, after a desperate resistance, which nothing but a bravery almost too daring could have overcome. The pirates, all but one, escaped by taking to their boats and jumping overboard, before the Alligator's boats reached them. Two other schooners escaped by the use of their oars, the wind being light.

Lieut. Allen survived about four hours, during which his conversation evinced a composure and firmness of mind, and correctness for feeling, as honourable to his character, and more consoling to his friends than even the dauntless bravery he before exhibited."

The Surgeon of the Alligator in a letter to a friend says: "He continued giving orders and conversing with Mr. Dale ,and the rest of us, until a few minutes before his

The Early Settlers

death, with a degree of cheerfulness that was little to be expected from a man in his condition. He said he wished his relatives and his country to know that he had fought well, and added that he died in peace and goodwill towards all the world, and hoped for his reward in the next."

Lieut. Allen had but few equals in the service. He was ardently devoted to the interest of his country, was brave, intelligent, and accomplished in his profession. He displayed, living and dying, a magnanimity that sheds lustre on his relatives, his friends, and his country.

PIRATES ENTRAPPED.

The British schooner Speedwell arrived at Nassau, N.P., in November, bringing in 18 pirates who had been captured by the Speedwell and her consort. The schooner had been disguised as a merchantman, and the pirates, taking her to be an easy prize, came carelessly alongside of her, for the purpose of boarding, when she gave them a hot fire, and threw them into confusion. Many jumped overboard and were drowned; and with these and the killed the loss of the pirates was about 15 or 16. The remainder of them, 18 in number, were taken prisoners and carried into Nassau.

SAILING OF COMMODORE PORTER.

Baltimore, Jan. 17th, 1823.

Yesterday Commodore Porter left this port in the steam galley Enterprize to join the squadron fitted out at Norfolk, for the purpose of suppressing piracy on the coast of Cuba. Every friend of humanity must wish that the efforts of the distinguished officer who has been selected for this command will be crowned with success. The means adopted are certainly the best calculated to effect the object. Frigates and sloops of war are totally inadequate, by means of their great draft of water; but the vessels which have been selected by Commodore Porter are precisely calculated to ferret the banditti from their lurking places. The

The Early Settlers.

aid of steam we think a most valuable addition to the squadron, and from the manner in which the Enterprize has been fitted out, we have every reason to believe she will completely answer the expectations formed. Commodore Porter has been indefatigable since he came here, and several of our citizens conversant in steam affairs volunteered their services to aid him in the necessary equipments for that department. We learn that she is provided with duplicates of every piece of machinery which might be carried away in action, and that able and experienced engineers were also procured for her.

In a very short time we hope to hear of the Commodore's arrival at his cruising ground, and we doubt not he will soon put an end to the ravages of those lawless barbarians.

The Early Settlers.

Governors of the Bahamas, from 1671–1937.

Johnson Wentworth	1671
Chillingworth	1673
Clark	1677
Lilburne	1684
Bridges	1687
Jones, Cadwallader	1690
Trott	1694
Webb, Nicholas	1694
Haskett, Elias	1700
Lightfoot, Ellis	
Birch	1704

(Bahamas occupied by the Spaniards 1704-1717)

Rogers, Woodes	1717
Phenny, George	1721
Rogers, Woodes, again	1728
Fitzwilliam, Richard	1733
Tinker, John	1738
Shirley, William	1759
Shirley, Thomas	1767
Browne, Montford	1774
Maxwell, John	1779
Dunmore, Earl of	1787
Forbes, John, Lieut.-Gov.	1796
Dowdeswell, W., Governor	1797
Hackett, John	1801

The Early Settlers.

Cameron, Charles	1804
Grant, M., General	1820
Smyth, Sir I. C.	1820
Balfour, B. T., Lieut.-Gov.	1834
Colebrooke, Lieut.-Col., Lieut.-Gov.	1837
Smith, Sir L., Governor	1838
Cockburn, Sir F., Governor	1840
Matthew, G. B., Governor	1844
Gregory, John, Governor	1849
Bannerman, Sir A.	1854
Baley, C. J., Governor	1857
Rawson, R. W., Governor	1864
Walker, Sir J. P., C.M.G., C.B.	1868
Hennessy, J. P., C.M.G.	1871
Robinson, Sir W. K., C.M.G.	1874
Callagan, T. F.	1880
Lees, Sir C. C.	1882
Blake, Sir Henry A.	1884
Shea, Sir Ambrose, K.C.M.G.	1887
Haynes-Smith, Sir W. F., K.C.M.G.	1895
Carter, Sir Gilbert T.	1898
Grey, Wilson, K.C.M.G.	1904
Haddon Smith	1912
Allardyce, Sir W. L.	1918
Cordeaux, Sir S.	1926
Orr, Major	1927
Clifford, Sir Bede, K.C.M.G.	1932
Dundas, Hon. C. C., C.M.G., O.B.E.	1937

DISTINGUISHED PERSONAGES.

The Governor of the Bahamas.

DUNDAS, HON. C. C. F., C.M.G., O.B.E.
Assistant District Commissioner, E.A.P., 1908.
District Commissioner, 1914.
District Political Officer (Hon. Rank of Major) G.E. Africa.
Provisional Administrator, 1916.
Senior Commissioner, Tanganyika Territory, 1920.
Acting Assistant Chief Secretary, 1924.
Acting Secretary for Native Affairs, 1926.
Colonial Secretary, Bahamas, 1929.
Acting Administrator, several occasions.
Appointed Chief Secretary, Rhodesia, 1934.
Acting Governor, 1934.
Appointed Governor of the Bahamas, June, 1937.
Descended from Viscount Melville. Title created 1802. (Great Britain).

Nassau, Lord Bishop of, The Right Reverend
JOHN DAUGLISH, M.A., St. John's College, Oxford;
Formerly Chaplain of the Royal Navy, 1905-1924;
Rector of Lympstone, Devon, 1924-1931;
Consecrated Bishop of Nassau, Jan. 25th, 1932.
No. of Churches in the Diocese - 87
        Priests - 18
    Communicants - 5840
      Members - 12,708

The Early Settlers

STREATFIELD, Very Rev. Robert Cornthwaite, M.A.,
Queen's College, Cambridge;
Dean of Nassau and Rector of Christ Church Cathedral.
Formerly Curate of S. Mary's, Peckham, 1925-26;
Domestic Chaplain to the Bishop of Southwark 1926-29.
Senior Curate of Wimbledon, 1929-34.
Installed as Dean, November 26th, 1934.

The Very Rev. BISHOP BERNARD, O.S.B.H, of the Bahamas,.
St. John's University, Minnesotta, U.S.A.
Formerly Pastor of St. Anselm's Parish, Bronx, New York,.
1907-1929;
Prefect Apostolic of the Bahamas, 1931;
Consecrated Titular Bishop of Camuliana, 1933.

Rev. HENSON BONAVENTURE, O.S.B.,
St. John's University, Minnesotta, U.S.A.
Prefect-Apostolorum, Bahamas;
Formerly Missionary in North Dakota, U.S.A., 1905-1920;
Appointed for the Bahamas, 1920.

TUTE, Sir Richard Clifford. Kt. Bach.
Educated, St. Peter's Royal School, York, and London University; Barrister-at-Law, Middle Temple. Entered Indian Civil Service, 1898; District and Sessions Judge, Allabad; Served throughout European War, retired as Major R.G.A. (1919); President District Ct. Sanana, 1920; President Land Ct. Jerusalem; Chief Justice, Bahamas 1931; Administer Government, 1932; Author of ,' A Commentary on Ottoman Land Code," etc. Sir Richard and Lady Tute, his wife, are so charmed with the climate of the Bahamas that they have built a palatial dwelling 200 ft. from a bathing beach where they take a daily plunge into the crystal waters facing their house.

TAYLOR, Sir Frederick Williams,
Also his wife, Lady Williams-Taylor, have been visiting the Colony for so many years that we are delighted when they arrive in the Colony for their winter stay. Sir Frederick Williams-Taylor was born in Moncton, N.B., 1863. Formerly General Manager of the Bank of Montreal; Director of the Canadian Steamship Co., Ltd.; Director of

The Early Settlers

the London, Liverpool and Globe Insurance Co.; Director and Member of the Executive Committee of the Royal Trust Co., Canada; a distinguished financier and a man of scholarly attainments. Awarded a Silver Medal by the Royal Society of Arts and held important positions in a dozen or more Corporations. Knighted in 1913. Received an Honorary Degree of L.L.D. conferred by the University of New Brunswick 1914. Owns a valuable estate in New Providence.

HOLT, Sir Samuel.

Of Canada, has built a palatial residence in the Island of New Providence which he occupies as his Winter home. A distinguished financier who has amassed a fortune in Banking business. Formerly: President of the Royal Bank of Canada; Montreal Trust Co.; Vice-President of the American Banker Associates; Director of the Canadian Pacific Railroad; Director of the Imperial Life Assurance of Canada; Director of the Sun Life Assurance Co. of Canada; President and Director of fifty or more Corporations. Born and educated in Dublin, Ireland, and came to Canada in 1875. Last, but not least, is a Member of the Anglican Church and Governor of McGill University.

RAE, Sir James Stanley.

Born 1881. Educated: Nassau Grammar School. Son of James Rae, Esq. (deceased) Stipendary and Circuit Magistrate. Descendant of Henry Rae, a Loyalist. Attorney-at Law, 1904, Middle Temple, London. Coroner, Island of New Providence, 1911. Justice of the Peace. Acted Attorney General, 1910. Stipendiary and Circuit Magistrate. District Commissioner British Honduras, 1914. J.P. British Justice of British Honduras. Chief Justice Leeward Islands. Knighted, 1933. Retired. Expected to reside in Nassau again.

MENENDEZ, Sir M. Raymond, Kt., Bach.

Educated: Taunton School and Emmanuel College, Cambridge, L.L.B., 1890; Barrister-at-Law, Inner Temple. Acted Stipendiary and Circuit Maistrate, Bahamas, 1892-94; Appointed District Commissioner, Lagos, 1894; Acted

The Early Settlers

Queen's Advocate, Lagos, 1896-1897. Chief Judicial Officer. Niger Coast, Protectorate, 1897; Puisne Judge, Nigeria, 1899; Acted Chief Justice on several occasions, Chief Justice, Nigeria, 1905.

JARRET, James Henry, K.C.
Educated: Lancing College; Barrister-at-Law, Gray's Inn; Served European War, 1914-1919; District Commissioner, Uganda, 1919; Magistrate, 1922-1924; Assistant Attorney General, 1926; Solicitor General 1927-1928; Crown Council, 1927; Attorney General, Grenada, 1929; Acted Administrator and Chief Justice, St. Vincent, 1930-1931; Attorney General Bahamas, 1933; Acted Chief Justice Administrator, 1934-1935; Colonial Secretary, 1935; Administrator 1936-1937; Chaiman: Agriculture and Marine Product Board.

GRIFFIN, John Bowes.
Educated: Trinity College, Dublin; M.A., L.L.D.; 1st Class Moderatorship, Gold Medallists; Prizeman; Barrister-at-Law, Inner Temple, 1936. Practiced Law in Uganda. Crown Council. Solicitor General on various occasions. Acted Attorney General. Appointed Attorney General, Bahamas, 1936; Acted Chief Justice, 1936. Chairman of the Development Board, 1937.

TAYLOR, Robert Walter, C.M.G., O.B.E.
Educated: Emmanuel School and King's College, London. Clk. Crown Agent's Office, London. Head Accountant Somaliland, 1906; Assistant Treasurer, Uganda, 1910; Assistant Treasurer Somaliland, 1914; Treasurer, 1915; Deputy Treasurer, Tanganyika Territory, 1922; Acted Chief Secretary, 1927; Governor's Deputy, 10th-27th May, 1927; Receiver General and Treasurer, Bahamas, 1936; Chairman, Board of Works, 1937.

DOLLY, Dr. Charles.
Came to the Bahamas about thirty-five years ago and was first to build a fine residence out West. Later on, he disposed of this residence to the late Mr. and Mrs. Doubleday, of New York. Afterwards, he built his present house, which two years ago was occupied by English

The Early Settlers

Royalty for a few months. He has a superb constitution, and although advanced in years, is very vigorous and exceedingly active. This country owes him a debt for the interest he has taken in inducing wealthy Americans to purchase land and to build winter homes along the Western sea front, and accordingly lands which were but a wilderness forty years ago have now become a beauty spot of the Island of New Providence.

OAKES, Harry, J.P.

Lived in Canada for the last twenty years, where he had wonderful achievements in the mining world. Discovered a gold mining region, which in a very short time made him one of the wealthiest men in Canada. His income is said to be not less than one million five hundred thousand pounds a year. Now settled in the Bahamas for the remainder of his life, and, is taking a wonderful interest in the Colony. Has given New Providence a 'Bus Service with no expectation of gaining a farthing from it, and unnecessarily finds employment for about five hundred labourers weekly. Is a Justice of the Peace of the Bahamas, and a Member of the Board of Public Works. Is one of the largest real estate owners in the Colony.

BAXTER, Guy.

Arrived in the Bahamas from England about twenty years ago and permanently settled in the Colony. Pioneer in the Real Estate movement. Having faith in the idea of Developing the waste lands in New Providence, was forced to invest heavily in the business. Mr. Baxter was right; for to-day, building of country seats is going on from one part of the Island to the other. Properties have gone up in value and will go higher as time goes on. Meanwhile, the old order in the Bahamas is fast hastening to a close, giving way to a continuous wave of development by the flowing of foreign wealth into the Colony.

DREXAL, Anthony.

Member of an old Banking business in Philadelphia. Daughter married Mr. Grundy, brother to Lady Clifford,

The Early Settlers.

wife of Sir Bede Clifford, K.C.M.G., late Governor of the Bahamas. Acquired a very valuable estate in the Colony, Member of the Nassau Royal Yacht Club.

LEVY, Austin.

A very practical type of man. Attracted to the Bhamas on account of its climate and quiet conditions and has consequently built a residence in the vicinity of Cable Beach in New Providence and is extending his building programme and other developments in Central Eleuthera. Has purchased from the Hatchet Bay Company's holdings, 2,000 acres of land, which he is now developing along agricultural lines in spite of some hindrances in the productiveness of the soil.

McLEAN, H. C.

Is the present Manager of the Royal Bank of Canada of Nassau, Bahamas. This branch of the Royal Bank of Canada was first established in 1912, and first did its business in the Higgs Building, Bay Street, under the management of the late Honourable George Gamblin. At first it was faced with local prejudices and interests on account of the influence of the old Nassau Bank which was firmly established and carrying on business in the City, but owing to its subsequent failure in 1918, the activity of the New Bank had greatly increased. In the meanwhile, the new building of the Royal Bank was erected and its business grew by leaps and bounds under the management of the Hon. George Gamblin. On the death of Mr. Gamblin, it fell under other managements. The appointment of the present very able Manager, H. C. McLean, was a commendable foresight in safeguarding the Banking interests on behalf of those whom it may concern, and, to-day, we can attribute the unparalleled business done by this bank to the wise management of Mr. McLean.

ERICKSON, Josiah.

A wealthy resident. He purchased the palatial residence on FitzWilliam's Mount from the owners of the estate of the late Charles E. Bethell, where he resides during the winter months. The dwelling overlooks the township and the ocean to the North. Mr. Erickson and his

The Early Settlers.

sons are operating the Salt Industry at Inaqua, one of the Eastern Islands of the Bahamas, lying in the roadstead of steamships passing through the Crooked Island Passage. The geographical position of Inaqua is such that although hurricanes pass over every other Island in the group, none ever strike Inaqua. The Ericksons are spending a large amount of capital in the development of the Salt Industry, which naturally gives employment to a large proportion of the inhabitants of Inaqua. The Salt Industry has been carried on by the inhabitants of the Bahamas since 1670. It was exported by them to the near-by Colonies of America in exchange for goods and foodstuffs required by the early settlers of the Bahamas for their daily use. It would be a blessing to the inhabitants of Long Cay, Rum Cay, Long Island, and the Island of Exuma if other wealthy Americans would be attracted to these Islands with the object of Developing the Salt Industry or some other Industry. We wish that the efforts of the Ericksons may be attended with success.

BIOGRAPHIES

of the Descendants of the Early Settlers, Loyalists, and other inhabitants in General.

ADDERLEY, Harold---Son of the late Harold Adderley. Educated: Queen's College, Nassau, New Providence, and completed his studies with his brother George B. Adderley, in England. Grandson of George B. Adderley, deceased, and a relative of Sir Augustus Adderley, England. Descended from Abraham Adderley, Loyalist. On the Staff of the Royal Bank of Canada, Nassau.

ADDERLEY, George B.---Son of the late Harold Adderley. Educated: Queen's College, and completed his studies in England. Grandson of George B. Adderley, deceased, and a relative of Sir Augustus Adderley, England. Descendant of Abraham Adderley, a Loyalist. Agent for the Northern Assurance Co., London, England.

ALBURY, Dr. Joseph Baird. ---Educated: Queen's College, Wycliffe College, Gloucestershire, England; St. Mary's Hospital, London; Natural Science Scholarship, M.R.C.S. (England); L.R.C.P. (London); Private Practice, Nassau; Medical Officer for Out-going Emigrants, and Board of Trade Department. The Moving Spirit of Boy Scouts, Bahamas. Acted Chief Medical Officer, Bahamas. Born in Nassau, son of the late Hon. Joseph Benson Albury, M.D., M.L.A., Nassau. Member of the Hon. Legislative Council, Bahamas. Descendant of James Baird, Loyalist.

ALBURY, Wilton, M.B.E.--- Is Inspector of Schools in the Bahamas, and belongs to one of the oldest Colonial families. In 1721, a John Albury was selected

The Early Settlers.

from among the inhabitants of the Colony as a "fit person to be recommended to His Majesty to be elected by the public to make an Assembly, or execute other public offices under the Government."

ALBURY, Gilbert---Is a retired Commissioner of the Civil Service of the Bahamas, and is descended from John Albury, one of the oldest settlers who came from England via Bermuda as a Colonist. In 1721, Governor George Phenney, with the assistance of his Council had selected from among the inhabitants of the Colony 27 "fit persons to be recommended to His Majesty to be elected by the Public to make an Assembly or execute other public offices under the Government." John Albury was one of the persons agreed on to be recommended.

ALBURY, Clan.—Son of Dewitt Albury. Educated: Queen's College. Secretary of Marine Product Board. Supervisor of the Tomato Export from the Bahamas and the Crawfish Industry. Real Estate owner. Descended from John Albury who was selected from among the inhabitants of the Colony by Governor George Phenney with the assistance of his Council, 1721, as a "fit person to be recommended to His Majesty to be elected by the public to make an Assmbly, or execute other public offices under the Government."

ALBURY, R. W. D.—A descendant of John Albury who was selected from among the inhabitants of the Colony by Governor George Phenney, 1721, as a "fit person to be recommended to His Majesty to be elected by the public to make an Assembly, or execute other public offices under the Government." Commission Agent for American and European firms. Agent for the Phoenix Assurance Co. of London.

ALBURY, Stanley V. S.---A descendant of John Albury, who in 1721, was selected by Governor George Phenney as a "fit and proper person to be recommended to His Majesty to be elected by the public to make an Assembly or execute other public offices under the Government." Was a Master in the public schools until appointed a Commissioner; finally Superintendant of the Bahamas General Hospital. Now retired from the public service on a pension. Commission Agent for Canadian and European firms.

The Early Settlers

ALBURY, Joseph J.— Born Harbour Island, Educated: Public Schools. Became Master Government School; Commissioner in all Districts. Descendant of John Albury, who was selected as a " fit person to be recommended to His Majesty to be elected by the Public for Harbour Island to make an Assembly, or execute public office under the Government."

ALBURY, Leonard. — Educated: Queen's College. Entered Civil Service, Bahamas, 1921. Clerk, General Post Office; Colonial Secretary's Department; Treasury Department and Supervisor of City Market, Nassau.

ALBURY, Roscoe.—Born 19th January, 1912, at Abaco. Educated at Public School, Abaco. A descendant of the old Settlers of Eleuthera. Clerk in the Establishment of J. P. Sands and Co., Nasasu.

ANDERSON, Hon. C. O.—Entered the Bahamas Civil Service as a Clerk at the Bahamas General Hospital, and later on, was appointed to the Post Office Department as a Clerk, where at length he became Postmaster General. He was a Member of the House of Assembly for over twenty years for the Western District, New Providence. Appointed a Member of the Board of Education. He is a Justice of the Peace for the Bahama Islands, and a Member of the Honourable Legislative Assembly.

ARMBRISTER, Hon. P. W. D., M.L.A., O.B.E.,—Born 8th Sept., 1862. Son of Dr. W. R. Armbrister, of Nassau (deceased). Educated: Nassau Grammar School. Resident Magistrate in practically all Districts in the Colony. Acted Stipendary and Circuit Magistrate. Receiver General and Treasurer; Acted Colonial Secretary. Justice of the Peace. Member of the Legislative Council. Retired from Civil Service.

ARTEAGA, Rosanda C.—Son of the late Charles E. Arteaga, who was the owner of valuable real estate in the Bahamas. Educated: Catholic School and Queen's College. Descendant of John Arteaga, Spanish. Merchant, Nassau, Bahamas.

ARTEAGA, Charles A.— Son of the late Charles E. Arteaga, who was the owner of valuable real estate in the Bahamas. Educated: Catholic School and Queen's College. Formerly associated with Kelly's, Ltd., and now with The William Brewer Co., Ltd., Nassau. Member of Nassau Yacht Club.

The Early Settlers

ASPINALL, A. E.—Has been for the last twenty years Agent for two of the largest Steamship Lines operating between New York, Nassau, Miami, Havana and Mexico. He succeeded the late Percival Solomon as Agent for the Ward Line---New York and Cuba Mail Steamship Service which afterwards was substituted by the Munson Steamship Company operating between New York, Nassau, Miami and Cuba, of which service he was also appointed Agent.

BERRY, Frank—Is the Manager of the Bahamas Realty Co., Ltd., and a Member of the Real Estate Board of New York City. He is a large real estate owner.

BETHELL, Charles P.—Is the son of the late John Bethell, Esq., Port Officer. He was educated at Queen's College and entered the Civil Serivce in 1912. He has moved along the different stages of appointments in the Colonial Secretary's Department, and now has the distinction of holding the Office of Assistant Colonial Secretary. Served with the British forces during the late World War, having left Nassau with the first Bahamas Contingent and became a Lieutenant in the British Army.

BETHELL, Charles W. F.—Son of the late Charles E. Bethell. Educated in England and was pursuing his studies at College on the death of his father which occurred in England, 1929. His father left a very large personal and real estate in the Bahamas and England. One of the successors of his father's estate, being too young to conduct the business in the Bahamas, the responsibility fell upon R. J. Robertson, his father's associate in business, who was Manager until the business was taken over by the present Charles W. F. Bethell, in 1933. Married Miss Patricia Kelly, a daughter of the late Allan Kelly, Esq., who had himself amassed a large fortune in business, and, who was also a descendant of James Kelly, a Loyalist, who came to the Bahamas from East Florida after the Revolutionary War of America in 1783. John Bethell, one of the old ancestors of Charles W. F. Bethell, was elected a Member of the first Legislative Assembly of the Bahamas for the Island of Eleuthera in 1728.

BETHELL, Peter.— Educated in England. The son of the late Charles E. Bethell. Associated in business with his brother, Mr. Charles W. F. Bethell, and is part owner of the very large real estate of his father.

The Early Settlers

BETHELL, John.—Is the son of the late Capt. John Bethell, Port Officer. He was educated at Queen's College, Nassau, and is Executor of the Estate of the late Sir James Young, or better known as "Young and Son." Also, Executor of the Estate of the late William Harris. On the death of the Testators, these estates were valued at about £100,000 each.

BETHELL, Aubry.—Born Harbour Island. Educated: Public School. Book Keeper, General Hardware Co.

BETHELL, W. H.—Born at Inagua, 1875. Educated: Public School, Inagua. Master of Public School, Inagua, 1897. Customs House Officer, 1901. Chief Clerk, Audit Office, 1912. Appointed Auditor General, 1925. Retired from the Public Service, 1935.

BINNIE, W. A.— Born and Educated in Scotland. General Agent for Imported Goods. Manager of the Firm of Pinder, Collins and Brown. Secretary, Hotel Montague Co., Nassau.

BOWLES, General William.— A Loyalist refugee settled in the Bahamas after the American Revolution. In evaluating his character, there is some data in the archives of Havana, Cuba, about his expeditions against Florida; one in 1788 and another in 1791. He led a third Expedition from Jamaica via the Bahamas, and received assistance from the latter place, 1799. Captured, 1802, for his daring exploits. Received a Royal Grant of 500 acres of land at Eleuthera. This conveyance was witnessed to by the Right Hon. The Earl of Dunmore, Governor of the Bahamas. The late Frederick H. Augustus Bowles and his brother Thomas Theodore Bowles, of Governor's Harbour, Eleuthera, were his great-grand-sons. The present Thomas Theodore Bowles, of Nassau, is a direct descendant of General William Augustus Bowles.

BRAYNEN, A. R.—Is a direct descendant of James Braynen, a Loyalist, who obtained a grant from the Right Honourable the Earl of Dunmore for 120 acres of land at Exuma in 1788. Member of the House of Assembly for Cat Island and Manager of the Cuba-Sinclair Oil Co., in the Bahamas. He has acted Chairman of the Agricultural Board and at one time Secretary to the Chamber of Commerce.

BRICE, Carl.—The son of the late Lorenzo Brice of this City, and is a Member of the House of Assembly for Long Island.

The Early Settlers

He is Exporter of Sisal Hemp and is Agent for the Dunlop Rubber Co., of England, and is also Agent for the Chevrolet Motor Cars, and is the Proprietor of the Central Gas Station. A Sponge Broker and Commission Merchant.

BRICE, Philip.---Son of the late Howard Brice, and the grandson of the Hon. D. A. Brice (deceased), who was a Member of the Executive Council of these Islands and a descendant of John Brice, a Loyalist. Philip Brice is the owner of large real estate in the Island of New Providence, and Manager of the Bahamas Trust Co.

BROOK, C. W.---Merchant, and a Member of the Whylly family which was an old Loyalist family of the Bahamas.

BROWN, Herbert.--- Manager of the Freight Department of the Firm of R. H. Curry and Co., Steamship Agents. Son of Sir Joseph Brown, who came to the Bahamas from Bermuda, and remained here to the end of his life. Sir Joseph was also Member of the House of Assembly, later, Member of the Executive Council, finally, Member of the Hon. Legislative Assembly.

BROWN, Christopher.--- Born in Nassau. Educated. Public School. Master Mariner and Senior Pilot of the Bahamas.

BROWN, Lester.—Born 2nd December, 1915, son of Willard Brown, Nassau, Bahamas. Educated: Queen's College. Clerk, John S. George and Co.

BURNSIDE, Nigel.—A retired Officer from the Public Service of this Colony. Had a distinguished career in the Civil Service. Acted Colonial Secretary for a number of years, and retired as Auditor General of the Bahamas. He is a Member of a noted family. One of his progenitors was Sir Bruce Lockhart Burnside, who was at one time Speaker of the House of Assembly. He has two sons and one daughter. His daughter, Miss Sybil Burnside, is the Chief Clerk in the Colonial Secretary's Department, while his two sons, John and Basil, are Merchants of the City.

BURNSIDE, John.—Son of the Honourable Nigel Burnside, I.S.O., and like his brother, is a Merchant of the City carrying on an extensive line of imported Hardware. Crockery and other goods. Lieutenant, Black Watch, during the World War.

The Early Settlers.

BURNSIDE, Basil.—Is a son of the Honourable Nigel Burnside, I.S.O., and is a Merchant of the City carrying an assortment of the best and finest quality of imported foreign goods. Agent, Royal Insurance Co., London. Officer of the Royal Air Force during the World War. One of the Executors of the Estate of the late William Harris, of Nassau.

BUTLER, Kenneth F.—The son of the late John Butler, who was a Member of the Firm of Messrs. G. B. Adderley and Co. He is one of the largest Wine Merchants in the City.

BUTLER, Herman.—Son of the late John Butler. Educated: Nassau Grammar Shcool. Auctioneer. Junior Member of the Firm of Duncombe and Butler. Fire Insurance Agent. Exporter of Barks, Sisal Hemp, Sponges, Dye Woods and Cotton. Descended from William Butler, a Loyalist.

CASH, Roland B.—Formerly Manager of the Lady Smith Shoe Store, is descended from William Cash, a Loyalist, one of the best families of Dunmore Town, Harbour Island. He was partner in business with the late Harold E. M. Johnson, which they carried on in this City for over thirty years. He is at present Assistant Manager of the Prince George Hotel.

CHIPMAN, H. N. — Is the grandson of Dr. Chipman, whose grandfather was a Loyalist who came from Nova Scotia to the Bahamas after the Revolutionary War of America. H. N. Chipman was elected a Member of the House of Assembly for Harbour Island at the last General Election in 1935, and formerly was a representative for the Southern District in New Providence. He is an astute business man and has exceptional ideas in the real estate world. He founded the new Village of Chippingham about 15 years ago, whose modern homes are a great improvement to former houses in the Suburban Districts of the Island.

CHRISTIE, Harold.— Is a descendant of Adam Christie, Esq., Loyalist, who was a former Colonial Secretary of the Bahamas. Harold Christie is a Member of the House of Assembly for Cat Island. His activities in developing the Colony as an attractive Winter Resort have brought great wealth and prosperity to the Islands. He is a large real estate owner and spends most of his time abroad in the interest of developing the Colony. Member of the Development Board.

The Early Settlers.

CHRISTIE, Percy.—Is a Member of the House of Assembly for the Western District, New Providence, and is the brother of Harold and Frank Christie; he shares with them the honour of being a descendant of Adam Christie, Esq., formerly Colonial Secretary of the Bahama Islands. He is the Proprietor of the Family Shoe Store and the Labour Leader of the House of Assembly.

CHRISTIE. Frank. — Is a Member of the House of Assembly for Abaco, and at one time represented Cat Island. Like his brother, Harold, is descended from Adam Christie, Esq., Colonial Secretary, a Loyalist. He is associated with his brother in the real estate business, and is the Manager of the Finance Company, the largest Loan Company in the Bahamas.

CLARIDGE, William Ivor.—Born May 2nd, 1908, Nassau. Educated: Queen's College, Bahamas. Son of the late William Frederick Claridge, Merchant. Large Real Estate owner. Clerk in the Firm of John S. George and Co., Nassau.

COLE, George.—Is the grandson of the late George Cole, Inspector of Schools. He was among the first contingents to join His Majesty's Forces in the World War in 1914. Is Proprietor and Manager of the Cole-Thomson Pharmacy.

COLE, A. K.—Is the son of the late George Cole, Esq., who came from England and remained in the Colony carrying on his duties as Inspector of Schools during his active life. His first appointment in the Civil Service was Secretary to the Board of Education; and later on, transferred to the Post Office Department as Chief Clerk. In 1914, appointed Assistant Comptroller of Customs and finally succeeded to that Office as Comptroller. He is a Member of the Honourable Legislative Assembly.

COLLINS, The Hon. Ralph.—Is the son of the late John E. Collins, of Los Angelos, California. He came to the Bahamas as a winter visitor along with his parents, and was so charmed with the quiet features of the Bahamas that he decided to make a permanent home in the Colony. Having a great foresight in business matters, he in 1901, inaugurated the Firm of Pinder and Collins, and a little later included the late Hon. John Brown as member, which Firm was the most prominent buyer of Sisal Hemp and Sponge for a number of years.

The Early Settlers

In 1930, he was appointed a Member of the Executive Council of the Bahamas which seat he now retains. In 1934, he was appointed Chairman to the Board of Education. Mr. Ralph Collins is a wealthy real estate owner, and has done much to relieve distress amongst the labouring classes of the Colony. He represents the District of Acklins Island in the Hon. House of Assembly, Bahamas.

CULMER, Dr. James, M.R.C.S., L.R.C.P.—Is the son of the late the Hon. J. W. Culmer, who descended from one of the oldest families of Eleuthera. The Culmers were among those settlers brought from England via Bermuda by Capt. Sayle in 1640. Dr. James Culmer was educated in England and took his Medical Course at Guy's Hospital, London. He was Chief Medical Officer of the Bahamas General Hospital for many years, retiring from that Office only a few years ago and is now carrying on a private practice in this City.

CULMER, Dr. William, M.R.C.S., L.R.C.P.— Is the brother of Dr. James Culmer. Educated in England. He studied medicine at Guy's Hospital, London. He practiced medicine in England, and is now retired. Spends the winter in the Bahamas and goes abroad in the summer. He is relative of David Culmer, a Loyalist, who obtained a grant of 57 acres of land from the Right Honourable Earl of Dunmore in 1788.

CURRY, Ormond H.—Is a Junior Member of the Firm of Messrs. R. H. Curry and Co., and a descendant of Robert Curry a Loyalist, who came to this Colony after the Revolutionary War of Independence in 1783. Member of the House of Assembly for Eleuthera, and a Member of His Majesty's Executive Council in the Bahamas.

CURRY, Robert Henry.—Born Nassau, Bahamas, 1861. Educated: Canada. Senior Member of the Firm of Messrs. R. H. Curry and Co. Member of the Honourable House of Assembly for Andros. He has represented the District for nearly forty years. A direct descendant of Robert Curry, a Loyalist (see list of Loyalists). Mr. Curry is a great traveller. Spends the Winter in his native land; and the Summer in Europe. Consul for Norway. Agent for Lloyds" Fire and Life Insurance Co. Agent for a great number of the world's largest Ocean Liners. He is a very wealthy real estate owner.

The Early Settlers.

DeGLANVILLE, Reginald.— Was educated at the Nassau Grammar School, and is the son of Rev. W. L. DeGlanville, deceased. Was called to the Bar in 1916. Acted Stipendary and Circuit Magistrate, Attorney General, and is Registrar General of the Bahamas.

DeGLANVILLE, Hugh.— Educated: Nassau Grammar School. Son of the late Rev. W. L. DeGlanville, of Nassau, Bahamas. Druggist by Profession.

DRUDGE, William George Albert.— Born, 16th December, 1898. Educated. Nassau Grammar School. Descended from John Drudge, Loyalist, who came to the Bahamas at the close of the Revolutionary War of America.

DUNCOMBE, Roger Kelsall.— Born, 1867. Son of Rev. W. W. Duncombe, deceased. Educated: Nassau Grammar School. Entered Bahamas Civil Service, 1890. Registrar of Records. Acting Coroner. Acting Supt. Bahamas General Hospital. Supervisor of Census. Assist. Registrar General. Descended from Roger Keysall, a Loyalist, who was granted 100 acres of land by the Right Hon. the Earl of Dunmore at Exuma, 1788.

DUNCOMBE, Frederick Arthur Cyril.— The grandson of the Rev. W. W. Duncombe, deceased ,who was formerly Rector of St. David's Parish, Long Cay. Mr. Roger Keysall, Loyalist, obtained a grant of 40 acres of land at Exua from the Right Honourable the Earl of Dunmore, Governor of the Bahamas and last Royal Governor of Virginia. We may say that the coming of the Loyalists introduced a new era in the Early History of the Bahamas. Their good manners, good government and strict adherence to religion had brought about the security and repose to the Colony which we are now enjoying. Mr. Duncombe was a Commissioner in the Civil Service of the Bahamas and is now the Acting Registrar General of the Bahamas.

DUNCOMBE, Robert. — His uncle was the Rev. W. W. Duncombe, Rector in charge of the Parish of St. David's, Long Cay, descended from Sir William Nehemiah Duncombe, of Great Britain, and Robert Duncombe, who had received a grant of land in the Island of New Providence from the Right Hon. The Earl of Dunmore, 1788. Educated: Nassau Grammar School, formerly on the Staff of the Firm of G. B. Adderley and John Butler, at present, Senior

The Early Settlers

Member of the Firm of Duncombe and Butler. Government Assessor in Valuating Lands. Agent of the Norwich Union Insurance Co. of Great Britain.

DUNCOMBE, Gurth.— Is the great-grandson of Rev. William W. Duncombe, late Rector of St. David's Parish, Long Cay. Descendant of the Keysalls, who were Loyalists settled at Exuma after the American Revolution, 1783, and is the family name of the Earl of Feversham, England. In recent years a member of this family came from England and visited Exuma where they found the Tomb of the Kelsalls at the Hermitage, bearing the inscription of: "Sacred memory of the death of several members of that family who died and were buried at Exuma." Gurth Duncombe is the Proprietor of the Bahamas Ironmongery, a very old firm known as "Young and Son," being a part of the estate of Sir James Young, deceased.

DUNCOMBE, Henry William Feversham Duncombe.---Son of the late Rev. W. W. Duncombe, who was formerly Priest in Charge of St. David's Parish, Long Cay, Fortune Island. Educated: Nassau Grammar School. Entered the Civil Service of the Bahamas in 1890. Later, received an appointment in the Civil Service in West Africa, from which service he retired on a pension. On his return to the Bahamas was reappointed by the Bahamas Government Commissioner for Inagua, and latterly transferred to Bimini as Commissioner.

EDWARDS. — The Edwards family of Rock Sound, Eleuthera, are the direct descendants of Peter Edwards, a Loyalist, who came to the Bahamas from St. Augustine, Florida, after the Revolutionary War in 1784. Brigadier-General Edwards, of England, arrived in Nassau in January of last year, with the object of tracing the movements of his ancestor, Peter, after the war, and succeeded in finding him in Florida in 1783, and in Nassau in 1784.

FARRINGTON, Reginald.— Is a Member of the Honourable House of Assembly for Harbour Island, and gained the seat in a contested Election which became vacant on the death of the late Allan Kelly, Esq., a wealthy real estate owner. Mr. Farrington is also a descendant of an old English family "the Anderson Farringtons" whose family vault is found on the South-west side of St. Matthew's Churchyard. The original home of the Farringtons is situate on the Hill top on the North side

The Early Settlers

of Shirley Street, adjoining the palatial dwelling of the Lord Bishop of Nassau. Mr. R. Farrington is the Manager of the Allan Kelly's Steamship Nassau-Miami Service. He married Miss Ena Kelly, the daughter of the late Allan Kelly, Esq.

FARRINGTON, R. J. A.—Educated: Nassau Grammar School, and, is descended from an old English family (the Anderson Farrington's family) whose Tombs with inscriptions to the memory of certain members of the family can be found in the South-western corner of St. Matthew's Churchyard. He was a Commissioner in the public service of the Colony for many years. Acted as Auditor of Public Accounts, Examining Officer and Warehouse Keeper and Superintendent of the Bahamas General Hospital.

FARRINGTON, Sydney.—Is a member of an old English family who settled in the Bahamas about 150 years ago. Some of his ancestors died in this Colony and were buried in the family Tomb in the South-west corner of St. Matthew's Grave Yard. He is a member of the Development Board, and Manager of the Pan-American Air-Ways. Lieutenant in Royal Air Force (Canadian) during the World War.

FERNANDER, Osmond Langford.— Born, December, 1896. Educated: Victoria School, Nassau. Son of James Robert Fernander, brother to Claude Stanford Fernander. Family of Spanish descent. In the language of the Spaniards—Fernandez.

FERNANDER, Claude Stanford.—Brother to Osmond Fernander. Born, January 16th, 1893. Educated: Victoria School. Merchant. Son of James Robert Fernander. This family originally came from Spain.

FISHER, Dr. Eric.—Educated: Nassau Grammar School. Veterinary Surgeon. Son of the Rev. Hartman Fisher, deceased, Rector of St. Agnes Church for over fifty years.

GAMBLIN, Dudley.—The son of the late Sir George Gamblin, who was late Manager of the Royal Bank of Canada, and son of James Henry Gamblin, of Somersetshire, England. Was on the staff of the Royal Bank of Canada, Montreal for a considerable time, and is now in the Bahamas Civil Service as Clerk in the Audit Department.

GARFUNKEL, Joseph.— Succeeded his father in business in Nassau about ten years ago. The wonderful growth of the busi-

The Early Settlers

ness demonstrates his master mind. The very large furniture establishment conducted by him obviates the necessity of the owners of modern homes sending abroad for their varied requirements of first-class furniture, etc.

GRAHAMÉ, R. B.—Born in Scotland. Chartered Accountant of Edinburgh, Scotland. Conducting a School of Accountancy, Nassau, Bahamas.

GRIFFIN, Wilbert.—Was born at Governor's Harbour, Eleuthera, and is the brother of Frederick Griffin. He is a Merchant at Governor's Harbour, Eleuthera. About 40 years ago there were about 60 families of Griffins at this settlement, fairly well to do, but on account of failure of the principal industry in 1898, most of the families left the Island to live in the United States, in consequence of which the settlement has gone back considerably, and only the commodious homes of the former planters now remain.

GRIFFIN, Frederick.— Was born at Governor's Harbour, Eleuthera, and is the descendant of John Griffin who in 1721 was one of a number selected from among the inhabitants of the Colony by Governor Phenny as being a "fit person to be recommended to His Majesty to be elected by the Public to make an Assembly, or, execute the public offices under the Government." He is a Merchant at Governor's Harbour, Eleuthera.

HALL, Charles R.—Born 1904. Educated: Boys' Central School. On the Staff of the Munson Steamship Co. Descendant of Joseph Hall, Sr., who was recommended to His Majesty to be elected by the public to make an Assembly, or execute other public offices under the Government.

HALL, Hershal Stanley.—Born 1894. Educated: Boys' Central School; formerly Merchant. Descendant of Nathaniel Hall, Loyalist.

HAMACHER, John H.—Born 1890. Educated: High School, Pennsylvania. Auto Engineer. Resident, Nassau, Bahamas.

HIGGS, Edwin T.—And his brother, Dr. Walter A. Higgs, M.R.C.S., L.R.C.P., London, are members of one of the oldest and best families in the Colony. They are the descendants of Samuel Higgs, a Loyalist, who settled in the Bahamas after the American Revolution in 1788. Mr. Edwin Higgs — Educated:

The Early Settlers

England. Sponge Broker and owns some very valuable real estate in this City. His brother, Dr. Walter Higgs, lives in London, England, and is a retired member of the Medical profession. One of the members of this family is a young Barrister-at-Law practising in Nassau, N.P.

HIGGS, G. W.—Born Nassau. Educated: Queen's College. Barrister-at-Law. Deputy Speaker, Hon. House of Assembly. Descendant of Abram Higgs, a Loyalist, who was appointed a Justice of the Peace by the Right Honourable the Earl of Dunmore, 1788.

HIGGS, Rex.—Born, Nassau. Educated: Queen's College. Employed recently, Customs Department. Acted Comptroller on several occasions. Resigned from Public Service. At present on the Staff of H. G. Christie's Real Estate Business.

HIGGS, George.—Grandson of George Higgs, deceased. Succeeded to the valuable estate of his grandfather on the death of his uncle, the late Lambert Higgs. A descendant of Samuel Higgs, a Loyalist, who was appointed a Justice of the Peace for Harbour Island by the Right Hon. the Earl of Dunmore, 1788. Chief Clerk in the General Hardware, Bay Street.

HIGGS, George. — Born in Nassau. Educated: Queen's College. Manager of the City Pharmacy. Descendant of Samuel Higgs, Loyalist, and Justice of the Peace for Harbour Island, 1788.

HIGGS, Hartman H.— Born 21st Feb., 1911. Educated: Public School, Spanish Wells. Son of Vincent Higgs. Part owner and Manager of Higgs and Collins, Aerated Waters. Clerk, Central Gas Station, Nassau.

HIGGS, Basil Dewees.—Born May 18th, 1918. Educated: Public School, Spanish Wells. A descendant of Samuel Higgs, a Loyalist, who was appointed a Justice of the Peace by the Right Hon. the Earl of Dunmore, Governor of the Bahamas, 1783. Clerk in the Firm known as J. P. Sands and Co., Nassau.

HILTON, Stanley.—Proprietor, Dry Goods Establishment, Bay Street. Brother to William Hilton and Thomas Hilton. Their grandfather, Dr. William Hilton, owned a large estate at Eleuthera. The Hiltons descended from an old English family who settled in New Hampshire, where they had received a grant of land known as "Hilton's Point." from Captain John Mason, Governor of Newfoundland, 1621.

The Early Settlers.

HILTON, William.—Is a descendant of William Hilton, of New Hampshire, who had a brother by the name of Edward. Edward Hilton was granted the land at Hilton's Point in New Hampshire, where they, in 1623, established a large business in canning Salmon, etc. William Hilton, of this City, is a Merchant on Bay Street, and is a large importer of foreign woollen and cotton goods. The Hiltons were some of the oldest settlers of Eleuthera.

JOHNSON, W. C. B.—Is the Senior Member of the House of Assembly, having been elected a Member of the House for half a century, which is a record for any member to serve for so long an unbroken period. Deputy Speaker for twenty-six years, and elected Speaker in 1935, following the death of the late Speaker, the Hon. Harcourt Malcolm, K.C., O.B.E. He has devoted the whole of his life to the welfare of the Colony and can still be seen at his desk from 7 a.m. to 5 p.m. daily, and appears to discharge his various duties very strenuously. Senior Member of the Firm of J. S. Johnson and Co. Agent for Lloyds, Underwriters, of London. Agent for Miami-Nassau Steamship Co.

JOHNSON, Mervyn.— Son of the late Sir George Johnson, a descendant of George Johnson, Loyalist, who obtained a grant of 100 acres of land at Eleuthera from The Right Hon. the Earl of Dunmore, Governor of the Bahamas, 1788. His father, Sir George Johnson, was a Member of the House of Assemoly for Rum Cay and Watlings; Member for Harbour Island; Leader in the House of Assembly for the Government. Appointed Member of the Executive Council and also President of the Hon. Legislative Council. Knighted by His Majesty, 1936. Mervyn Johnson, born in Nassau, New Providence; educated: Queen's College. Studied Law under the late Harcourt Malcolm, Barrister-at-Law, K.C., O.B.E. After practising at the Bahamas Bar, entered Middle Temple, London, where he successfully passed Law examination. Barrister-at-Law. Appointed Assistant Registrar General of the Bahamas. Acted Stipendary and Circuit Magistrate.

JOHNSON, Thaddeus (deceased).—Was a Leading Merchant in Nassau up to the time of his death. Owned that valuable property known as "The Johnson House"; extensive residence in Dowdeswell Street, valuable property on East Bay Street, a Country Seat known as Cedarville and other holdings in real estate. A Lumber Merchant, and conducted the largest wholesale and retail business in the Island. Had four sons: Errol, Allan, Thaddeus and

The Early Settlers.

Bertram. Five daughters: Mrs. W. Albury, Mrs. D. S. D. Moseley, Mrs. Morton Turtle, Mrs. P. M. Lightbourn, and Mrs. Carl Brice. Thaddeus Johnson, Sr., was a man of sterling character and very popular among the inhabitants.

JOHNSON, William T. B.---Son of Dr. T. B. Johnson, of Harbour Island (deceased), who was descended from George Johnson, a Loyalist. Formerly employed by the Firm of Messrs. Young and Son for many years, but at present, on the Staff of R. H. Curry and Co., Steamship Agents.

JOHNSON, Joseph.---Is the son of the Hon. W. C. B. Johnson, Speaker of the Honourable House of Assembly. He is on the Staff of the Firm of R. H. Curry and Co., Steamship Agents. Junior Member of the Firm of J. S. Johnson and Co. Agent for Lloyds' Underwriters.

JOHNSON, Dr. Hugh.---Is a descendant of George Johnson, a Loyalist. He is the son of the late Dr. A. T. W. Johnson, of Harbour Island, and is practising Dentistry in this City.

JOHNSON, Allan L.---Son of George Henry Johnson, and brother of the late Sir George Johnson. Formerly a Merchant, but at present on the Staff of R. H. Curry and Co., Steamship Agents.

JOHNSON, Dewees O.---Son of Dr. T. B. Johnson (deceased), of Dunmore Town, Harbour Island, who was descended from George Johnson, a Loyalist. So much esteemed was his father by the inhabitants of Dunmore Town, that they have erected a Monument in the Centre of a public street in the Township to his memory. A Commissioner in various Districts, is now retired on pension and lives at Governor's Harbour, Eleuthera.

KELLY, James K. A.--- Is descended from James Kelly, a Loyalist, who came to the Bahamas after the Revolutionary War of Independence in 1783. He contested a seat in the House of Assembly for the Islands of Grand Bahama and Bimini in 1937, and was elected by the inhabitants as their representative by a large majority vote. Also President of William Brewer, Co., Ltd., one of the largest Wine Merchants in the Bahamas.

KELLY, Charles J.---Is a descendant of James Kelly, a Loyalist, who came to the Bahamas after the Revolutionary War in 1783, and obtained a grant of 300 acres of land at the Island of Eleuthera from the Right Honourable the Earl of Dunmore in 1788. Charles Kelly is the largest lumber dealer in the Colony, and is a Ship Owner.

The Early Settlers

KELLY, Newel. — Like the other members of the Kelly family, is descended from James Kelly, who came to the Colony at the conclusion of the Revolutionary War, 1783. He is connected in many local enterprises and is interested in the real estate business. Agent for the General Accident Assurance Corporation, Ltd., of Scotland.

KELLY, Bert. — Born, Nassau. Educated: Queen's College, Agent and Manager of the Ford Motor Co., of the Bahamas. Agent for the Goodyear Rubber and Tyre Co., of Nassau. Descendant of James Kelly, a Loyalist.

KELLY, C J., Jr. — Is the son of Charles Kelly, Sr., and is associated with his father in the lumber business known as "Kelly's Lumber Yard."

KELLY, Audley. — Educated: Queen's College, Nassau. Merchant, associated with the Firm of William Brewer and Co., Nassau. Descendant of James Kelly, a Loyalist.

KELLY, Trevor. — Is the son of Mr. Charles Kelly, and is associated with his father in the Lumber business known as "Kelly's Lumber Yard."

KELLY, Kenneth. — Is the eldest son of Mr. Charles Kelly, and is a Merchant carrying on a large hardware business on Bay Street.

KEMP, Thomas Theodore. — Born 13th June, 1912. Entered Civil Service, Bahamas, August, 1931. Clerk, Receiver General and Treasurer's Department. Descended from the old Kemp family of Eleuthera.

KEMP, Frederick Arnold. — Born in Bahamas. Educated: Central School, Nassau. Started Clerk with the Firm of Pinder, Collins and Brown, in Sponge and Sisal Business. Wine Merchant. Associated in Real Estate Business in the Bahamas. Belongs to the old family of Kemps, who owned a large estate at Eleuthera, and in the Eastern District of the Island of New Providence.

KEMP, Rev. Henry E. — A descendant of the Kemps of Eleuthera. They owned one thousand acres of land at Kemp's Bay, about 20 miles to the south of the settlement of Rock Sound, also land at Kemp's Bay, Andros. Rev. Kemp was formerly a Merchant in the City, but gave up business for the Ministry. He had lived in Canada for many years, returning to his native land about twenty years ago. He is the Proprietor of a large Apartment House on Frederick Street, also owns valuable property on East Bay Street.

The Early Settlers.

KNOWLES, Tracy J.—Is a direct descendant of the Early Colonists who came here in 1640, and is a wealthy real estate owner. He does an extensive business in the Sponge industry, and is one of the largest importers of foreign manufactured goods in the Colony.

KNOWLES, Harry.—Born in Nassau. Educated at Public School. Pilot. Descended from John Knowles, who was among the Colonists of 1640.

KNOWLES, Stanley.— Is a descendant of one of the early settlers. He is the son of the late Uriah Knowles, of Long Island, and a Merchant of the City, also a real estate owner. Descendant of Samuel Knowles, Loyalist.

LIGHTBOURN, R. M.—Is the Proprietor of the most up-to-date and attractive Pharmacy in the Island of New Providence. He is a very large real estate owner and owns the Lucerne Hotel, Frederick Street. The Lightbourns of the Bahamas and Bermuda are of the same family. They are also descendants of Paul Lightbourn, Esq., who obtained a grant of 700 acres of land from the Right Hon. the Earl of Dunmore, Royal Governor, Bahamas, 1784.

LIGHTBOURN, Nelson E.—Is the son of Mr. R. M. Lightbourn. Educated: Queen's College, Nassau. Is Assistant Comptroller of Customs. Was Chief Clerk in the Electrical Department for a number of years, and has recently acted Port Officer in conjunction with his duties as Assistant Comptroller of Customs.

LIGHTBOURN, Howard L.— Educated: Queen's College. Manager of Gas Station. A descendant of Paul Lightbourn, Esq., a Loyalist.

LIGHTBOURN, Hugh.—Is the youngest son of Mr. R. M. Lightbourn, and is associated with his brother Percy Lightbourn in business. Eucated: Queen's College, Nassau.

LIGHTBOURN, Cyril.—Is the son of Mr. R. M. Lightbourn, and is associated with his father in business. Educated: Queen's College, Nassau.

LIGHTBOURN, Percy. — Is the Proprietor of the Colonial Pharmacy, which is one of the very best in the City. He specialises in French Perfumeries. He is the son of Mr. R. M. Lightbourn. Educated: Queen's College, Nassau.

LIGHTBOURN, George.—Son of the late James Lightbourn, of Audit Department. Educated: Queen's College. Assistant Manager of William Brewer Co., Ltd., Nassau.

The Early Settlers

LIGHTBOURN, H. L.—Born, Nassau. Educated: Queen's College. Son of the late James Lightbourn, of the Audit Department. Manager, Electric Supply Co., Nassau.

LOFTHOUSE, Charles.—Is the Manager of the most up-to-date Drapery Establishment in Nassau. The best Scotch and English Woollen Goods can be bought at his place of business. He is the grandson of the Rev. Thomas Lofthouse, deceased. His father, the Hon. T. H. C. Lofthouse, was a Member of the Honourable Legislative Assembly.

LOWE, J. Estwick.— Born, May 20th, 1913, Abaco. Educated: Privately. Son of John A. Lowe, Preacher of the Gospel. Clerk in the Firm of John S. George and Co., Nassau.

LOWE, Eldred. — Born at Abaco, and is descended from Edward Lowe, a Loyalist. Merchant at Abaco, and Surveyor of Lands.

MALCOLM, Kirkwood. — Is the son of the late Kirkwood Malcolm; was educated at Queen's College, and is a descendant of Michael Malcolm, a Loyalist. He is the Proprietor of the Malcolm's Garage of Nassau. Agent for Firestone Rubber Co., U.S.A.

MALONE, J. V.— Formerly employed by the Board of Education. Master of one of the Board Public Schools. Acted Commissioner of Long Island; recently appointed Commissioner of Inagua and Mayaguana. Married a daughter of the late Uriah Knowles, of Long Island, a wealthy real estate owner.

McCARTHY, John F.—Is a large real estate owner and takes a great interest in the Tomato Industry.

MAURY, Peter.—Is the son of the late John Maury who was one of the wealthiest men in the Bahamas. He owned a large estate in Palm Beach, (Florida), Grand Bahama and Nassau, New Providence. His son Peter is a partner in the business of Roberts-Maury, Co., Nassau, and part owner of Prince George's Hotel which adjoins the Royal Bank of Canada.

MAURY, Marcel. — Is the brother of Peter Maury, and a partner in the business of Roberts-Maury, Co., and part owner of the Prince George's Hotel.

MAURA, William Henry Handford,---Has Spanish ancestry on the one side and English on the other. One of his ancestors was Hosé Maura, Consul General for Spain in the

The Early Settlers

Bahamas and Charles Marshall, Esq., on his maternal side, was Speaker of the House of Assembly in 1753. W. H. H. Maura is a large importer of Canadian Manufactured Goods and carries on an extensive Lumber Business. President of the Nassau Sponge Exchange Co., Ltd., and is himself a Sponge Broker.

MAURA, John.—Born in Nassau. Educated: Queen's College. Son of W. H. H. Maura. Assistant to his father in the Sponge Business.

MAURA, Rev. Bertram, B.A.— Educated: Queen's College and in Canada. Now carrying on Religious Work in Canada. Son of W. H. H. Maura, Bahamas.

MAURA, Montague. — Born Nassau. Educated: Queen's College. Son of W. H. H. Maura. Lumber Merchant, Sponge Broker, and Agent for the West India Company of Canada. He is the Manager of his father's business in Nassau.

MAURA, Bruce.— Shares the honoured ancestry of his brother, W. H. H. Maura, and was one of the first thirty contingents to leave the Bahamas via Jamaica in 1914, to join His Majesty's Forces in the late European War, and was one of the lucky ones to return home at the close of the War in 1918.

MAURA, Edward.—Born, Nassau. Educated: Queen's College. Clerk in the Bahamas Ironmongery.

MAURA, Lionel.—Born, Nassau. Educated: Queen's College. Clerk of the General Hardware Co.

McKINNEY, Herbert. — Proprietor of Messrs. John S. George and Co., who conducts the largest Hardware business in the Island of New Providence. This business was formerly carried on by the late Edward George and is the oldest business establishment in the City. Is a member of the Electrical Board and acted Chairman on several occasions. Descendant of Benjamin McKinney, a Loyalist.

McKINNEY, Basil.— The son of Herbert McKinney, is a Member of the House of Assembly for Andros Island. Associated in business with his father. Educated in England.

McKINNEY, Edward H.— Retired Commissioner. Acted Stipendary and Circuit Magistrate on many occasions and Inspector of Sisals. Acted Assistant Comptroller of Customs for several years.

MOORE, The Hon. Walter K. Is one of our distinguished citizens, and is a descendant of Peter Moore, a Loyalist, who

The Early Settlers

came to the Colony from East Florida, after the close of the revolutionary War of Independence. His achievement in the business life of the Colony is outstanding, and has for many years been the largest exporter of Sisal hemp and marine products. In 1912 he was elected a Member of the House of Assembly for Grand Bahama and Bimini which seat he held till 1935. In 1930 was elected a Member of the Executive Council, and in 1936 was appointed a Member of the Hon. Legislative Council of which he is now President. In 1937 he had the honour to be one of the representatives to attend the Coronation of King George VI. on behalf of the Bahamas.

MOORE, Walter K., Jr.—Son of the Honourable Walter K. Moore, C.B.E., M.E.C., M.L.A. Is a member of the Nassau Royal Yacht Club, also Manager of the Sisal Hemp and Marine Products establishment which is owned by his father. Descended from Peter Moore, Loyalist.

MOORE, Ernest.— Born in Nassau. Educated: Queen's College, Nassau, and in Toronto, Canada. He is associated in business with his father, the Hon. W. K. Moore, C.B.E. Is also a Member of the Royal Nassau Yacht Club. Descendant of Philip Moore, a Loyalist.

MOORE, Edwin Labron.— Chief Engineer and Superintendant of the Electrical Department. Descendant of Phillip Moore, Loyalist.

MOORE, Roger.— Born in Nassau. Educated: Queen's College. Chief Clerk in the Office of Marine and Products Board. A descendant of Peter Moore, Loyalist.

MOSELEY, Oswald.— Is the son of D. S. D. Moseley, and the grandson of Mr. Edwin Moseley, late Proprietor of the "Nassau Guardian." He is the Acting Cuban Consul, Agent for the Sun Life Assurance Co., of Canada, and for the Commercial Assurance Co., of London.

MOSELEY, Daniel.— Is the son of the late Edwin Moseley, Editor of the "Nassau Guardian." Clerk to the Honourable Legislative Council, and was a Member of the House of Assembly for Inagua. Proprietor of Moseley's Book Store.

MURPHY, George. — Was elected one of the Members of the House of Assembly for Exuma in 1935. He is one of those men who adheres to the principle "Example is better than Precept." It is universally known that he is a great asset to the Colony, and takes a keen interest in the welfare of his constituents. He encour-

The Early Settlers

ages and helps them to better their conditions, in short, takes special interest in their everyday life. Mr. George Murphy is a wealthy real estate owner, very astute in business, and always of a pleasant countenance. Kind and generous. It is owing to men of Mr. Murphy's calibre amongst us that this Colony is outstanding in prosperity. He wisely manages the Montagu Hotel, which at one time, that is, before he took over the management, was near becoming a failure. Now it seems to have been a gilt-edged investment to its shareholders and the Government.

MUNROE, Charles.---Born in Nassau. Educated: Boys' Central School. Commenced as a Clerk with the firm of R. H. Curry and Co. Later with R. T. Symonette Ship Yard. Proprietor and Manager of the Ship Yard, East Bay Street.

NEWBOLD, Leonard A.---One of the few living descendants of Paul Newbold, who was chosen to be one of the representatives for Eleuthera at an Assembly holden in Nassau, 29th Sept., 1729, who was on the Committee appointed to enquire into the state of affairs of the Bahama Islands, 29th Sept., 1729, by John Colebrooke, Esq,. Chosen Speaker of the Assembly. Leonard A. Newbold is a Clerk in the firm of Messrs. Victor and Stafford Saunders, now of Nassau.

PARKS, Frank.--- Is a descendant of George Campbell Parks, a Loyalist, who came to the Colony in 1783, after the War of Independence in America. Merchant, conducting a large assortment of woollen and dry goods business in the City.

PARKS, Joseph. --- Is the brother of Frank Parks, and is the Manager of a Clothing Establishment on Bay Street. Descended from an old Loyalist family.

PARKS, Allan.---Is a brother of Frank Parks, and is a Commission Merchant of this City; he too is descended from the old Loyalist family of Parks.

PINDER, Brice.— The son of the late William J. Pinder, who during his life time was a Member of the House of Assembly for Long Island. The Pinders were very important in the early days of the colonization of the Bahamas. A William Pinder was one of the persons chosen to be one of the representatives for the Town of Nassau, on the 29th Sept., 1729, being the 1st proceedings of the newly created House of Assembly for the Bahamas. The family name of Brice carries us back to John Brice, a Loyalist, who came to these Islands after the American Revolution and settled at Long Island. Mr. John Grey Brice, the father of the late Hon. D. A. Brice, died at Long Island in 1879.

The Early Settlers.

PINDER, Warren. — Born, Spanish Wells. Educated: Spanish Wells. Promoter of Local Enterprises. Manager of the business known as "Commission Merchants," Nassau. Real estate owner.

PINDER, Percival. — Born, July 10th, 1916. Educated: Government School, Abaco. A descendant of Salem Pinder, one of the earliest settlers in the Colony. Clerk in the firm of John S. George and Co., Nassau.

PINDER, Randolph.—Born at Spanish Wells, Bahamas. Educated: Public School. Chief Clerk, Bahamas Ironmongery.

PINDER, Frederick. — Educated: Public School, Spanish Wells. Merchant, Sisal Dealer. Descended from the old Pinder family of the Bahamas.

PRITCHARD, William E.—Is a retired Merchant of this City and is a descendant of William E. Pritchard, a Loyalist. He is a wealthy real estate owner and the father of Asa Prichard, Merchant; W. E. G. Pritchard, Merchant; Reginald Pritchard, Lawyer; and Artemas Pritchard, Lawyer; all of the City of Nassau.

PRITCHARD, Asa.— Son of William E. Pritchard, Esq., a retired member of the old firm of Messrs. Pritchard and Bro. He was a Member of the House of Assembly for Eleuthera, a seat which he again contested at the General Election but was unfortunately defeated on account of the combined strength of three other candidates. He is a good politician. Some district would do well to send him back to the House. Mr. Pritchard is a wholesale importer of Foreign Manufactured Goods.

PRIITCHARD, W. E. G.—Is the son of William E. Pritchard, Esq., a wealthy retired Merchant of this City, who himself is a descendant of William Pritchard, a Loyalist, who obtained a grant of 80 acres of land at Abaco from the Right Honourable the Earl of Dunmore, Governor of the Bahamas, in 1788. W. E. G. Pritchard is a prominent Merchant on Bay Street, carrying a very large stock of imported manufactured goods.

PRITCHARD, Herbert. — Is the eldest son of the late Olando Pritchard. Educated at Queen's College. Is the brother of Frank Pritchard, and was a partner in the business known as A. and F. Pritchard. He is also a descendant of William Pritchard, a Loyalist.

PRITCHARD, Frank.---Is the son of the late Olando Pritchard, who was the owner of considerable real estate, and the brother of W. E. Pritchard, of the firm of Pritchard and Bro.

The Early Settlers.

Mr. Frank Pritchard was educated at Queen's College, and carried on the business known as "A. and F. Pritchard." Is a Sponge Broker, Auctioneer and Commission Merchant. He is a descendant of William Pritchard, a Loyalist, who came to this Colony in 1783.

PYFROM, Canon George.--- Born, Governor's Harbour, Eleuthera. Educated: Dorchester College, England. Many years Priest in Charge Anglican Church at Long Island. Transferred, Rector of St. Agnes' Church, Nassau 1935. Descendant of Peter Pyfrom, of Eleuthera, a Loyalist.

PYFROM, Jerome E.---Is the son of the late Jabez Pyfrom, of Governor's Harbour, Eleuthera. He is a wealthy real estate owner and the most successful pineapple grower in the Bahamas. This industry was introduced into the Colony by Governor Woodes Rogers in 1718, and up to the year 1896 was the greatest asset to the Colony. Its death blow occurred in consequence of the annexation of Puerto Rico and the Phillipine Islands by the United States of America on the conclusion of the Spanish American War in 1898 when a high tariff went into force in the United States against the importation of pineapples from foreign Colonies. Descendant of Peter Pyfrom, Loyalist.

PYFROM, Sydney.--- Son of Jerome E. Pyfrom, and conducts an up-to-date fruit business on Bay Street. Descendant of Peter Pyfrom, a Loyalist.

PYFROM, William.--- Brother to Sydney Pyfrom, is associated with him in the fruit business. Descended from Peter Pyfrom, a Loyalist.

ROBERTSON, R. J.---Born in Scotland, N.B. Is a member of the firm of Robertson and Symonette, formerly the Manager of the firm of Bethell and Robertson. President of the Nassau Acquatic Club.

ROBERTS, G. W. K.---In 1935 contested his first Election campaign for a seat in the Bahamas Legislature and was elected a Member of the House of Assembly by a very large popular vote. His activities are centred chiefly in the Lumber business, and carries one of the largest stocks of imported Lumber in the Colony. He is a very young man and displays in his personality the making of a great man. He belongs to one of the oldest Colonial families in the Bahamas. One of his ancestors, John Roberts, was elected by the inhabitants of Harbour Island to a seat in the first House of Assembly of the Bahamas at a General Election held in 1729.

The Early Settlers

ROBERTS, J. W.— Born at Abaco. Educated: Public School. Member of the House of Assembly for Abaco. Past owner of the Prince George Hotel. Wealthy real estate owner.

ROBERTS, Capt. George— Born at Harbour Island. Educated: Public School, Harbour Island. Port Officer,, Immigration Officer, Marshall Admiralty Court. Real estate.

ROBERTS, G. G.—Born at Abaco. Educated: Public School. Merchant. He is a descendant of John Roberts, who was chosen to be a representative for Harbour Island at an Assembly holden at Nassau, 29th Sept., 1729: Woodes Rogers Governor.

ROBERTS, Newton Clyde.— Born 1910, Spanish Wells. Educated: Public School and Government High School, Nassau. Clerk, Colonial Secretary's Office, Nassau.

ROBERTS, Layfettee.—A descendant of John Roberts, who was chosen to be one of the representatives for Harbour Island at an Assembly holden in Nassau, 29th Sept., 1729. Interested in private loans and real estate business.

ROGERS, Leon K.—Born 11th July, 1912. Educated: Government School. Entered Civil Service Bahamas, 1929. Clerk, Customs Department, Post Office Department; Clerk to Superintendent, Bahamas General Hospital; Clerk, Public Board of Works. Acted Commissioner, Grand Bahama.

RUSSELL, A. Roy.— Member of the House of Assembly for Abaco, and is a descendant of John Russell, a Loyalist. He is the Manager of the British American Insurance.

RUSSELL, Edison.—Unsuccessfully contested Abaco, Bahamas House of Assembly, 1937. Born at Abaco. Descendant of John Russell, Esq., Loyalist, who obtained from the Right Hon. the Earl of Dunmore 3,000 acres of land at Abaco. Assistant Manager, Prince George Hotel, adjoining the Royal Bank of Canada.

RUSSELL, A. T.— Born at Abaco. Educated: Abaco. Merchant, East Street. Descended from John Russell, a Loyalist, he obtained over 3,000 acres of land at Abaco from the Right Hon. the Earl of Dunmore, Governor of the Bahamas, 1783.

RUSSELL, Thomas Elma.— Born 3rd July, 1902; son of Walter Russell, Hope Town, Abaco. Educated: Public School, Hope Town, Western Central School, Nassau. Employed by Board of Education as School Teacher. Hope Town, Cherokee Sound, Abaco. Manager and Accountant, Central Gas Station, Nassau.

The Early Settlers.

RUSSELL, Herbert J.—Was a Member of the Honourable House of Assembly for the Eastern District. Chairman of the Prison Board and Contractor for the sale of Ice which is owned by the Government. Justice of the Peace for the Bahama Islands.

RUSSELL, Randall A.—Born at Abaco. Educated: Public School, Abaco. Employed by the Government since 1924. Master Mariner. A descendant from John Russell, a Loyalist, who was granted 2,000 acres of land at Abaco by the Right Hon. the Earl of Dunmore, 1788.

SANDS, Harry P.— Barrister-at-Law, Bahamas, is a direct descendant of Peter Sands, who was selected as a "fit person to be recommended to His Majesty to be elected by the public for the Island of Eleuthera to make an Assembly, or, execute public offices under the Government." Nephew of the late Sir James P. Sands, of the Bahamas.

SANDS, Arthur.—Brother of J. P. Sands, is a Member of the House of Assembly for the City. He is the Manager of the Lumber Department of J. P. Sands and Co.

SANDS, James P.—Is the son of the late Sir James P. Sands, and is the Manager of the firm of J. P. Sands and Co. In 1721, Peter Sands, the ancestor of the Sands family in this Colony, was selected from among the inhabitants as one of the "fit persons to be recommended to His Majesty to be elected by the public to make an Assembly, or, execute other public offices under the Government." He was one of six to represent the Island of Eleuthera.

SANDS, Stafford.—Brother of Mr. James P. Sands, is the Manager of the City Meat Market Establishment. He was the Manager of the firm of Pinder, Collins and Brown, and also on the Staff of the Royal Bank of Canada, Bahamas. Agent for the Liverpool and London and Globe Insurance Co., Ltd.

SANDS, Neville.— Is another brother of James P. Sands, and is the Manager of Kelly's, Ltd., which is one of the wealthiest firms in the Bahamas. Formerly Secretary of the Board of Agriculture.

SANDS, Alfred B.—Is also a brother of James P. Sands, whose business establishment is located on Bay Street, and is an importer of some of the finest woollen goods in the Colony.

SANDS, W. H.—Descendant of Peter Sands, who settled at Eleuthera in 1640. He was one of the six Eleutherians whom Governor George Phenny had selected from among the inhabi-

The Early Settlers

tants of the Colony as "fit persons to be recommended to His Majesty to be elected by the Public to make an Assembly, or execute other public offices under the Government." Mr. Sands is an importer of some of the best woollen goods to enter the Colony from the United Kingdom.

SAUNDERS, William T. — Born at Harbour Island; descendant of Benjamin Saunders, who was selected from among the inhabitants of the Colony as a "fit person to be recommended to His Majesty to be elected by the public to make an Assembly, or, execute other public offices under the Government." He is associated with the business firm known as "The City Lumber Yard," of Nassau.

SAUNDERS, Victor.—Likewise his brother Stafford Saunders, are descended from Benjamin Saunders, who was selected by Governor George Phenney from among the inhabitants of the Colony as a "fit person to be recommended to His Majesty to be elected by the Public to make an Assembly, or, execute other public offices under the Government." These brothers are very retired in their dispositions and do not appear to have aspired to political honours, but rather attend strictly to the large business which they are now conducting.

SAUNDERS, Edward.—Is one of the most enterprising Merchants in the Colony. He has never aspired to Legislative Honours like his brother, the late J. L. Saunders, but has given his attention strictly to business. He is a large importer of French Wines, Canadian, American and English manufactured goods.

SAUNDERS, William T. — Born in Nassau. Educated: Queen's College. Proprietor of Establishment consisting of woollen goods imported from England, also silks, linen goods and hosiery. Descended from Benjamin Saunders, who was selected from among the inhabitants of the Colony by Governor George Phenney, 1721, as a "fit person to be recommended to His Majesty to be elected by the public to make an Assembly, or, execute other public offices under the Government."

SAWYER, R. W.—Is a descendant of the Sawyers who settled at Eleuthera in 1640. In the meantime, this family branched off to the other Islands in the Bahamas. He has been a Member of the House of Assembly for over twenty years and was again returned as a Member for Eleuthera at the General Election in 1935. Chairman of the Board of Education for many years, during which time rendered invaluable service to the Board by fostering the activities of Education.

The Early Settlers

SAWYER, Eugene.—Is a direct descendant of one of the oldest families in the Colony. The Sawyer family came from England via Bermuda in 1640. He is a wealthy real estate owner and does an extensive business in imported foreign goods.

SAWYER, William A.— Descendant of one of the oldest families in the Bahamas. Richard Sawyer was among the batch of Colonists who accompanied Capt. Sayle to Eleuthera in 1640. Employed by the Munson Steamship Co., Nassau.

SAWYER, Henry V.— Born 13th July, 1903, Abaco, Bahamas. Clerk, J. P. Sands and Co., Nassau. Descendant of the Sawyers who settled at Eleuthera, 1640.

SCAIFE, Commander John Andrew Hanson.— Born, Constantinople, Turkey, August, 1888. Editor, Bahamas News. Entered Navy as a Cadet in January, 1903, served in old three-decker H.M.S. Britannia, officers' training ship. During the World War served with Submarines in North Sea and in the Dardanelles campaign. Was captured from E.7 by the Turks and made a prisoner from September, 1915, until end of war. Was invested by His Majesty King George V. at Buckingham Palace as an Officer of the Most Distinguished Order of the British Empire, Military Branch.

SAWYER, Dr. Raymond. — Youngest son of R. W. Sawyer. Educated: Queen's College and in England; studied Dentistry at the University of Pensylvania; Practising Dentistry in the Island of New Providence.

SAWYER, Carl.—Son of R. W. Sawyer. Educated: Queen's College. Carried on business in Bahamas for a number of years, which he gave up to live in Miami; now Manager of his Steamship business known as the Miami-Nassau Mail Steamship Service.

SEARS, Edward D.—Son of Edward L. Sears. Educated: Queen's College, Nassau, Bahamas. Served in the late European War, Lieutenant, Canadian Artillery. Sponge Merchant.

SIMMS, Moses.—Amongst the first batch of Colonists who came to the Colony in 1640. Son of Moses Simms, was chosen to be a representative for the Town of Nassau at an Assembly holden in Nassau, 29th September, 1729; Woodes Rogers, Governor. Joseph P. Simms, a descendant of Moses Simms, is a large real estate owner of the Bahamas.

SMITH, William.— Loyalist. Came to the Bahamas 1785 at the close of the Revolutionary War. Pembroke C. Smith is the direct descendant of William Smith

The Early Settlers

SMITH, John.—Is the son of Thomas Smith, and is Chief Clerk in the Honourable House of Assembly and Assistant Manager of the firm of Bethell-Robertson and Co., Ltd., one of the largest wholesale business houses in the City. Descendant of Thomas Smith, Loyalist.

SMITH, H. A.—Is a descendant of Thomas Smith, a Loyalist who came from East Florida after the Revolutionary War, in 1788. He is an importer of American and Canadian choice meats. Descendant of Thomas Smith, Loyalist.

SOLOMON, Hon. A. K., K.C.—Is one of the most distinguished Lawyers at the Bahamian Bar. Being the son of a gentleman, the late Julius Solomon, Esq., Magistrate, has inherited from both his father and mother those fine qualities which are marked in his personality. In 1916, became a Member of the House of Assembly, and appointed by the House as its Legal Adviser, but as such he never subjugated a principle against the dictates of his conscience, irrespective of the source from which a matter might emanate. In 1921, was appoined a Member of the Executive Council, and in 1935, was re-elected a Member of the House of Assembly for the Southern District. His constituency recognizing his good services to the District as their representative returned him to the House by a great popular vote in 1935. In 1920, was appointed by the Secretary of State for the Colonies, Stipendary and Circuit Magistrate. He has acted as Attorney General on several occasions, as well as Chief Justice of the Bahamas. In 1926, was made a K.C., and has been Chairman of the Board of Public Works, the Board of Pilotage, and is Chairman of the Electrical Board. In 1937, he had the honour to be one of the representatives to attend the Coronation in London of King George VI. on behalf of the Bahamas.

SOLOMON, Eric.—Is a Member of the House of Assembly for Exuma. He served in His Majesty's Forces in the World War, and attained to the rank of Captain in the Canadian Army. He was for many years Chairman of the Electrical Board, rendering valuable service to that Department. He is a Fire Insurance Agent, and Agent for the C.P.R. Steamship Co., and also a real estate owner. He is one of the Proprietors of of the business known as "Solomon Bros.", Nassau.

SOLOMON, Cyril.—Is an associate with his brother in the Steamship and the business known as "The Pipe of Peace," and is partner in the real estate of Solomon Bros., Insurance Agents.

The Early Settlers

SOLOMON, Neville Stafford.—Son of the late Julius Solomon, Magistrate (deceased). Educated: Nassau Grammar School; entered Bahamas Civil Service 1912. Later, was appointed Supervisor of Customs on the West Coast of Africa; at length, retired on pension. Again re-appointed as Receiver General of the Bahamas, 1927. Now retired from the Civil Service, and lives abroad.

SUTTON, Arthur Bruce.—Son of Charles Sutton (deceased) Inspector of Police. Formerly a Member of the Honourable House of Assembly for the Eastern District. Clerk to many Lumber Firms in the Bahamas.

SUTTON, Theodore.—Son of Charles Sutton (deceased) and the grandson of Charles Sutton, Sr. (deceased), Inspector of Police. Attached to the Staff of the Royal Bank of Canada.

SWEETING, G. R.—Is a descendant of the old Colonists of Sweetings who came to the Bahamas in 1640. A large importer of foreign manufactured goods, and the owner of valuable real estate.

SWEETING, Paul.—Educated: Boys' Central School, under his father, the late Thomas W. Sweeting, Head Master. Formerly on the Staff of the Royal Bank of Canada of Nassau. Assistant Manager of Munson Steamship Company, Nassau. Descendant of Richard Sweeting, Justice of the Peace at Harbour Island, 1785, who was a Loyalist.

SWEETING, Samuel Roger.—Educated: Public School, Abaco and Jacksonville, Florida. Formerly Merchant; now on the Staff of the firm of W. H. Sands, Nassau. Real estate owner, Abaco. Descendant of Henry Sweeting, a Loyalist.

SWEETING, Allan D.—Educated: Victoria School, Nassau. Born 21st Dec., 1900. Descended from Samuel Sweeting, a Loyalist. Chief Clerk in the firm of John S, George and Co., Nassau.

SWEETING, Charles M.—Born Oct. 3rd, 1893, Nassau, Bahamas. Educated: Victoria School. Descended from Samuel Sweeting, Loyalist, who came to the Colony at the close of the Revolutionary War of America, 1784. Clerk in the firm of John S. George and Co., Nassau.

SWEETING, William.—Son of the late Dr. C. C. Sweeting, who was a Member of the House of Assembly for the Eastern District, Abaco, and the City. Educated: Queen's College. He was formerly on the Staff of the Colonial Secretary's Department, and has recently been transferred to the Treasury De-

The Early Settlers.

partment. He is a descendant from Henry Sweeting, a Loyalist, and Richard Sweeting, brother to Henry, Justice of the Peace for Harbour Island in 1785.

SWEETING, Stanley A.—Born Nov., 1891. Educated: Victoria School, Nassau, Bahamas. Living in Miami, Florida. A descendant of Samuel Sweeting, Loyalist.

SYMONETTE, R. T.— Is a Member of the House of Assembly for the Eastern District. Commodore of the Nassau Yacht Club, and is Proprietor of the Rozelda Hotel, the Nassau Dock Yard, and a business on Bay Street. Is a wealthy real estate owner, and is the senior member of the firm of Robertson and Symonette; one of the founders of the Prudential Life Assurance Co., and President of the Chamber of Commerce.

SYMONETTE, W. J.— Born, Current, Eleuthera. Educated: Central School. Head Master of School, Inagua. Commissioner Mangrove Cay, Andros. Later, Chief Clerk, Treasury Department, Civil Service. Merchant.

TAYLOR, Zachary.— Is the descendant of Archibald Taylor, a Loyalist. He conducts a drapery business in George Street, and is a large real estate owner.

TAYLOR, Frederick. — Educated: Queen's College, Nassau, Merchant, brother to Zachariah Taylor, Merchant, both being descended from Archibald Taylor, Loyalist. Owners of a large estate, Long Island.

THOMPSON, Charles.— Only son of the late Austin Thompson, Postmaster General of the Bahamas. Was formerly on the Staff of R. H. Curry and Co., Steamship Agents, afterwards appointed Cashier in the Treasury Department. Acted Receiver General and Treasurer on several occasions, and temporary Member of the Executive Council of the Bahamas.

THOMPSON, Bruce Kilroy.— Belongs to an old Bahamian family of marked distinction. Richard Thompson, Sr., was nominated and appointed a Member of His Majesty's Council by Governor Woodes Rogers in 1718. In 1729, Richard Thompson, Sr. and Richard Thompson, Jr. were present at a Council Meeting held by Governor Woodes Rogers. At the first General Election held by the inhabitants of all the Islands in 1729, John Thompson, Sr. and John Thompson, Jr. were elected to two seats out of four to represent Harbour Island thus, the Thompsons in the early history of the Government of the Bahamas held seats both in the Upper and Lower

The Early Settlers.

Branches of the Legislature. Mr. Bruce Thompson was once a Member of the House of Assembly for the Western District, and owns considerable real estate. He has a son, now an undergraduate of the University of Cambridge.

THOMPSON, T. A.— Master of the Western Central School. Descended from the Thompsons who played a conspicuous part in the formation of the first Elective Assembly which met in New Providence, 29th September, 1729.

THOMPSON, Wallace.— For many years Master of the Victoria School. Now retired from the public service. A descendant of the Thompsons who were members of the first House of Assembly in the Bahamas.

THOMPSON, R. G.— Is a Merchant conducting a large up-to-date grocery, meat and fruit business in George Street.

TURTLE, Wheatly. — Educated: Queen's College. Last Manager of the Bank of Nassau. Manager of the estate of the late Herbert I. Claridge. Son of J. F. Turtle, who was himself Manager of the Bank of Nassau.

TURTLE, Morton.—Educated: Queen's College. Building Contractor. Real estate owner. Son of J. F. Turtle, former Manager of the Bank of Nassau.

UNDERWOOD, Carlton F. — Born, March 5th, 1906, Spanish Wells. Educated: Public School, Nassau. Descendant of Augustus Underwood, a Loyalist. Clerk in the firm of J. P. Sands and Co., Nassau.

WATKINS, Rupert. — Was born at Rock Sound, Eleuthera, and is a descendant of John Watkins who was one of a number selected from among the inhabitants of the Colony in 1721 as being a "fit person to be recommended to His Majesty to be elected by the Public to make an Assembly, or, execute the Public Office under the Government." He is engaged in the tomato industry and real estate business, also a Commission Merchant. Real estate owner, Eleuthera.

WEECH, George.— Educated: in England, and is a descendant of George Weech, a Loyalist. Was formerly a Member of the Hon. House of Assembly for the City. Has served on most of the Public Boards of the Colony. Is the oldest Merchant in the City, and owns very valuable real estate on the Harbour Front.

The Early Settlers

WEECH, Vernon.---Only surviving son of George Weech, depicts the character of his father in his friendly disposition. Merchant, conducts business on the Water Front of the Township, and is the last male descendant of the old Loyalist, George Weech.

WILSON, William M.--- Educated: Public School, Ragged Island. Commission Agent to many foreign firms. President, County Garden Club. Descendant of William Wilson, Loyalist.

Letter of Loyalty and Devotion
on the
Coronation of King George VI.,
from
The Bahamas.

SENT TO HIS MAJESTY THROUGH THE GOVERNOR, SIR BEDE CLIFFORD, K.C.M.G.

Following is the text of an Address which was sent to His Majesty the King through His Excellency the Governor:—

Nassau, N. P.
Bahamas.
14th April, 1937.

An address written on the Coronation of King George VI.
By
Arnold Talbot Bethell, University of Cambridge,
On behalf of the Natives of the Bahamas.

To the King's Most Excellent Majesty.

Sire:
Most Gracious Sovereign:

It gives the natives of the Bahamas a great pleasure to transmit a written address through His Excellency the Governor of the Bahamas, Sir Bede Clifford, K.C.M.G., who is about to leave the Colony to attend the festivities of the Coronation of Your Majesty in London on the 12th day of May, 1937.

May it please Your Majesty to accept this our expression of loyalty and devotion to the Throne as is herein set forth by us.

It now gives us great pleasure to address Your Majesty on this auspicious occasion.

This, being the day of the Coronation of Your Majesty the King is a day of great rejoicing amongst the nations of the British Empire. And we in our Island homes of the Bahamas are most happy to offer to Your Majesty our best wishes for happiness and long life.

Our prayers today are that Your Majesty shall be imbued with the spirit of love for all his subjects throughout the Empire; that he will maintain the Sword of Justice with mercy, and that under Divine guidance his throne shall endure for ever, and his Kingdom shall know no end.

And, lastly, that You may be saved and delivered from Your Enemies; and that the King of all Kings, and Governor of all things shall abate their pride and assuage their malice and confound their vices.

God Save The King.

Fullname Index

ADAMS, John 60
  Samuel 35-36 38
ADDERLEY, A F 115
  Abraham 102-103 184
  Augustus 184 G B 190
  193 George B 184
  Harold 184 Henry 150
AGASSIZ, Prof 121
ALBURY, 126 Basil
  114 Benjamin 75 130
  Clan 185 Dewitt 185
  Gilbert 185 J Baird 111
  John 70 130 184-186
  Joseph 75 129-130
  Joseph Baird 184
  Joseph Benson 184
  Joseph J 186 L B 113
  Leonard 186 Martha 75
  Mary 75 Mary B 113
  Matthew 130 Miriam 75
  Paul 114 R W D 185
  Roscoe 186 Sarah 75
  129 Stanley V S 185 W
  199 Wilton 184 Wilton G
  113 Wm 129
ALEXANDER, John 106
  William 107
ALLAN, Ethan 39
ALLARDYCE, W L 176
ALLEN, John 102 Lt
  172-173
AMHERST, Gen 31
AMIDAS, Capt 17

ANDERSON, C O 111
  186 David 104 John 107
  Leah 75 Mary 75 Peter
  75
ARANHA, Wm N 114
ARGAL, Capt 21
ARMBRISTER, James
  106 108 131 P W D 111
ARMSTRONG, John 107
  Thomas 105 Wm 103
ARNOLD, 39 Benedict
  50-51 Gen 50
ARTEAGA, Charles A
  186 Charles E 186 John
  186 Rosanda C 186
ASPINALL, A E 187
BACON, 10
BAIN, Alexander 150
  Terry 119 Wm 135
BAINES, Annie 113
BAIRD, James 104 109
  131 184
BALDWIN, Juba 108
  Magdalene 104
BALEY, C J 176
BALFOUR, B T 176
BALLIOU, Isaac 102
BALTIMORE, Lord 26
BANCROFT, O L 113
BANNERMAN, A 176
BANNISTER, Kathleen 115
BARCLAY, John Wallace
  104 106

The Early Settlers

BARLOW, Capt 17
BARNETT, 126 Hannah 75
  Richard 109 Samuel 75
  Thomas 69 75 Thomas
  Sr 71
BARROW, Isabella 104
BARRY, Geo 102
BARTHOLOMEW, 18
BARTON, Edward 109
  William 108
BASDEN, Robert 103
BAXTER, Guy 181
BEAK, Anna 109 John 70
BEAKER, George 106
BEASEY, Francis 69
BECK, Catherine 75
  Patience 75 Richard 75
  William 75
BEDFORD, Constance M
  115
BEEN, Andrew 85 Elizabeth
  85
BEGBIE, Alexander 103
BELL, Ann 75 James 75
  John 131 Margaret 107
BELOU, Cane 72
BELTON, Jonathan 107
BENNET, John 72
BENZIE, John 104 107
BERKELEY, Lord 27
BERNARD, Bishop 74 178
  Lord Bishop 117 Rev
  Bishop 118-119
BERRY, Frank 187 Timothy
  104
BETHEL, George L 114
BETHELL, 88 150 Ann 85
  89-90 Anne 88 Arnold
  Talbot 217 Aubry 188
  Benjamin 89 Bethia 85
  Catherine 89 Catherine
  Elizabeth 90 Charles 89-
  90 Charles Alexander 88
  Charles E 89 182 187

BETHELL (cont.)
  Charles P 111 187
  Charles Percival 111
  Charles Samuel George
  89-90 Charles W F 187
  David 88 Elizabeth 85 89
  Jeremiah 89 Joanna 89
  Johanna 85 John 72 85
  88-89 128 187-188
  Jonathan 89 Jonathan
  Winer 89 Mary 85 Nath'l
  85 88-89 Noah 85 88-90
  109 Patience 89 Patricia
  187 Peter 187 Prenza
  Jonathan 85 Sarah 85
  88-89 Susannah 89
  Thos 88-89 W H 188 W P
  112 Wm 88 Winer 85 88
  89 107
BETHNELL, 127
BETHUNE, Peter 108
BILL, Ben 75 Hannah 75
  John 75 Mary 75
  Susannah 75 Thos 75
  108
BINNIE, W A 188
BIORNE, 9
BIRCH, 175
BIRD, Thomas 103
BISLEY, Mary 75 Timothy
  75
BISSEY, Francis 75 John 75
  Sarah 75
BLAKE, Henry A 176
BLANCHARD, Andrew 105
BLAY, Elizabeth 75 John 75
  Mary 75 Phenny 75 Rose
  75
BODE, Charles 143 Charles
  M 142 Lillian 115
BONAMY, Bromfield 102
BONAVENTURE, Father 117
  Henson 178 Rev Father
  74

The Early Settlers

BOON, Thos 102
BOOTH, Capt 157 Wm 156
BOURN, Capt 163
BOWE, Roger 103 Wm 103
BOWEN, C A 112
BOWER, Ann 75 Benjamin 75 John 75 Martha 75 Mary 75 Nathaniel 75 William 75
BOWLES, Elizabeth 109 Frederick H Augustus 188 Thomas 109 Thomas Theodore 188 William 188 William Augustus 188
BOYD, John 101 131
BRADDOCK, John 104
BRADFORD, James 154 William 109
BRADWELL, Jacob 85 Mary 85
BRAMHALL, John 108
BRAYNEN, A R 115 188 James 102 108 188
BREWER, Wm 186 199-201
BRICE, Carl 188 199 D A 189 205 Howard 189 John 102 189 205 John Grey 205 L C 116 Lorenzo 188 Philip 189
BRIDGES, 175
BRISBAINE, James 131
BRISBANE, James 106
BROCKLEY, William 100
BROMHALL, John 106
BROOK, C W 189 George I 134
BROOKS, Peter 128
BROWN, Ann 143 Christopher 189 Henry V 114 Herbert 189 John 131 191 Joseph 189 Lester 189 Martha 75 Michael 105 Sarah 75

BROWN (cont.) Susannah 106 Thomas 103 105-106 Walter 101 Willard 189 William 75 143
BROWNE, Montford 175
BRUCE, Herbert 89
BUCKLEY, John 101
BUDDON, William 155
BUGNON, Capt 162
BULLARD, Ann 85 Charles 85 Eliza 85 Esther 85 Mary 88 Nathaniel 70 85 Philip 103 Solomon 85
BULLOCK, Benjamin 69 75 John 75 Mary 75 Sarah 75
BUNCH, George 131 William 109
BUNTING, Isaac 108
BURGESS, Joseph 91
BURGOYNE, 50-52 Gen 49
BURKE, 37 Edward 35
BURNETT, John 104
BURNS, James 107-108
BURNSIDE, Basil 189-190 Bruce Lockhart 189 James 144 John 189 Nigel 111 189-190 Sybil 111 189
BURRAS, Ann 20
BURROWS, Nicholas 103 William 103
BURRUM, Edward 75 James 75 Mary 75 William 75
BUTLER, Col 53 Herman 190 John 190 190 193 Kenneth F 190 William 104 190
BUXTON, 136
CABOT, 9 16
CALDWELL, James 106
CALICO, Jack 95

The Early Settlers

CALLAGAN, T F 176
CALLIE, Alexander 131
CALVERT, Cecil 26 George 26 Henrietta Maria 26 Leonard 26
CAMERON, Charles 176 Donald 102
CAMPBELL, Alexander 105 Archibald 126
CAREY, Abraham 86 Elizabeth 100 John 72 86 Mark 86 100 Mary 85 Richard 86 Sarah 85 William 85
CARGILL, Ann Mary 105
CARLETON, Gen 41
CARMICHAEL, John 131
CARR, Wm 101
CARRIER, Thomas 107
CARROLL, Thomas 107
CARTER, Capt 171 Elizabeth 75 Gilbert T 176 Jane 75 Peter 75 Thomas 91
CARTES, Peter 106
CARTIER, James 22
CASH, 127 Gwendolin 114 Joseph 153 Robert 130 Roland B 190 Thomas 129 Thomas Sr 130 William 108 190 Wm 130
CATERET, 27
CAUFIELD, C C 117 Charles 143
CHAMBERLAIN, Joseph 124
CHAMPLAIM, 22
CHARLES, Ann 75 I 26 84 Ii 27-28 84 William 75
CHARLOW, John 86 Joseph 86 Martha 86 Thos 86
CHARLTON, William 102
CHAVERS, Sarah 106

CHILCOTT, Luke Augustus 102
CHILLINGWORTH, 175
CHIPMAN, H N 115 190 Lois 111
CHRISTIAN, Elizabeth 104
CHRISTIE, Adam 130-131 190-191 Charlotte 108 Frank 115 191 H G 197 Harold 190-191 Harold G 115 Percy 191 Percy E 115
CHRYSTIE, William Mina 108
CIMBERLIN, James 75 Mary 75
CLARENDON, Lord 27
CLARIDGE, Herbert I 215 William Frederick 191 William Ivor 191
CLARK, 175 George 54
CLARKE, Edith S 112 John 107 William 102
CLAYBOURNE, 26
CLEAR, Henry Milton 114
CLEARE, John 129 Thomas 129
CLEMENTS, James 104
CLIFFORD, Bede 176 182 217 Lady 181
CLINTON, 56-57 Gen 40 42 59 Gov 61
CLUTSAM, Samuel 108
COAKLEY, John 107
COCHRAN, John 105
COCKBURN, F 176
COCKSHIS, Thomas 106
COFFIN, Videlicet William 158 William 159
COLBY, Richard 104
COLE, A K 111-112 191 George 191
COLEBROOK, Lt Gov 138

The Early Settlers

COLEBROOKE, Gov 138
  John 72 205 Lt Col 176
  Lt Gov 138
COLLIE, Alexander 107
COLLINS, John E 191 R G
  116 Ralph 111 191-192
COLUMBUS, 11-16
  Christopher 10
CONNOLLY, Honor 108
CONOLLY, Judith 108
COOKE, John 105
COOPER, H R 112
COPELAND, Patrick 83
CORDEAUX, S 176
CORNISH, John 102 105
  126
CORNWALLIS, 48 55-58
COTTINEAN, Capt 55
COVERLEY, Jane 76 Mary
  76 87 Nathaniel 76
  Thomas 76 Wm 76
COVERLY, Nathaniel 70
COX, Charles 100
  Florentine 72 I V 114
  James 76 Sarah 76
  Timothy 108
CRAIMEL, Robert 106
CRISPIN, Silvester 105
CROMWELL, Oliver 84
CROSSKILL, John 102 107
  131
CRUDEN, John 107 Mary
  106
CRUIKSHANK, John M 113
CULMER, Charles 131 Chas
  108 Constant 108 Daniel
  86 104 David 192 J W
  192 James 192 John P
  114 Judith 86 Mary 86
  Thomas 86 William 192
CULVER, Abraham 104
CUMMING, Robert 109
CUNNINGHAM, Annotte 134
  Robert 102

CURRY, 126 Benjamin 130
  Cosiah 76 John 128-129
  John Jr 76 John Sr 128
  Joseph 107 129 Martha
  76 Mary 76 O H 111 115
  Ormond H 192 R H 115
  189 192 199 205 214
  Richard 76 104 128 130-
  131 Robert 102 106 192
  Robert Henry 192
  Thomas 128
CURTIS, Andrew 76 Charity
  76 Elizabeth 76 Faith 76
  Frances 76 Henry 76
  Neptune 76 107 Richard
  76 107 Susanna 76
  Thomas 76 William 104
CUSHING, Jeremiah 108
CUTHBERT, Rebecca 103
DALBY, Daniel 106
DALE, 172 Eleanor 18
  Thomas 21 Virginia 18
DAMES, Charles 101 103
  Samuel 100
DANIELS, Charles 104
DANS, Maria 107
DARLING, Rebecca 107
DARVIL, James 100
  Marmaduke 76 Mary 76
  Zachaeus 76
DARVILL, 125
DARVILLE, Sophia 106
DAUGLISH, John 177
DAVIS, Arthur 91 Catherine
  102 Charles 140 George
  107 Jane 103 107 John
  16-17
DEAN, Hugh 103 105 John
  Conyers 143 Peter 101
  103 131
DEBRUHL, Michael Samuel
  108
DECARGIGAL, Don Juan 74

The Early Settlers

DECASTRO, Don Pedro 153
  Pedro 153-154
DEGLANVILLE, Hugh 193 R
  J A P G 112 Reginald
  193 W L 193
DEGRASSE, 57 Adm 56
DELAFAYETTE, Marquis 52
DELANCY, Stephen 108
DELAWARE, Lord 20-21
DELEON, Ponce 123
DEMONTS, Sieur 22
DENNESTONE, John 103
DEVEAUX, Andrew 74 101
  103 109 126 Edward Sr
  131 John 109
DICKENSON, John 86 Mary
  86
DICKSON, John 109
DIEHL, Patricia S 13
DILLET, Stephen 135
DIMOND, Capt 163
DIXON, Elizabeth 142 Philip
  132
DOLEY, Daniel Jr 143
DOLLY, Charles 180
DORKINS, Lawrence 100
DORSET, Earl Of
  Southampton 20
DORSETT, Mary 86
DOUBLEDAY, 180
DOUGLAS, John 103
DOUGLASS, John 102 131
DOWD, Seth 107
DOWDESWELL, W 175
DOWNHAM, James 76
  Thomas 72 76
DRAKE, Francis 16-17
DREXAL, Anthony 181
DRISCOLL, Lawrence 76
  Mary 76 Sarah 76
  Thomas 76
DROMGOOLE, Paul 109
DRUDGE, John 106 193
  Wm George Albert 193

DRYSDALE, Alexander 103
DUBOIS, Isaac 104
DUMARESQUE, Philip 106
  130
DUMORESQUE, Phillip 131
DUNCAN, Henry 107
DUNCOMBE, F A C 112
  Frederick Arthur Cyril
  193 Gurth 194 Henry
  William Feversham 194
  Robert 108 193 Roger
  Kelsall 193 W W 193-
  194 William Nehemiah
  193 William W 194
DUNCOME, Nehemiah 76
  Samuel 76 Susannah 76
  William 76
DUNDAS, C C 176 C C F
  177 Charles 110
DUNMORE, Gov 88 Lord
  73-74
DUNN, John 108
DUPUCH, A E J 115 L G
  116 Mary V 112
DYER, R P 119
EDWARDS, 194 John 105
  Peter 107-108 131 194
ELDING, Anna 76 Edward
  72 Hannah 76 Reed 76
ELDON, Alfred 112 S A 111
ELIZABETH, Queen 17-18
ELLORBY, Thomas 105
ELTON, Capt 163
ERICKSON, 183 Josiah 182
ERSKIN, Lord 62
EVANS, Amelia 86 Elizabeth
  86 John 86 Joseph 86
  108 Ruth 76 William 86
EVAS, Samuel 145
EVE, Joseph 103 131
  Oswald 131 Oswell 103
  William 107
EVELYN, John 106
FAIR, William 102

The Early Settlers

FALCONER, John 108 142
FARQUHARSON, Carles 106
  George 107 Goerge 131
FARRINGTON, Anderson
  194-195 Ena 195 R 195
  R J A 195 Reginald 115
  194 Sarah Anderson 144
  Sydney 195 William 144
FERGUSON, Ancel 105
  Anne 129 Donald 105
  John 102 104 106 131
  Kenneth 104
FERNANDER, Claude
  Stanford 195 James
  Robert 195 Osmond
  Langford 195
FERNANDO, Mary 76
  William 76
FIFE, Andrew 76 John 76
  Phenny 76
FINE, Frederick 108
FISH, Sarah 106
FISHER, Abraham 76
  Elizabeth 76 109 Eric
  195 Hartman 195 John
  76 Martha 76 Philip 162
FITZMAURICE, Dr 113
FITZWILLIAM, Richard 152
  175
FITZWILLIAMS, Rich'd 154
FLOWERS, George 104
FLYNS, Dennis 105
FORBES, Dugald 101 John
  175 Sophia 106 Thomas
  107
FORD, James 107
FORESTER, John 82
FORREST, 20
FORSYTH, Rear-adm 126
FOSTER, Thomas 104
FOWLER, Dennis 109
FOX, 125 Charles James 62
  George 28 James 76
  John 76 102 106 Joseph

FOX (cont.)
  76 106 Martha 76 Mary
  76 Nancy 76 Samuel 105
  Sarah 76
FRANK, Moses 128
FRANKLIN, Benjamin 52 60
FRASER, Edward 76 Eliza
  76 John 76 Susannah
  76 Thomas 76 Wm 76
FRAZER, John Lewis 109
FREEMAN, Capt 172 Setts
  106
FRENCH, John 109
FRIAR, Anthony 107
FRITH, Catherine 76 Jasper
  76 John 76 Samuel 69
  71-72
FROBISHER, 16 Martin 17
FROSBACK, Frederick 107
FRY, Philip 107
FRYAR, Anthony 105
FURNELL, Organ 152 Peter
  152 154
GAGE, Gen 36-40
GAMBIER, Deborah 141
  Elenor 103 Samuel 103
GAMBLE, George Augustus
  107 131 William 104
  Wm 131
GAMBLIN, Dudley 195 G D
  112 George 182 195 J
  James Henry 195
GARFUNKEL, Joseph 195
GARRARD, William 105
GASCOIGNE, Charles 77
  Frances 77 Moses 77
GATES, 21 51 Gen 52 Maj-
  gen 50 Thomas 20
GEORGE, 65 Edward 203 Ii
  28 Iii 35 59 131-132
  John S 189 191 202-203
  206 213 King 44 46 68 V
  King 211 Vi King 204
  212 217

The Early Settlers

GERMAIN, Lord 48
GIBBONS, Edward 104
  Jemmima 77 Mary 77
  Samuel 77
GIBBONY, Edward 108
GIBBS, George 131
GIBSON, Alexander 102
  Charles I 113 John 103
GIGNAC, Elsie G 115
GILBERT, Humphrey 16-17
GILCHRIST, William 105
GILDERT, James Jr 157
GILLET, Thomas Wood 105
GLASS, Solomon 105 107
GLINTON, Henry 104
GLOVER, Col 47
GOLDSMITH, Jesse 102
GOODIE, John 131
GORDON, William 132 Wm 131
GOSNOLD, 18
GOUDET, Peter 72
GOULD, Ann 140 Henrietta 144 William 144 William Thomas 140
GRAHAM, Eliza 77 Esther 77 James 77 Nancy 77
GRAHAME, R B 196
GRANT, Gilbert 104 109 Joseph 53 Lt Gen 99 M 176 Michail 131 Robert 107
GRANVILLE, H 18
GRAY, Geo 101 George 101 108 131 James 107
GRAYHAM, Alexander 102
GREEN, 39 55-56 Elizabeth 106 Gen 47 57 Nath'l 45
GREENAGE, Abraham 104
GREENIDGE, J F 113 Jerome F 113
GREGOR, Lt 171
GREGORY, John 176
GRENVILLE, Richard 16

GREY, Wilson 176
GRIFFIN, Benjamin 77 Frederick 196 George 77 Hannah 77 J Bowes 111-112 John 70 77 196 John Bowes 180 Mary 77 Miriam 77 Thomas 77 Wilbert 196 William 77
GRIFFITH, John 106
GRIMES, John 152 154
GRUNDY, 181
GUTTIEREZ, Pedro 15
HACKETT, John 175
HADDON, Smith 176
HAKLUYT, Richard 19-20
HALE, Elizabeth 77 Matther 77 Nathan 47 Sarah 77
HALL, Benjamin 72 Catherine 77 Charles R 196 Henry 107 Hershal Stanley 196 Jane 77 John 77 106 Joseph 77 Joseph Sr 69 196 Mary 77 Nat 103 Nathaniel 103 106 131 196 Patience 77 William 77
HALLIDAY, Robert 102
HAMACHER, John H 196
HAMILTON, 53 John 101 Wm Henry 101
HANDCOCK, John 38
HANHAM, Thomas 19
HANNA, John 105
HANOCCK, 43
HARBARD, John 85
HARDY, Mary 108
HARKNESS, George 106 106
HARMBRISTER, P W D 186
HARNOTT, Margarett 77
HARRIS, I 150 Wm 188 190
HARRISON, John 104 108
HARROLD, Alexander 102 105

The Early Settlers

HARVARD, John 85
HARVEY, Henry 142 John 24
HASKETT, Elias 175
HASKEY, William 107
HAVEN, Stephen 107
HAWES, Jacob 160
HAWKINS, John 16-17 Susannah 108
HAXTON, R B 112
HAYMAN, Richard 107
HAYNES, Edward 105 William 105
HAYNES-SMITH, W F 176
HENDRICKS, John 108
HENNESSY, J P 176
HENRY, Iv Of France 22 Patrick 37 54 Vii King Of England 9-10
HENZELL, Robert Thompson 104
HEPBURN, James 103 126
HERKIMER, Gen 49
HESTER, William 158-159
HEWITT, Sarah 99
HIGGS, 127 Basil Dewees 197 Edwin T 196 G W 115-116 197 George 197 Hartman H 197 Lambert 197 Rex 197 Samuel 102 129 131 196-197 Vincent 197 Walter 197 Walter A 196
HILTON, Edward 198 Stanley 197 Thomas 197 William 197-198
HODGSON, Ann Bigland 101 Thomas Sr 103
HOGAN, John 103
HOLDSWORTH, Stephen 107
HOLLAND, Clement 110
HOLLIDAY, Robert 107 131
HOLMES, Anthony 104 John F G 114 Mary 128 Reuben 109
HOLT, Samuel 179
HOOKER, Thomas 25
HORN, John 104
HORNBY, Geoffry 142 Stanley Byng 142
HORNYGOLD, Benjamin 91
HOWARD, Thomas 17
HOWE, Gen 40 42 47 James 103 126 Lord 45-46 49 Thomas 102
HOWELL, Ann 77 John 77 Moore Sanderson 77 Susannah 77
HUDSON, 27 Henry 26 Sarah 108
HUGHES, Lionel S 114
HUMBER, Robert 103
HUME, James 102
HUNLOKE, Thomas 131
HUNT, Robert 101 106 131
HUNTER, Andrew 77 Elizabeth 77 Joseph 102
HUOSNE, 100
HUTCHESON, 158-159 Annie 25
HUTCHINSON, 36 Gov 35
INDIAN, Pocahantas 20 Pocahantes 20 Pocahontas 21 Powhatan 20
INGRAHAM, 127 Ann 86 Benjamin 86 Bethia 86 Catherine 86 Duke 86 John 129 Joseph 70 72 86 Kenneth R 114 Mary 86 Miriam 86 Rebecca 86 Sarah 86 William 86
IRVING, James 77
ISABELLA, Queen 11
JACKSON, Calvin 77 Capt

The Early Settlers

JACKSON (cont.)
  162 Hannah 77 Mildred 77
JAMES, King 19 Wm 105
JARRET, James Henry 180
JARRETT, J H 110 James Henry 111
JARROED, Jacob 72
JASPER, Sgt 42
JAY, John 60
JEFFERSON, Thomas 43
JENKINS, Griffin 107
JENNINGS, John 77 Sarah 77 Susannh 77
JOHN, Earl Of Dunmore 132
JOHNSON, 127 A T W 199 Alexander 103 Allan 198 Allan L 199 Bertram 199 Catherine 77 Count 150 Dewees O 199 Edward 84 Errol 198 George 102 198-199 George E 114 George Henry 199 George Jr 141 George Sr 141 Harold E M 190 Hugh 199 J S 198-199 Joseph 199 Mary 77 Mervyn 112 198 Nathaniel 77 Samuel 77 Samuel Jr 129 Sarah 77 T B 199 Thaddeus 198 Thaddeus Sr 199 Thomas 77 107 W C B 115 115 198-199 William T B 199
JOHNSTONE, 100 James 104 John 106 Lewis 103 Mary 104 Nathaniel 129 Robert 101 Thomas 130 William 102
JOLLIE, Martin 102
JONES, Cadwallader 175 John 104 Margaret 102

JONES (cont.)
  Paul 54-55 William 69 Wm 128 131 154
JORDAN, John 105
KEINHART, William 105
KELLY, Allan 187 194-195 Audley 200 Bert 200 C J Jr 200 Charles J 199 Charles Sr 200 Ena 195 Hugh 104 J K A 115 James 102 109 131 187 199-200 James K A 199 Kenneth 200 Newel 200 Patricia 187 Trevor 200
KELSALL, Ann 107 John 107 Roger 103
KEMP, Anthony 86 Benjamin 86 130 Frederick Arnold 200 Henry E 200 Jane 86 John 86 John C 108 Martha 86 Mary 86 Thomas I 111 Thomas Theodore 200
KERR, James 131 John 104
KERSEY, John 107 Mark 106
KEWIN, John 77 Margaret 77 Mary 77 Ruth 77
KEYSALL, 194 Roger 193
KIERCHER, Jacob 107
KING, C H 113 Capt 94-95
KIRK, Francis 107
KNIGHT, Ann 77 Edward 77 Jane 77
KNOWLES, Alexander 77 Ann 77 86 Daniel 86 Eliza 86 Elizabeth 86 H F 113 Hannah 86 Harry 201 James 104 John 86 201 Judith 86 Martha 86 Mary 86 Robert 86 Samuel 86 105 108 201 Sarah 77 86 Stanley 201

The Early Settlers

KNOWLES (cont.)
    Thomas 86 Tracy J 201
    Uriah 201-202 Viola T
    112
LAFAYETTE, 57 Gen 56
LAFOUNTAINE, Julien 76
    Sarah 76
LAMPIN, Thomas 133
LANCASTER, F G 113
LANE, James 107-108
LANGTON-JONES,
    Commander 116
LAURENS, Henry 60
LAWFORD, Samuel 71-72
    152-154
LAYDON, Ann 20 John 20
LEARY, Susannah 108
    Thomas 70
LEE, Ambrose 107 Gen 47
    Richard Henry 43
LEES, C C 176
LEITCH, George 131
LEMON, Benjamin 77 John
    77 Mary 77 Rebecca 77
    Richard 77
LESVIS, Judith 105
LEVY, Austin 182
LEWIS, 100 John 107
LIEF, 9
LIGHTBOURN, Cyril 201
    George 201 H L 202
    Henry 130 Howard L 201
    Hugh 201 J L 112 James
    201-202 N E 112 Nelson
    E 201 P M 199 Paul 109
    109 201 Percy 201 R M
    201 Thos 130 Wm 114
LIGHTFOOT, Ellis 175
LILBURNE, 175
LINCOLN, Abraham 135
    Ann 77 Earl Of
    Southampton 20 Gen 50
    Martha 77
LINDOP, R A Erskine 113

LINTON, Robert 105
LOCKE, John 27
LOCKHART, Wm 105 126
LOCKWOOD, Capt 148
LOFTHOUSE, Charles 202
    T H C 202 Thomas 202
LONGLEY, John 107
LORD, Benjamin 108
LORINER, Alexander 106
LORRIMORE, John 131
LORRINER, Alexander 105
LORY, Thomas 72
LOVE, Ebenezer 108
LOVECK, George 105 107
LOVELL, John 105
LOW, Eliza 86 Elizabeth 87
    Frances 86 Gideon 86
    John 87 Martha 86 Mary
    86 Matthew 86 Sarah 86
    Thomas 86
LOWE, Doris R 112 Edward
    102 202 Eldred 202
    Gideon 128 J Estwick
    202 John A 202
LYFORD, William 106 Wm
    101
MACARTHUR, Archibald
    101
MACKARTHY, Martin 109
MACKAY, John 103
MACKEY, Samuel 102
MADDOCKS, Nancy 104
MADOC, Prince 9
MADURAS, 152
MAIR, Alexander 106
MAJOR, Mary 105
MALCOLM, Harcourt 198
    Kirkwood 202 Margaret
    112 Michael 202
MALCOM, Michael 104
MALONE, J V 202
MANSON, Henry H 114
MANTANZAS, 172
MANUEL, Thomas 106

The Early Settlers

MARION, 57
MARKS, James 104 John 105
MARR, Henry 144
MARSHALL, Chas 108 203 David 78 Margery 78
MARTIN, John 99 103 131 Nicholas 102 131
MARTINANGET, Abraham 103
MASON, Elizabeth 108 John 25 197
MATTHEW, G B 176
MATTHEWS, William 104
MAURA, Bertram 203 Bruce 203 Edward 203 Hose 202 John 203 Lionel 203 Montague 203 W H H 203 William Henry Handford 202
MAURY, John 202 Marcel 202 Peter 202
MAXFIELD, James 171
MAXWELL, John 175
MAYCOCK, Sweeting 105
MCALISTER, Hector 104 Margaret 126
MCALLISTER, Margaret 104
MCCANN, Daniel 104
MCCARTHY, John F 202 Lawrence 105 Saml 100
MCCARTNEY, Timothy 112
MCCOWAN, John 105
MCDONALD, Alexander 107 Donald 42 104 John 103 103 126
MCEVOY, Martin 107
MCFARLANE, John 105
MCINNES, Miles 107
MCINTOSH, John 103 105 108
MCKAY, Alexander 102 Daniel 102 Malcolm 102

MCKEE, Alexander 105 John 104 Michael 105
MCKELVEY, Sarah 108 108
MCKENZIE, Alexander 77 Ann 78 Anthony 78 Daniel 103 Eliza 77 Elizabeth 78 George 109 131 Hannah 78 78 John 78 101 Joseph 78 106 Mary 78 Mildred 78 Roderick 78 Thomas 77
MCKINEN, Samuel 104
MCKINEY, Benjamin 103
MCKINNEY, B H 115 Basil 203 Benjamin 107 203 E H 114 Edward H 203 Herbert 203 203 Joyce 115 Lenora 115
MCKINS, David 105
MCLEAN, Alexander 104 H C 182
MCLEOD, Rose 107 William 104
MCMEYERS, Christian 106
MCNEAL, 124
MCNEIL, Margaret 104-105
MCQUEEN, Alexander 107
MEADOWS, John M 150
MENENDEZ, 150 M Raymond 179
MENZIES, James 131
MEREDITH, Robert 161
MICKLITHWAIT, Richard 102
MIDDLETON, William 108 108
MILLAR, R M 113
MILLER, Bainhear 107 George 106 John 101 131 Patrick 105 Wm 131
MILLS, John 99
MINNS, Mary 103
MINORS, Drover 108 James 108 Rose 108 Thos 108

The Early Settlers

MINOS, Elizabeth 78
  Joseph 78 Martha 78
  William Pierce 78
MISICK, James 105
MITCHAEL, John 78 Ruth
  78 Sarah 78 William 78
MITCHELL, Edward
  Seymour 112
MITCHELSON, James 104
MONBRAY, John 104
MONTCALM, 32-33
MONTGOMERY, Gen 41
MOODIE, Robert 101
MOORE, Diana 100 Edward
  L 114 Edwin Labron 204
  Ernest 204 Hattie J E
  115 John 130 Joseph
  Morris 105 131 Peter
  203-204 Philip 103 108
  204 Phillip 204 Roger
  204 W K 111 204 Walter
  K 203-204 Walter K Jr
  204
MORELEY, Benjamin 78
  John 78 Mary 78
  Samuel 78 Susannah 78
MORGAN, 51 55 Gen 50
MORLEY, Edward 109
  William 103
MORRIS, John 101-102
  Robert 49
MORTON, Howard 78 John
  78 Sarah 78 Warren 78
MOSELEY, D S D 199 204
  Daniel 204 Edwin 204
  Oswald 204
MOSS, James 134 141 156
  John 100 William 103
  108 141 156-157 Wm
  102 131
MOTER, Abednego 78
  Esther 78 Jeremiah 78
  Johannah 78 Ruth 78
  Shadrach 78

MOTTE, Hannah 106
MOULTRIE, Col 42
  Frederick R 114 John
  101
MOUNSEY, Athanias 78
  Daniel 78 George 78
  Thomas 78
MOWBRAY, John 103
MOXELEY, W 116
MOXEY, Benjamin 109
  Humphrey 78 Jonathan
  78 Mary 78 Samuel 109
  Sarah 78 William 105
MUCADELL, Salvadore 105
MUIR, John 100 Thos 100
MULATTO, Boy William 161
MULLINS, Elizabeth 106
  Patrick 104
MULTRYNE, John 109
MULYNE, John 126
MUNROE, 127 Charles 205
MURDOCK, 161 Thos 160
MURPHY, Ann 106 George
  116 204-205
MURRAY, Alexander 101
  109 131 Edward 109
  131
MYSICK, James 108
NEEKS, Thomas 109
NEGRO, Cymbello 156-157
  Domingo 157 Jack 89
  Lucy 89
NEILLY, Christopher 102
  107
NEIMO, 124
NESBIT, Charles Rogers
  158
NESBITT, C R 159
NEWBOLD, Eliza 87 Hall 70
  Leonard A 205 Mary 87
  Paul 72 205 Samuel 87
  Sarah 87
NEWMAN, Elizabeth 78
  Hannah 78 John 78

The Early Settlers

NEWMAN (cont.)
 Joseph 78 Josiah 78
 Rosanna 107 Samuel 78
 William 109
NEWPORT, Capt 20
NEWTON, Benjamin 107
NICKLETHWAITE, Henrietta 107
NICOLLS, Emerald E 112
NIMMO, Alexander 144
 Peter 144
NIXON, Joshua 103
NODLINGS, George 107
NORTH, Lord 37 58 Thomas 109 Thos 101
O'CONNELL, Cardinal 74 Daniel 136
O'HALLORAN, John 131
O'NEAL, James 102
OAKES, Harry 181
OGLETHORPE, 29 Gen 28
OLIVER, Benjamin 87
 Charles 87 John 87
 Mary 87 Thomas 87
ONIEL, James 105
ORR, Maj 176
OSWALD, 60
OUTLAW, George 106
OUTTEN, John 108
OWENS, Charles 171
PALFREY, J G 116
PANTON, William 103
PARKER, Capt 38 Eleanor 108
PARKINSON, William Dorsett 114
PARKS, Allan 205 Frank 205 Geo Campbell 101 George Campbell 205 Joseph 205 Mark 130
PASTEUR, Charles 105
PATERSON, O'lof 102
PATRICK, Samuel 129

PATTON, Elizabeth 144
 George 144
PAYNE, John Jacob 108
 Mary Bell 108 Mary Matilda 108 Thomas 43 156-157
PEARCE, Joseph 129
 Thomas 129 William 153
PEARIS, Margaret 102
 Richard 102 109
PEEL, Robert 20
PEET, James Herbert 112
PEMBERTON, H 113 James 107
PENN, Adm 28 John 106
 William 28
PENNYBACKER, Conrade 103
PENNYBAKER, John 126
PENSHAW, John 87 Mary 87 Sarah 87 Susannah 87
PERCH, Lawrence 108
PETTEE, 127
PETTY, John 106 108
 Matthew 102
PHEEMER, Samuel 100
PHENNEY, George 185 210
PHENNY, 70 George 69 175 209 Gov 71 196
PHILIPS, John 105
PHILLIP, 17
PHILLIPS, Maj-gen 51-52
PICKERING, Col 37
PIERCE, George 114
PINCKNEY, Charles 141
 Thomas 141
PINDER, 126 Brice 205
 Elizabeth 78 Eric P 114
 Frances 78 Frederick 206 H 116 John 78
 Joseph 109 Mary 78
 Michael 78 Moody 108-109 Percival 206

The Early Settlers

PINDER (cont.)
  Randolph 206 Richard
  87 Ridley 102 Salem 78
  206 Sarah 78 Seaborn
  72 Susannah 78 Thomas
  78 Timothy 78 Vivian N
  112 Warren 206 William
  69 72 78 William J 205
PITCAIRN, Maj 38
PITT, 31 37 William 35
PLENIS, Benedict 105
POOL, F 116
POOR, John 107
PORTER, Commodore 173-174
POWELL, Sarah 106
PRATT, Abraham 104 108 131
PRESCOTT, Col 40
PRICHARD, Asa 206
PRIITCHARD, W E G 206
PRINGLE, James 104-106
PRITCHARD, A 206-207
  Aretmas 206 Asa 206 F
  206-207 Frank 206-207
  Herbert 206 Olando 206
  Reginald 206 W E 206 W
  E G 206 William 102 106
  207 William E 206
PRUDEN, 127
PURDY, Capt 160 George 160-161
PUTMAN, 46 Israel 39 45
PYE, Deborah 78 James 78
  John 78 Mary 78 Sarah
  78 William 78
PYFROM, Canon George
  117 207 Jabez 207
  Jerome E 207 Peter 108
  207 Sydney 207 Wm 207
QUEEN, William 106
RAAB, Gerhart 108
RACKMAN, 96-98 John 95

RAE, Henry 179 James
  Stanley 179 John 118
RAGALA, John 103
RAINE, Sarah G 113
RAINGER, John 105
RALEIGH, 17-18 Walter 17 22
RAMAGE, Capt 170
RAMER, Robert 131
RANGER, John 129
RAWSON, R W 176
RAY, Henry 104 Phebe 107
READING, Roger 72
REARDEN, Margaret 102
RECKLEY, John K 108
REES, William 106
REEVES, Cleveland H 113
REISTER, Ernest 104
REVERE, Paul 38
RHAMING, John 104
RHODEN, Grace 108
RHODES, William 131
RICHARDS, John 131
RICHTER, Charles 106
RICKER, Capt 169
RIDLEY, James 105
RIEDESSEL, Baron 51-52
RIGBY, William 104
ROBERTS, 126 Benjamin
  78 129-130 E P 113
  Elizabeth 79 G G 208 G
  W K 115 207 George 78
  130 208 George
  Campbell 113 J W 115
  208 James 128 Jane 78
  John 72 78-79 106 128-129 129-130 207-208
  Joseph 78-79 129
  Lafayette 208 Madge K
  115 Martha 78-79 129
  Mary 78-79 Merriham 78
  Newton Clyde 111 208
  Richard 79 129 Ruth 78-

The Early Settlers

ROBERTS (cont.)
  79 Theodora S 114 Wm 129
ROBERTSON, Mary 104 R J 187 207 Thos 130-131
ROBERTSONE, Thos 130
ROBINSON, Mary 103 W K 176
ROCHAMBEAU, Gen 56
ROCKINGHAM, Lord 58-59
RODE, Edith 115
RODGERS, Michael 107
ROGERS, Leon K 208 P G 116 William Whelston 72 Woodes 65-67 69 71 91 127 175 207-208 211 214
ROKER, Thos 102 108 131
ROLLE, Dennis 101 103 John 133 Lord 124 133
RONLAND, Charles 87 Chas Jr 87 Elizabeth 87 Mary Coverley 87
ROOKER, Jonah 100
ROSE, James 104 106
ROSS, Alexander 101 131 Betsy 49 James 171 Ruth Myers 79 Sarah Myers 79 Susannah Myers 79 Thomas 106 131 Wm 79
ROWLAND, John 104
ROWORTH, Samuel 105
ROXBURGH, Anthony 103
RUMER, Robert 101 125
RUSH, Mary 100
RUSSEL, 126 John 103
RUSSELL, A Roy 208 A T 208 B R 115 Benjamin 79 130 Benjamin Jr 130 Daniel 79 128 Edison 208 Elizabeth 79 Herbert J 209 Howard W 114 John 105 208-209

RUSSELL (cont.)
  Joseph 129 Nathaniel 128 Randall A 209 Sarah 79 Thomas 129 Thomas Elma 208 Walter 208 Wm 130
SABINS, Capt 169
SAINTLEDGER, 50 Gen 49
SALCEDO, 15
SALTER, David 114
SAMSON, James 103 109
SANDERS, Charley 109
SANDIP, Edward 20
SANDS, 210 Alfred B 209 Arthur 209 Arthur H 115 Charles 87 Harry P 209 J P 186 197 209 211 215 James P 209 John 87 Mary 87 Mary A 113 Neville 209 Peter 209 Peter Jr 87 Peter Sr 87 Robert H 114 Ronald G 114 Samuel 87 Sarah 87 Stafford 115 209 W H 209 213 William 87
SAUNDER, 126
SAUNDERS, Benjamin 69 79 108 129-130 210 Catherine 79 Edward 210 Eliza 79 Henry 79 J L 210 James 130 Jane 79 Jean 79 John 79 128 130 John L 114 Martha 79 Mary 79 Nathaniel 79 129 Nathaniel Jr 128 Peter 70 Ruth 79 Samuel 79 Sarah 79 Stafford 205 210 Thomas 72 Thomas Sr 129 Thos 69 79 Victor 205 210 William T 210
SAWNEY, Gov 91
SAWYER, Ann 87 Carl 211 Daniel 129 Eugene 211

The Early Settlers

SAWYER (cont.)
　Henry V 211 John 87
　130 Mary 87 R W 115
　150 210-211 Raymond
　211 Richard 87 211
　Samuel 130 Sarah 87
　William A 211 Wm 87
SAYLE, Capt 82 84 192 211
　William 83
SCAIFE, John Andrew
　Hanson 211
SCHREINER, Chrysostom
　117-119 126
SCHUYLER, 50 Philip 41
SCOTT, James 79 Margaret
　79 Robert 108 Wm 103
SEARS, Edward D 211
　Edward L 211 Hannah
　79 Martha 79 Thos 79
SELON, Peter 106
SEYMOUR, Andrew 155
SHAFTESBURY, Lord 27
SHEA, Ambrose 176
SHEARS, Elizabeth 108
　Philip 103
SHELBORNE, 59-60
SHIRLEY, James 100 103
　Thos 101 175 Wm 175
SHOEMAKER, Joseph 106
SHORT, Hannah 105
SIMM, 125
SIMMERY, 100 Wm 100 102
SIMMS, Aim 79 James 79
　Joseph P 211 Mary 79
　Moses 79 211 Moses Sr
　72 William 109 Wm 130
SIMONS, Elizabeth 79
　Nathaniel 79
SIMPSON, John 103
　Thomas 102
SISSON, Capt 164
SKINNER, Andrew 102

SLAVE, Ann 133 Bell 134
　Elizabeth 133 Harriet
　134 Sally 134
SMITH, 20-21 Alice 112
　Amelia 102 106 Doris M
　115 Elizabeth 104
　Florence 115 George 105
　H A 212 Henry 104 John
　19 23 79 212 Joseph
　104 131 L 176 Mary 79
　P E 113 Pembroke C 211
　Richard 79 Robert 79
　Samuel 79 Thos 102 105
　131 212 Wm 109 211
SMYTH, I C 176
SOLOMON, A K 111 115
　212 Cyril 212 E V 116
　Eric 212 Julius 212
　Neville Stafford 213
SOMERS, George 20
SOUTHALL, Peter 108
SOYONS, Dr 113
SPATCHES, Anthony 79
　Arthur 79 Eliza 79 John
　79 Mary 79 Mary
　Huggins 79 Susannah
　79 William Sr 71 Wm 79
SPENCE, Robert 101
　Thomas Sr 69
SPENCER, Mary 87 Moses
　87 Thomas 87
SPIERS, Alexander 106
STAGE, Frederick 102
STANDISH, Miles 25
STANLEY, Bruce 89 Lord
　142
STARK, John 39
STENFORT, Anthony 103
STEPHENS, John 102
STERLING, Robert 108 131
STEVENS, Eleoner 105
　James 101 108 131
　Thomas 105

The Early Settlers

STEWARD, Catherine Elizabeth 90
STEWART, Alexander 104 Ann 79 Col 57 Icodan 79 Jeremiah 106 John 106 Margaret 79 Mary 79 Nancy 79 Rebecca 79 Roderick 79 Samuel 79 Sarah 79 William 79
STIPPER, William 108
STOODLEY, E A 112
STORR, John 105 143
STOUT, Joseph 101
STOW, James 79 John 79 Mary 79
STRACHAN, G B 113
STREATFIELD, Rev Canon 120 Robert Cornthwaite 178
STRUDER, John Martin 105
STUART, E H 112
STUBBS, Richard 102 Wade 102 131
STURRUP, Kersey 107 109
STYLES, John 131
SULLIVAN, Gen 53 John 37 Maj-gen 38
SUMNER, Henry L 113
SUPPLE, John 79
SUTHERLAND, Daniel 104
SUTTON, Arthur Bruce 213 Charles 213 Charles Sr 213 Lilly 113 Theodore 213
SWAIN, Elisha 108
SWEETING, 126 150 Allan D 213 Benjamin 80 C C 213 Charles M 213 Eliza 79 Elizabeth 80 G R 213 Henry 104 213-214 Letitia 80 Margery 79 Martha 79-80 Mary 79 Nathaniel 79 Paul 213 Rebecca 130 Richard

SWEETING (cont.) 109 131 213 Richard Sr 214 Samuel 80 106 129-130 213-214 Samuel Roger 213 Sarah 79-80 Stanley A 214 Thomas W 213 Thos 79-80 Thos Jr 79 William 80 213 William A 112 Wm 130
SYMONETTE, R T 115 205 214 Stafford 114 W J 214
TALFAIR, William 102
TATNALL, Johh Nulywn 103 Josiah 130-131
TATNELL, Josiah 101
TAYLOR, Alexander 103 Archibald 105 131 214 Charles Fox 107 Chas Fox 102 Dudley A W 114 Duncan 105-106 Frederick 214 Frederick A 112 Frederick Williams 178 Joseph 105 R W 111 Robert Walter 180 Thomas 92 Zachary 214
TEDDER, Joseph 129 Joseph Jr 129
TEDEL, John 80 Joseph 80 Mary 80
TELFAIR, Wm 131
THAYER, James 143
THOMASON, William 107
THOMPSON, 126 Ann 80 90 102 Austin 214 Bruce 215 Bruce Kilroy 214 Catherine 80 Charles 214 Charles S 111 Eliza 80 Elizabeth 80 F 130 Florence 130 James 80 John 70 72 80 John Jr 69 72 214 John Sr 214 Joseph 80 142 Margery 80 Martha 80 Mary 80

236

The Early Settlers

THOMPSON (cont.)
  Priscilla 80 R G 215
  Rebecca 80 Richard 80
  109 129 214 Richard Jr
  69 214 Sarah 80 T A 215
  Thomas 80 102 Thomas
  A 113 Thos D 80 Wallace
  215 William 80 141
  William Jr 70 80 William
  Sr 70 80
THORWALD, 9
TINKER, Jeremiah 107
  John 142 175
TODD, Alexander 102 108
TOUYN, Capt 100
TOWNSON, Susannah 108
TRIMMINGHAM, John 84
TROTT, 175
TUBLEY, David 104
  Elizabeth 104 Helena
  104 John Joachin 104
TUCKER, Rush 107
TULBY, David 126
TURNBULL, Walter 103 131
TURNLEY, Richard 92
TURTLE, J F 215 Morton
  199 215 Wheatly 215
TUTE, Lady 178 Richard
  Clifford 113 178
TWING, William 124
TYACK, Thomas 107
TYRON, Gov 36 45
UNDERWOOD, Augustus
  104 Carlton F 215
VALENTINE, John 103
VALLEAN, Josiah 105
VANE, 96-98 Chas 91 94-95
VANZEYLEN, Frederick C
  114
VENEBALES, Bishop 120
VENERABLES, Addington R
  143
VERGINNES, 60

WALDRON, Louisa 106
WALKER, Alice 80 Ann 80 C
  R 115 Chas 80 Chief
  Justice 68 Elizabeth 80
  J P 176 John 80 Thomas
  80 92
WALLACE, A S 113 James
  104 James H 112 John
  106
WASHINGTON, 39 45-49
  52-53 56-57 59 Gen 38
  42 44 58 61-62 Geo 41
WATER, Thomas 108
WATERS, Thomas 105
WATKINS, Benjamin 80 87
  Hannah 87 Hodon 87
  John 69 71 215 Martha
  80 Mary 87 Mary
  Susannah 87 Rupert
  215 Sarah 80 Venus 109
  Wm 87
WATSON, John 104
WEATHERFORD, 127
  Martin 106 131
WEATHERLY, Martha 87
  Mary 87 May 87 Saltus
  69 Wm 87
WEBB, Nicholas 175
WEECH, George 102 108
  215-216 Vernon 216
  William 150
WEIR, John 105 Robert 106
WELLS, E 140 E S 112
  Frances 140 Henry 106
  John 103 103 140 Mary
  Hamilton 140 Wm 102
WEMYSS, Peter 103 131
WENTHROP, Gov 83
WENTWORTH, John 63
  Johnson 175
WESLEY, John 29
WEST, John 24
WHIPPO, John 140

The Early Settlers

WHITE, James 108 John 18
  Nathaniel 84-85
WHITEHEAD, Roland 80
WHITNEY, Capt 92
WHYLLY, Alexander
  Campbell 131
WIGG, Edmund Rush 105
WILCOX, William 105
WILKINS, Ann 102 Samuel
  106
WILKINSON, Adj-gen 51
WILLIAMS, Amos 108
  Burton 103 Henry 103
  126 Roger 25 Samuel
  103 Wm 103 Wilson 103
WILLIAMS-TAYLOR,
  Frederick 178 Lady 178
WILLIAMSON, Thos 103
  105
WILSON, Randal 100
  Randall 104 Robert 104
  Samuel 103 William 106
  126 216 William M 216

WILSON (cont.)
  Wm 102 131 Wm Jr 102
WINTHROP, John 25
WOLFE, 21 30 32-33 Gen
  31 James 31 108
  Pocahantas 21
WOOD, John 102
WOODSIDE, John 100
WRIGHT, Ann 81 Lord 124
  Marmaduke 106 Mary
  81 Sarah 81 Wm 81
WYLLY, Alexander Campbell
  102 107 William 104
YATES, Jeremiah 81 Lt Gen
  99 Sarah 81 Thomas 19
YEOMAN, Seth 105 Sett 107
YOUNG, Elizabeth 81 James
  188 194 Joseph 106
  Kessiah 81 L W 115
  Richard 81 106 Thomas
  81 109 Thos 81 William
  81 152 154
ZANNICAL, Charles 105

www.ingramcontent.com/pod-product-compliance
Lightning Source LLC
Chambersburg PA
CBHW050140170426
43197CB00011B/1910